HOW TO
GET RID OF A
PRESIDENT

HOW TO
GET RID OF A
PRESIDENT

History's Guide to

Removing Unpopular, Unable,

or Unfit Chief Executives

DAVID PRIESS

PublicAffairs
New York

PublicAffairs
Hachette Book Group
1290 Avenue of the Americas, New York, NY 10104
www.publicaffairsbooks.com
@Public_Affairs

Printed in the United States of America
First Edition: November 2018

Published by PublicAffairs, an imprint of Perseus Books, LLC, a subsidiary of Hachette Book Group, Inc. The PublicAffairs name and logo is a trademark of the Hachette Book Group.

The Hachette Speakers Bureau provides a wide range of authors for speaking events. To find out more, go to www.hachettespeakersbureau.com or call (866) 376-6591.

The publisher is not responsible for websites (or their content) that are not owned by the publisher.

Editorial production by Christine Marra, Marrathon Production Services. www.marrathoneditorial.org

Book design by Jane Raese
Set in 12-point Adobe Caslon

Library of Congress Control Number: 2018958064

ISBN 978-1-5417-8820-6 (hardcover), ISBN 978-1-5417-8821-3 (ebook)

LSC-C

10 9 8 7 6 5 4 3 2 1

In memory of David Woods,
who dedicated his life to
supporting and defending the Constitution
and inspired others to do the same.

Contents

HOW TO
GET RID OF A
PRESIDENT

Introduction

President-Eject

A regular and orderly change of rulers [is] the strongest
guarantee against the approach of tyranny.[1]
—JAMES BLAINE

STIFLING AIR FILLED Philadelphia's crowded Pennsylvania State House, now Independence Hall, during the summer of 1787.

The distinguished men who had assembled there to revise the new country's inadequate Articles of Confederation struggled through their discomfort. The stakes could hardly be higher: the structure for national governance they had crafted during their long and costly war had clearly begun to fail them in time of peace. They needed to improve what they had, or their fragile experiment would break up.

Among the most significant problems with the existing government the Constitutional Convention would address was the lack of an effective chief executive.

THOMAS PAINE IN early 1776 had sparked a tidal wave of anti-monarchical sentiment with *Common Sense*, his pamphlet that took the colonies by storm. From that point on, the War of Independence stood for not only the protest against taxation without representation but also the inherent righteousness of republicanism over kingly rule.

Victory had delivered both a new country and a new sense of political order. Fears of planting the seeds for another monarchy, which the Americans had just thrown off, loomed large. Consensus in the separate states gelled around the idea that any strong central government would open the door to future oppression. Silas Deane, later a delegate to the Constitutional Convention, in 1782 wrote to Benjamin Franklin that "it would be absurd in Men pretending to be free, to use no other freedom than that of choosing Masters, and of flying from one Tyrant, to another."[2] Yet astute Americans saw that their makeshift confederation, lacking both taxing authority and reasonable enforcement powers, remained too weak to function effectively.

That tension between anti-monarchical sentiment and the palpable need for a stronger administrative leadership fell to George Washington, James Madison, Franklin, and dozens of other delegates to resolve as they worked to forge a new constitution that summer. Calls for a national executive authority, while no longer universally discarded, prompted energetic debate. James Wilson of Pennsylvania first proposed on June 1 that a single person hold executive power. South Carolina's Charles Cotesworth Pinckney and John Rutledge seconded the motion and spoke in favor of the one-man idea, respectively.[3] The motion quieted most others in attendance, including the man presiding over the discussions. Only a few years had passed since then-general Washington had stepped away from power, despite some calls for him to take over as King George. Now he sat in silence, probably just as aware as his colleagues in the room that he was more likely than anyone in the thirteen former colonies to first occupy any proposed executive position.

Edmund Randolph of Virginia finally voiced the fears of pure republicans and much of the young nation, objecting to one-man rule with the claim that it inherently contained "the fœtus of monarchy."[4] The next day, Franklin similarly named the danger the delegates now flirted with: "There is scarce a king in a hundred who would not, if he could, follow the example of Pharaoh, get first all the peoples money, then all their lands, and then make them and their children servants forever. It will be said, that we don't propose to establish Kings. I know it. But there is a natural inclination in mankind to Kingly Government. . . . I am apprehensive therefore, perhaps too apprehensive, that the Government of these States, may in future times, end in a Monarchy."[5]

THE NEED FOR a strong executive clearly remained controversial, even at the Constitutional Convention, because many Americans then simply had no way to imagine how vesting national power in one person *could* end well. Few positive role models existed. Franklin, the most worldly of the delegates assembled in Philadelphia, on June 4 reminded his colleagues of the recent history of the United Netherlands. There, as he summarized it, the popular stadtholder had devolved into a hereditary position and seemed bound to become just another king. "The Executive will be always increasing here, as elsewhere," he lamented, "till it ends in a monarchy."[6] Virtually everywhere these American wise men looked, they saw an unacceptable absence of liberty, an unacceptable abuse of executive power, or (more often) both.

The delegates fretted about the apparently universal tendency for leaders to amass power at the expense of the legislature and the people—and, consequently, stay in charge too long. South Carolina's Pierce Butler, for example, noted that "in all countries the Executive power is in a constant state of increase."[7] Virginia's George Mason opposed the single executive concept—both during the Constitutional Convention and well afterward, as a leading "anti-federalist" during the ratification debates—fearing an oppression worse than that which the colonies had thrown off. "We are not indeed constituting a British Government," he said, "but a more dangerous monarchy, an elective one."[8]

Eventually, of course, the delegates found their answer, now enshrined in the Constitution of the United States—the president of the United States. This single person would hold impressive powers: faithfully executing the laws, pardoning criminals, nominating judges, making treaties, and leading the armed forces as commander in chief. The best method of selecting this federal CEO prompted much debate. Navigating between the rocks of popular-will demagoguery (which, they worried, could result from direct election by the people) and puppet-presidency impotence (which, they worried, could result from election by the legislature), they devised a cumbersome electoral college system. By the founders' logic, the people would choose their leader, but only indirectly.

Candidates for this powerful office would face no qualification tests beyond birth as a natural-born citizen, residency in the United States for fourteen years, and an age of at least thirty-five years.

WE TAKE FOR GRANTED that voters can kick the incumbent out and choose someone else as their leader. It's the simplest and cleanest way to get rid of a president, and it has happened to ten of the first forty-five presidents. But it almost wasn't so.

Delegates to the Constitutional Convention debated both the length of the president's term and whether he would face reelection at all. Pennsylvania's Gouverneur Morris said if the people were to elect the chief executive, they would never fail to prefer a man of distinguished character and of "continental reputation."[9] But Morris recognized that good men sometimes break bad. So he spoke sharply against language that would keep the chief executive in office for seven years, but leave him unable to run for reelection. Denying a leader the incentive of additional terms, he asserted, would "destroy the great motive to good behavior, the hope of being rewarded by a re-appointment."[10] The delegates agreed, spurring sharp debate over how long the president ought to serve. Rufus King, thinking fixed terms would unduly restrain the popular will, said that "he who has provided himself to be the most fit for an Office, ought not to be excluded by the constitution from holding it."[11] Maybe, King suggested, power should be held indefinitely, as long as the occupant of the office maintained "good behavior," to be assessed by the legislature.

Wiser heads argued for more debate. Madison declared that any plan letting Congress constantly judge "good behavior" would undermine the separation of powers he had been lobbying for. Mason weighed in, calling any presidential service plan without a fixed term "a softer name only for an Executive for life" and "an easy step to hereditary Monarchy."[12] The men in Philadelphia took some time to get there, but this back-and-forth eventually got them to settle on a four-year term, with *no* restriction on reelection. Arguments from delegates like Alexander Hamilton for property or experience requirements failed to make it into the Constitution. The American people at the ballot box, mediated through electors from each state, would henceforth decide which candidate proved most worthy of the highest office in the land.

That's how we got the presidential term as we know it, with regular elections to allow us to remove the chief executive if we feel like it. But the feasibility of the new Constitution was not tested initially. It was clear to the convention delegates who the first president would be, irrespective of what the terms of the appointment were: only the former commander in chief of the Continental army could bring to the new position both unparalleled gravitas and near-universal acceptance across the newly independent states. Consequently, Washington took office with the electoral college's first unanimous vote, an outcome repeated just once when he coasted into a second term four years later. It was a wholly unrealistic beginning for a presidential system, which would never see such unanimity again.

Most of America seemed happy to keep their hero in the nation's highest office. When the first president should hand over the reins was left to the whim of one man and one man only: Washington himself. His service would end when *he* chose to retire to his beloved Mount Vernon, which is exactly what he did in 1797. Leaving the top office after two terms set an example. Only Franklin Roosevelt in 1940, leading the country out of the Great Depression while the Second World War spread across Europe and Asia, sought a third and then a fourth consecutive term. Many others wanted more time in office, but were removed by voters at the next opportunity.

THE DELEGATES' ELECTORAL structure has worked, with only three substantive tweaks. In 1804, the Twelfth Amendment revised procedures to account for the development of political parties and joint president–vice president tickets. In 1951, the Twenty-second Amendment prohibited future presidents from reelection if they had already served two full terms or, if they became president during another's term, more than ten years in the office. And in 1961, the Twenty-third Amendment granted electors to the District of Columbia.

Apart from these exceptions and the shift in electors' role from deliberative agents to rubber-stamp representatives of each state's popular vote, we still choose our presidents essentially as intended back in that summer of 1787. We weigh the candidates' relative merits, then we pick one to lead us. Once selected, that incumbent president gains great benefits, chief among them a platform like no other in the world to allow his or her message to dominate political discourse and various media. The evolution of the "imperial presidency" in the twentieth century grants the officeholder many more levers of influence than the founders envisioned. Hamilton would smile at this growth of executive power; many others would not.

But the anti-Federalist spirit has never been quashed in American public life. Just as the presidency has grown in power—and, perhaps, majesty—so the means of curtailing a president and even removing him or her have quietly evolved as well.

THE UNITED STATES has developed several safety valves through which unpopular, unable, or unfit leaders can be flushed—some constitutional, others rather less so.

Looking at how we've come to eject presidents across more than two centuries—using means from the partisan to the personal, the institutional to the ad hoc, the fair to the foul—shines a different light on the American political experience. The overwhelming focus politicians, pundits, and scholars put on *electing* leaders needs to be balanced by attention to the odd mix of elegant and distasteful ways those leaders have *left* office. Through design or improvisation, presidents have been (or can be) ousted by voters, rejected by their own parties, removed in place by opponents or subordinates, dismissed preemptively, displaced by death, taken out by force, declared unable to serve, or impeached and removed.

There may be abundant pomp and circumstance attending the arrivals of new presidents, but the more lasting lessons about the health and happiness of the body politic can be found in the nature and style of their departures.

Chapter One

Rejected by the Party

How can you challenge an incumbent President
of your own party and not be divisive?[1]
—GERALD FORD

I F POLITICS MAKES strange bedfellows, then the brief sleeping arrangements that paired John Tyler and the Whig Party show how political bedfellows can be pushed off the mattress and onto the cold, hard floor.

Tyler had served as a Virginia State delegate, US representative, and the governor of Virginia before taking a US Senate seat in 1827. A champion of states' rights, he often supported Andrew Jackson during that president's first term (1829–1833), largely out of shared opposition to a big, know-it-all federal government that would impose its will on the states. Tyler's support waned, however, during Old Hickory's second term when the president sought congressional backing to use force, if needed, against South Carolina for nullifying a federal tariff. Ever paranoid about the feds telling his constituents what to do, Tyler declared, "I owe no responsibility, politically speaking, elsewhere than to my State."[2] Jackson saw his law authorizing the use of force passed, with only one senator saying no. That sole vote was his fellow Democrat Tyler; all of the bill's other opponents had walked out of the chamber in protest.[3]

Tyler forged a working relationship with leading anti-Jacksonians in Congress, and the odd pairing crafted and passed a compromise tariff in 1833 to avert probable civil war and the use of force against South Carolina.[4] Later that year, the Democratic Party lost Tyler. He was enraged again at Jackson, this time for removing federal funds from the Bank of the United States. In the 1830s, when so much of the nation's growth depended on available credit, that was a huge deal. Tyler voted with the emerging Whig Party to censure Jackson. Its leader, Henry Clay, enthusiastically accepted the new ally into the Whig fold, despite their complete disagreement over most other pressing political issues.[5]

A few years later, Tyler found himself alongside presidential candidate William Henry Harrison, the supposed hero of the battle of Tippecanoe, as the Whigs' vice presidential choice. He served as a stereotypical ticket-balancer. Harrison came from the North, so Tyler would represent the South. Harrison had defeated Clay for the nomination, so Tyler would represent the Clay faction of the party.[6] The fact that his actual positions clashed with party orthodoxy was breezily overlooked. One early indicator that this wasn't going to end well was the fact that his own state's delegation refused to sponsor him at the party convention.[7] Even his most generous biographer admits that "no one with his views should have run for the Vice-Presidency on the Whig ticket."[8] But by pairing Harrison with Tyler, the Whigs would win the White House for the first time to the festive cheers of a catchy campaign slogan: "Tippecanoe and Tyler, too!"

The new vice president expected so little action in his job that he left for his residence in Williamsburg, Virginia, after his swearing-in ceremony on March 4, where he stayed until Harrison died on April 4, 1841—just thirty-one days later.[9] At that, Tyler returned to Washington and assumed the powers of the highest office. But nobody was really sure if he was now, in fact, the president.

THE CONSTITUTION'S TEXT lacked clarity on what should happen if the chief executive proved unable to do his job because of, say, death. The relevant (and, per the custom of the time, annoyingly overcapitalized) language appeared in article 2, section 1: "In Case of the

Removal of the President from Office, or of his Death, Resignation, or Inability to discharge the Powers and Duties of the said Office, the Same shall devolve on the Vice President. . . ." Many politicians and scholars of the era took this to mean the vice president should take on the former president's powers and duties without actually *becoming* the president. Others thought "the Same" referred to the immediately preceding words "the said Office," meaning the vice president should inherit the full presidency.

So the messy dilemma for Tyler, his cabinet, the Congress, the courts, and the American people to resolve was: Did they have a new president or merely an acting one?

One man who could speak with credibility about the office, congressman and former president John Quincy Adams, left no doubt where he stood. "I paid a visit this morning to Mr. Tyler, who styles himself President of the United States and not Vice-President, which would be correct style," he wrote in his diary. "It is a construction in direct violation both of the grammar and context of the Constitution which confers upon the vice-president, not the office but the 'powers and duties of said office.'"[10] Many congressmen concurred. Even Tyler's cabinet members, Harrison appointees whom the new leader had asked to remain in place, addressed their new boss with this mouthful: "Vice President, Acting President."[11]

Tyler, of course, thought he was fully the chief executive, and that everybody had damn well better start treating him that way. He certainly acted like a president: taking the oath of office, receiving the heads of executive departments, meeting with foreign ambassadors, and issuing a statement that looked a lot like an inaugural address.[12] Tyler ended Harrison's practice of accepting the cabinet's majority-vote decisions as his own. "I shall be pleased to avail myself of your counsel and advice," he told them in their historically awkward first session together. "But I shall never consent to being dictated to as to what I shall and shall not do. I, as president, will be responsible for my administration. I hope to have your co-operation in carrying out its measures; so long as you see fit to do this, I shall be glad to have you with me—when you think otherwise, your resignations will be accepted."[13]

The new president's action accomplished two things. First, Congress grudgingly acknowledged his status. Vice presidents thereafter would more easily take over as full presidents in their own right upon the death of their predecessors, using the so-called Tyler precedent. This norm held sway for almost 130 years, until the Twenty-fifth Amendment clarified and codified vice presidential accession. Second, Tyler's energetic grasping of the reins of power also placed him within a circular political firing squad. In winning the battle to be considered the chief executive, he lost support from most politicians within his own adopted party, which controlled the House and Senate.[14] As a firm states' rights advocate, Tyler considered most of the Whigs' stances on federal power unconstitutional.[15] So no one should have been surprised when, early on, the president sparred with his party leader and supposed ally Clay, who thought Congress should drive the national agenda.

Tyler's son claimed that a meeting between the two powerful men early in the term concluded with his father fuming, "Then, sir, I wish you to understand this—that you and I were born in the same district; that we have fed upon the same food, and breathed the same natal air. Go you now, then, Mr. Clay, to your end of the avenue, where stands the Capitol, and there perform your duty to the country as you shall think proper. So help me God, I shall do mine at this end of it as I think proper."[16]

He vetoed Clay's national bank bill in August 1841, spurring a boisterous protest outside the White House.[17] The Whigs took a deep breath and hit reset, sending up Pennsylvania Avenue a new bill that had been revised to address Tyler's specific objections. Nevertheless, after first indicating he would sign this second bill into law, the president vetoed it, too.

That's when all political hell broke loose.

"THE CONDUCT OF Mr. Tyler," wrote Senator Thomas Hart Benton, "produced its natural effect upon the party which had elected him— disgust and revolt."[18]

Until this presidency, an incumbent chief executive had neither seen his cabinet quit en masse, nor suffered ejection by his own party, nor faced an impeachment resolution in the House of Representatives, nor sought but failed to gain renomination. John Tyler's veto of the second bank bill brought him the historic distinction of achieving all four.

On September 11, 1841, all but one cabinet officer took him up on that offer he'd made back during their initial meeting, by resigning. Only Secretary of State Daniel Webster, Clay's rival within the party, stood with the besieged president. The Whigs may have thought they could force Tyler himself to resign, which, under the succession law of the time, would bring the president pro tempore of the Senate, a Clay ally, to power. But the president nominated replacements before Congress ended its session, giving legislators little choice but to confirm them quickly before adjourning.[19]

During a Whig caucus meeting before they left town that month, Clay ripped into Tyler, who, he said, "will stand here, like [Benedict] Arnold in England, a monument of his own perfidy and disgrace."[20] They then took their outrage out to the public gardens adjoining the Capitol and evicted Tyler from the party. "The conduct of the President has occasioned bitter mortification and deep regret," the lawmakers' manifesto declared. "In no manner or degree," they said, could they be "justly held responsible or blamed for the administration of the executive branch of the government."[21] Tyler became the first president without a party since the pre-partisan George Washington. Unlike the father of his country, however, Tyler had no history of revolutionary heroics, no reservoir of national gratitude to draw on.

And yet Tyler somehow still felt he had earned a renomination for the 1844 election. He certainly wouldn't get it on the Whig ticket, whose state conventions as early as summer 1842 had started endorsing Clay. So the president turned to his colleagues from a decade earlier, the Democrats, whom he'd shamelessly begun appointing to government jobs instead of Whigs. As the election got closer, his cabinet was almost wholly a Democratic one. "The name of Tyler will stink in the nostrils of the people," one Whig fumed, "for the history of our Government affords no such palpable example of the prostitution of the executive patronage to the wicked purpose of bribery."[22] The party of Jackson nevertheless had no interest in seeing Tyler on their 1844 ticket, well aware that any party foolish enough to nominate this embattled president faced humiliating defeat at the polls. Democrats grabbed the federal jobs he offered and politely cooperated on compatible legislation, but they wouldn't even recognize Tyler as a candidate at their national convention.[23]

Never one to give up, Tyler engineered the only way he'd win any nomination that year: a rival-free convention for himself in Baltimore.[24] Several weeks later, however, he could deny reality no longer. His support remained far too narrow and shallow, so he withdrew. Tyler managed to reinforce his pariah status in 1861, when he supported Virginia's secession from the very Union he once led. Then he was voted into the Confederate States of America's House of Representatives. When he died before taking his seat, as the Civil War raged on, politicians back in Washington did what most of them had done while he was chief executive: they ignored him.

To this day, John Tyler remains the only American president whose death the government has never formally recognized.[25]

P RESIDENTS NEED NOT be thrown out at the polls on Election Day to find themselves dislodged from the White House. History shows us that a chief executive's own political allies can remove that incumbent when they perceive him as unpopular or unfit. Refusing to nominate a president for a second term or, better yet, getting the incumbent to realize that he should walk away before it comes to an embarrassing vote at the convention does bring the party significant pain. But many politicians have calculated that discarding their own party's toxic president by internal action is better than waiting for the voters to do it.

This dynamic remained absent for the first half century or so of American politics. George Washington, who didn't represent any formal party, set a precedent by stepping away from reelection after two terms. Successor after successor followed suit, keeping the support of their parties until they either left office after eight years (Jefferson, Madison, Monroe, Jackson), lost the next election (both Adamses and Van Buren), or met the grim reaper (Harrison).

John Tyler, if only in this one respect, was a trendsetter: he began a six-president cascade of men who failed to appear on their party's ballot in the general election after their first term. One, Zachary Taylor, literally had no choice; like Harrison, he died in office. The others, by staying alive through their four-year terms, could have carried their parties' banners again on the next Election Day. Not one did, as national agonizing over slavery and other tensions within each of the major parties made it difficult for any president to build and sustain a governing coalition.

Of those five chief executives, only James Polk left with a solid reputation and a ledger of successes. He'd told Democrats upon his nomination in 1844, "I shall enter upon the discharge of the high and solemn duties of the office, with the settled purpose of not being a candidate for re-election,"[26] and he stayed true to his word. It was just as well: only three months after what would have been his second inauguration, he died at age fifty-three. The three presidents who followed Polk—the forgettable series of Millard Fillmore, Franklin Pierce, and James Buchanan—share three characteristics. First, historians routinely rank them among the nation's absolute worst. Second, and related to that, they took no responsibility for resolving the national moral failure of slavery. And third, no matter how they had attained office, they, like future presidents Chester Arthur and Lyndon Johnson, found themselves spurned by their own parties.

T HE WHIGS HAD learned in 1840 that a celebrity candidate seemed to have an easier route into the White House than a party regular so in 1848, they nominated General Zachary Taylor, a recent hero of battlefields in the Mexican-American War.

Despite his lack of solid political principles or any apparent passion for the job (just two years earlier, he'd said with apparent sincerity, "I am not and shall never be an aspirant for that honor"), Taylor won the election over Democratic candidate Lewis Cass.[27] In July 1850, he became the second straight Whig general-to-president who couldn't make it to the next election alive; Vice President Millard Fillmore took his place. Fillmore had risen to prominence in New

York's Anti-Mason Party, dedicated to exposing and opposing Free-
mason fraternal organizations, but switched allegiance to the Whigs
in the 1830s. In the first year and a half of the administration, intra-
party rivals had manipulated Taylor better than Fillmore did, leaving
him with little to do but preside over the Senate and stew over his
fate in a useless job.[28]

But as president he was prepared to avenge perceived slights.
Ahead of their expected dismissal, all the cabinet members whom
Fillmore had inherited from Taylor offered their resignations, which
were quickly accepted by the new president. He asked them to re-
main in place for one month. They agreed to stay—for one week.[29]
Fillmore would proceed to fire more previous political appointees
than any of his successors had; more than half of those at the State
Department, for example, had to find new jobs.[30]

The biggest development during Fillmore's presidency was the
Compromise of 1850. This set of bills admitted California to the
Union as a free state, allowed the organization of the Utah and New
Mexico territories without reference to slavery, resolved both the
Texas state boundary and the Lone Star Republic's remaining debt,
abolished the slave trade in the District of Columbia, and reaffirmed
the Fugitive Slave Law that required the return of slaves escaping
across state lines. Fillmore signed each bill, believing this package of
measures had fixed what he considered an annoying issue that kept
getting in the way of his other initiatives.[31]

The compromise bills delayed a war between the states, but at a
cost. They not only perpetuated slavery but split the Whigs further
apart, as most Northerners refused to abide by the Fugitive Slave
Law.[32] Congressional elections in November 1850 increased the
Democratic opposition's majorities in both the House and the Senate.[33] The rest of the president's term was so bad that the highlight
might have been the start of Commodore Matthew Perry's voyage
to Japan to open that country to American trade, even though he
didn't arrive until Fillmore left office.

NOT LONG AFTER rising to become the chief executive, Fillmore declared he wouldn't run again in the 1852 election. He reiterated that

in 1851.[34] But the trappings of presidential power and the pleas of his remaining party faithful convinced him to retract that pledge and make a late entry into the field of candidates.[35] He portrayed his about-face as a noble personal sacrifice for the good of the party and the country, and during the spring of that election year eight Whig state conventions endorsed him.[36]

As delegates gathered for what a leading historian of the era calls the "longest, most rancorous, and most debilitating Whig national convention ever to meet," the first tally had Fillmore in the lead. More than forty ballots later, he had dropped to second place, where he remained until the fifty-third and final ballot crushed his hopes.[37] Like a vinyl record stuck in a groove, the party instead nominated yet another former military man, General Winfield Scott, whom Democrat Franklin Pierce defeated both at the polls and, overwhelmingly, in the electoral college. That crushing loss delivered the coup de grâce to the Whig Party itself, which wouldn't compete nationally again.[38]

Fillmore didn't know when to give up. He ran for president again in 1856, returning to his nativist roots on the xenophobic "Know-Nothing" ticket that exploited anti-Catholic prejudices. He lost, badly, barely topping 20 percent of the overall vote and winning electoral votes from just one state.

For any president, the White House can seem a dark, lonely place. Franklin Pierce's unimpressive term saw the executive mansion at its darkest and loneliest.

He remains one of the lesser known American leaders, and for good reason. He managed primarily to exacerbate sectional tensions through the disastrous Kansas-Nebraska Act. Historians rank his presidency about as low as you can get, often among the bottom two or three. And yet, as dour as his administration was, Pierce's personal story is even more dismal. When you're having a bad day, reflect on the life of Franklin Pierce and hug someone.

Sent to a boarding school a dozen miles away as a child, Pierce grew so homesick that he walked all the way back home one Sunday when age twelve. His father, Revolutionary War general Benjamin Pierce, allowed his son a peaceful dinner before getting in the carriage to take young Frank back. They didn't get far. Along the rainy road, the general kicked him out and made him walk the rest of the way, alone.[39] Despite the tough love, Pierce developed into an affable and eloquent attorney and politician. Success in local and state positions in New Hampshire led him into the US House of Representatives and the Senate as a Democrat in the 1830s.

As leader of a New England regiment, he went off to war in Mexico in 1846 and rose to the rank of brigadier general. He left the conflict with a significant knee injury and a reputation for fainting during battle. Alcohol comforted him while in the field, giving his later political opponents an epic quip. Pierce, they laughed, was "the hero of many a well-fought bottle."[40] After the war, he brought his damaged knee and bruised ego back into legal work in New Hampshire.

His personal life brought sorrow. Pierce's first son, born in New Hampshire, didn't live long enough to be named. Epidemic typhus killed his second son before his fifth birthday. At least Benjamin, his third and last son, fared better. At age eleven in 1852, the boy they called "Bennie" even got to see his forty-eight-year-old father surprise most everyone by getting the Democratic nomination for president. And then Pierce beat Whig nominee Winfield Scott in the general election, buoyed into office in part by a fawning biography written by his friend Nathaniel Hawthorne, already a best-selling author with blockbusters like *The Scarlet Letter* and *The House of the Seven Gables*.[41]

Pierce's good fortune in the campaign didn't last through the transition. The president-elect, his wife, and young Bennie attended a relative's funeral in Boston and then visited with family in nearby Andover for a few days. Proceeding by rail back to New Hampshire, their single-car train suddenly lurched off the track, flipped over, and tumbled into a field. The adults suffered only minor injuries, but they were devastated by what they witnessed—the lifeless, crushed body of Bennie, whose head was all but severed.[42] Pierce's wife's long-standing melancholia developed into years of severe depression. She spent much of her husband's time in office either trying to speak to Bennie via letters—and, some claim, séances—or not talking at all; certainly not much to the president himself.[43]

Pierce took to wearing black gloves, against the style of the times, and became increasingly religious. The struggle within festered. He had sought the presidency in large part to improve Bennie's life prospects; now, as Pierce biographer Roy Franklin Nichols put it, the job seemed less an honorable duty than "an impending horror." It's hard to disagree with Nichols that "much of the difficulty which he experienced in administration during the next four years may be attributed to this terrible tragedy and its long-continued after effects."[44]

PIERCE'S EARLY CHOICES show a lack of deep reflection. He didn't seem to think through cabinet selections well, because he managed to annoy even leaders within his own party such as Senator Stephen Douglas.[45] Several prominent Democrats, in fact, bailed out and joined the emerging Republican Party instead.

His wife's condition and, perhaps, Pierce's own may have even set in motion a series of events leading to his acceptance of Douglas's Kansas-Nebraska Act, which opened those two territories to the option of slavery and, in so doing, drove violent pro- and anti-slavery zealots to marshal forces in what became known as "Bleeding Kansas."

Mayhem erupted not only in Kansas but also in the US Capitol, where representatives attended sessions armed with pistols and a senator was beaten mercilessly with a cane.[46] Pierce rejected any personal responsibility for the wholly predictable violence and death provoked by the ill-advised legislation he had signed into law.

Nonetheless, the law's effects weakened Pierce politically and helped lead to his undoing. On one side of the party, Douglas undercut Pierce's bid for renomination by quietly building support among pro-slavery Democrats in the South and West. "Shrewd, cunning Douglas!" commented one anti-Nebraska editor. "Poor, deluded, duped Pierce!"[47] On the other side, Pierce's own ambassador in London, former secretary of state James Buchanan, used his absence from the United States to duck any blame for the Kansas-Nebraska Act and lift his own candidacy.[48] Pierce for some reason wanted to stay in the White House, and the Democratic convention briefly gave him hope. The first ballot placed him within reach of front-runner Buchanan. But he never picked up strength; the energy for him just wasn't there within his own party. Fifteen ballots later, the president's ambition died and he threw in the towel. He gave the supporters he did have to Douglas to try to stop Buchanan's momentum,[49] but failed at that, too.

Being removed from contention by his own party stung Pierce. Buchanan, the nominee, didn't even bother to seek the incumbent's aid in the campaign.[50] Pierce would return to the bottle in a vain effort to drown his personal and professional sorrows, supposedly telling a friend, "There is nothing left to do but get drunk."[51] Tuberculosis took his wife's life in 1863. Six years later, Pierce died of cirrhosis—helped along, perhaps, by the heavy guilt since Bennie's death—without a single family member present.[52]

WHEREAS PIERCE HAD emerged from relative obscurity to take power as a dark-horse candidate in 1852, James Buchanan had been preparing most of his life for the nation's highest office. The Pennsylvanian's impressive political career—state legislator, US representative, ambassador to Russia, US senator, secretary of state, ambassador to the United Kingdom—contrasts sharply with the disaster his presidency became, such that by the end of it he, too, was unceremoniously dumped by his party.

President Polk had asked Buchanan to lead the State Department, which he did studiously and ably, though complaining most of the time. "I am an overworked man," he wrote to a friend, describing the job as requiring ten to fifteen hours of work each day. "I have not read thirty consecutive pages in any book since I came to the Department of State."[53] He and Polk respected each other's skills but grated on each other personally.[54] Not all Democrats warmed to Buchanan; party founder Andrew Jackson called him "an inept busybody."[55] But as a Northerner who managed to overcome his dislike of slavery enough to support Southerners' right to share in new western territories, he attracted many supporters for the 1848 presidential nomination before ultimately declining their appeals for him to enter the fray.[56] In 1852, most of Polk's former cabinet rallied behind Buchanan, who led the Democratic convention balloting by a wide margin at one point but lost to Pierce. [57]

The party turned that around four years later and picked Buchanan. The opposition Whigs had collapsed and offered no opponent to Buchanan, but two other parties did: the new Republicans (who put forward former army officer and adventurer John Frémont) and the Know-Nothings (who chose former president Millard Fillmore). Frémont and Fillmore gave Buchanan a greater challenge than expected, together winning almost 55 percent of the popular vote, but the electoral vote elevated Buchanan anyway.

His administration was maladroit. "The night is departing," the new president had told friends. "To secure this, all we of the North have to do is permit our southern neighbors to manage their own domestic affairs, as they permit us to manage ours."[58] That didn't prove a recipe for success. Buchanan, for example, believed the Supreme Court's Dred Scott ruling, confirming slaves as property and banning federal regulations of slavery, had resolved the slavery discussion. Instead, it inflamed the North.

Back at Buchanan's inauguration ball, the Russian ambassador had said to the French ambassador's wife that Washington in early 1857 resembled Paris just before the Revolution of 1830, where, at a similar ball, the French king had been told, "Sire, we are dancing on a volcano."[59] As war approached, Buchanan opined that neither Congress nor the president had any constitutional authority to compel Southern states to stay in the Union.

BUCHANAN HAD ANNOUNCED early on that one term would be enough for him, but many inside and outside the Democratic Party doubted he meant it.[60] In December 1858, his annual message to Congress sure sounded like a man setting the stage to run again. He wrote about pulling through the worst of the Kansas debacle, weathering a financial panic, getting the United Kingdom to renounce the right to search US vessels, and making progress on commercial treaties in the Far East. He faced a Congress, however, uninterested in working with him on much of anything. In fact, legislators didn't pass even routine treasury bills, much less take on more ambitious programs or make any substantive efforts to prevent the pending national crisis over slavery and secession.[61]

In October 1859, it got worse. John Brown and a group of abolitionist insurgents captured the armory at Harper's Ferry, then in Virginia, hoping to spark a slave revolt. Federal forces defeated them, but the incident drew even more attention to the ethical vacuum of slavery, bolstering the fortunes of the Republican Party and dividing Democrats.[62] Congress essentially ignored the president's message about the raid, which included his continued deference to an increasingly dysfunctional legislature.[63] Buchanan dithered, writing to President Polk's widow, "I am now in my sixty-ninth year and am heartily tired of my position as President." He let anti-slavery Democrats leave to join the Republican Party, saw Douglas expand his following among remaining Northern Democrats, and watched Southern Democrats like Jefferson Davis lay the foundation for their own pro-slavery party.[64]

Buchanan's friends nevertheless thought he was the man for the country's moment and planted stories in the press that he had developed interest in receiving the nomination.[65] Although he denied the claims, everything in his more than three decades in politics suggested that a call for him to step in to save his party and his country would gain his cooperation. He remained oddly optimistic well into 1860, telling his colleagues, "The present issue is transitory and will speedily pass away."[66] Ultimately, the Democratic Party couldn't settle on a single candidate for president in 1860, so Douglas and John Breckinridge both ran.

Even after the Democrats lost to Republican Abraham Lincoln, Buchanan firmly stood his ground on, well, not standing on firm ground. He told Congress in December 1860 that secession was "neither more nor less than revolution," and therefore unconstitutional. But he added that the federal government had no power to "coerce a State into submission."[67] He had boxed himself into a corner from which he could only helplessly watch events unfold, justifying the Democrats' desire to remove him from the White House no matter the cost.

F OR MOST OF his war-torn first term, Abraham Lincoln's reelection looked unlikely. Even after a group of disappointed Republicans split off, held their own convention, and put forward a separate nominee, a secret movement arose within the mainline Republican Party to remove Lincoln from the ticket in 1864 and "concentrate the union strength on some one candidate who commands the confidence of the country, even by a new nomination if necessary."[68]

Lincoln had appealed for loyalty in a typically folksy way. "I have not permitted myself, gentlemen, to conclude that I am the best man in the country," he said after his renomination in June 1864, "but I am reminded, in this connection, of a story of an old Dutch farmer, who remarked to a companion once that 'it was not best to swap horses when crossing streams.'"[69] Disgruntled officials remained unconvinced and began grassroots work to engineer a removal from within. They circulated a call for the party faithful to convene as needed in September: "I think we have a pretty good start in New York and the N. E. States, Pa., Del., and Ohio and Michigan," wrote one. "If a break be made there, it compels Lincoln's surrender."[70]

Only the Union army's battlefield successes in the autumn of 1864 prompted a surge in support for the incumbent's "National Union" ticket with Democrat Andrew Johnson. And then, on Election Day, the American people (as in 1812) chose not to remove the president during wartime.

Lincoln's death in April 1865 brought to office Johnson, who was so spectacularly undermined while president that he earns a special section of his own in the next chapter. After that, Ulysses Grant served two full terms. Rutherford Hayes served but one, repeating Polk's steadfast, credible renunciation of a second term from the very start.[71] "He had announced at the time of his election that in no circumstances would he accept a re-nomination," wrote longtime White House staffer William Crook, who claimed he'd heard Hayes say, "I believe the second-term idea is opposed to the principles of Republican government."[72] His desire to step aside sat well with party leaders, one of whom declared that Hayes "couldn't be elected if no one ran against him."[73]

That left the Republican nomination in 1880 wide open. James Garfield rose to the top of the ticket as a compromise during a stalemated convention. By then, the party had split into two factions: the Stalwarts, who looked back fondly on the glory days of party patronage and pocket-lining during the long Grant administration, and the anti-corruption Half-Breeds, so named because Stalwarts considered them less than fully Republican. Garfield, the first sitting member of Congress to win the White House, affiliated more with the Half-Breeds. And he looked to have a pretty good chance at reelection, too, based on the early performance of his administration. But death stole his chance, elevating to the presidency the least likely man yet to occupy the Oval Office.

THE AMERICAN PUBLIC can be remarkably forgiving of its presidents. Think of Bill Clinton. Despite lying about his sexual relationship with a White House intern and getting impeached by the House of Representatives, he left the presidency with a higher approval rating than he had upon entering.

More than a century before Clinton, Chester Arthur seemed worthy of similar absolution. Never had a man brought such low public expectations with him into the office and then gone on to redeem himself so much while in it. The turnaround was admirable, even historic. Yet Arthur failed to convince his own party to renominate him.

ARTHUR HAD COME into the vice presidency as a surprise, never before elected to any office and woefully unprepared for a national one. He was a party hack, both a recipient and dispenser of New York Republican patronage, most often at the behest of the party's flamboyant power broker, Senator Roscoe Conkling. "As a politician," one author notes, "he bore the same relationship to a statesman as a mechanic does to a scientist or a printer to a poet."[74] Arthur, as collector of the Port of New York for almost eight years, controlled many jobs and much money, which he used to support the era's dirty political spoils system. As such, he planted his roots firmly in the Stalwart camp of Republicans, who managed very well under lax oversight during President Grant's eight-year administration. But the less Stalwart-inclined Hayes, who succeeded Grant in 1877, fired Arthur in July 1878.

At the party convention in 1880, the vice presidential nomination surprisingly came to Arthur, in an attempt to ensure Stalwart support in the general election.

"The Ohio men," Arthur informed his mentor Conkling, "have offered me the Vice Presidency."

"Well, sir, you should drop it as you would a red-hot shoe from the forge," came Conkling's reply. Arthur explained he was there to consult, not to take orders, spurring Conkling to blurt out, "What, sir, you think of accepting?"

"The office of Vice President is a greater honor than I ever dreamed of attaining," Arthur admitted. "In a calmer moment you will look at this differently."

"If you wish for my favor and my respect you will contemptuously decline it."

"Senator Conkling," Arthur said proudly, "I shall accept the nomination and I shall carry with me the majority of the delegation." Conkling stormed off.[75]

Arthur thus began as vice president without the support of the man most responsible for putting him in the position to be considered for that job. Also, no vice president, before or since, has faced the burden Arthur bore four months later. Not only was the president shot and killed, but the assassin had endorsed Arthur after his foul deed.[76]

While doctors tried to keep Garfield alive, dire predictions commenced, especially as Arthur hunkered down in New York City with none other than Conkling.[77] Former president Hayes wrote in his diary, "The death of the president at this time would be a national calamity." Another Republican asked, "Are we not passing through greater peril than we can comprehend? Is there any safety but prompt resignation of Arthur? . . . How fatal a mistake was made in Chicago in the nomination for the second place. The prayer for poor Garfield is *universal*."[78]

As official White House business stacked up week after week, Garfield held on for eighty days. Arthur, who had openly lamented his situation upon hearing about the shooting, began impressing some skeptics. He managed to avoid looking eager for the presidency by firmly refusing a request in late August from some cabinet members to step in for Garfield at their meetings.[79] The press noticed his forbearance.

BY THE TIME Garfield finally died on September 19, 1881, prompting his vice president to make his way to Washington as the twenty-first president of the United States, Arthur was increasingly seen less like an evil and energetic party boss and more like a well-mannered gentleman who'd just gotten into something beyond his limited abilities.[80]

In his brief inaugural address, Arthur reassured the nation with some of the best words of his presidency: "Men may die, but the fabrics of our free institutions remain unshaken."[81] He also gained points early on by distancing himself from Conkling, who had quit his Senate seat several weeks before the shooting. The new president offered his former patron no post through which he could control jobs and money, only a Supreme Court position, which Conkling refused.[82]

Most importantly given that the public had viewed him as the poster child for corruption, Arthur used his first major address to support civil service reform. He vowed not to remove any competent federal official on a personal or partisan whim, and he stuck to that pledge.[83] When Congress passed the Pendleton Civil Service Reform Act in early 1883, he signed it and later enforced its provisions.[84] Although the law left some 90 percent of federal government positions unprotected from political hirings and firings and thus remained one small step for reform, it was one giant leap for Chet Arthur.[85] The Civil Service Commission brought into existence through the law later tipped its hat to the president, noting,

"Our function cannot be successfully discharged without the constant, firm, and friendly support of the President. That support has never failed."[86] His single largest failure was probably his inability to dispose of the federal budget *surplus*—not bad for a man almost universally seen as the most ill-prepared president the nation had yet produced.

Many pundits and much of the public seemed to appreciate Arthur's administration. Mark Twain, for example, wrote, "I am but one in 55,000,000; still, in the opinion of this one-fifty-five-millionth of the country's population, it would be hard to better President Arthur's Administration."[87] But most Republicans, who controlled his renomination chances, disagreed. The president had alienated many of them by vetoing the pork project–saturated river and harbor bill.[88] And his commitment to prudent civil service reforms, while annoying Stalwart Republicans affiliated with former president Grant and Roscoe Conkling, didn't go far enough to convince former senator James Blaine of Maine and other reformers they should forgive his past dark deeds.[89]

As the presidential election year of 1884 began, Arthur had fallen into a vicious cycle. The lack of robust support from within his own party depressed him. His lack of energy, in turn, encouraged Republicans to look to others for the next nomination. This slow spiral of personal lethargy and political drift may have started way back with his horror at having to replace the respected Garfield, but it certainly grew worse with the diagnosis in 1882 of a fatal kidney condition as the cause of his frequent illnesses, irritability, and nausea.[90] While it was "natural that President Arthur should have wanted the nomination," wrote White House aide William Crook, the incumbent put forth "singularly little effort" to obtain it, refusing even to meet with one prominent Republican who reportedly stood ready to deliver votes that would secure his reelection bid.[91]

The party convention in June began with the president in second place behind Blaine.[92] Arthur refused to allow exchanges of cash during the convention, rejected an offer to gain eighteen delegates as a trade for giving the postmaster general slot to their preferred man, and declined opportunities to dole out federal jobs to family members of other delegates leaning his way.[93] As a result, his own party swapped Arthur out for the popular Blaine, who went on to lose to Grover Cleveland in the general election.

The president's last major act in office was merely ceremonial, dedicating the completed Washington Monument in February 1885. Before the following year was out, he'd be dead at age fifty-seven.[94] He wouldn't have made it through even half of his term had he been nominated by his party and elected by a forgiving general public.

FOR MORE THAN fourscore years afterward, parties gave incumbent presidents who wanted to run for another term their wish. Some of these were actually close calls: Republican William Howard Taft nearly lost his renomination bid in 1912 to his predecessor-on-a-comeback, Theodore Roosevelt, and prominent Democrats in 1948 actively considered ditching Harry Truman.

But then, finally, a president eligible for and wanting his party's renomination didn't get there. Oddly, it was a man who in the previous few years had driven the most ambitious economic and social program since FDR's New Deal.

LYNDON JOHNSON TOOK over for the murdered John Kennedy in November 1963 and went on to crush Barry Goldwater in the 1964 presidential election. He employed both the late president's legacy and his own monumental powers of persuasion to produce the body of legislation collectively called the "Great Society," which Doris Kearns Goodwin describes as "more laws, more houses, more medical services, more jobs to more people."[95]

The good times didn't last long. By September 1966, societal tensions at home and the lack of a visible end game for the conflict in Vietnam had reduced Democratic support enough for him to tell an advisor, "My own party is turned against me, and the Republicans are chiming in. We probably need a fresh face."[96] Public approval of Johnson's handling of the war dropped to 40 percent by March 1967.[97] Students liked him even less; they announced they would shut down any presidential attempt to speak publicly in a big city, anywhere in the country. Even the Secret Service saw a dramatic rise in the number of letters threatening Johnson's life.[98] "How is it possible," he would ask, "that all these people could be so ungrateful to me after I had given them so much?"[99]

The nation's economic problems exacerbated the president's political ones. The Great Society and the escalation in Vietnam didn't come cheap; the budget deficit looked poised to approach $20 billion in 1968.[100] The real tipping point for Johnson's chances at renomination came on January 30 with the Tet Offensive by the North Vietnamese and Viet Cong. This wave of attacks against both military and civilian targets exposed the vulnerability of the highly militarized South Vietnam, and Tet convinced an increasing number of Americans the continued escalation of a distant war had not worked. Johnson couldn't hide his disgust. "I did not expect the enemy effort to have the impact on American thinking that it achieved," he later wrote. "Hanoi must have been delighted; it was exactly the reaction they sought."[101] The Tet Offensive sent the president's approval ratings into a tailspin—50 percent of respondents polled soon afterward disapproved of his Vietnam policy and only 35 percent expressed approval.[102]

He nevertheless started the race toward his second election as the front-runner, winning the first Democratic primary in New Hampshire on March 12 over anti-war candidate Eugene McCarthy. Much like the Tet Offensive itself, however, the Johnson victory in New Hampshire felt empty because McCarthy finished much stronger than expected. Smelling blood in the water, Robert Kennedy, with whom Johnson had a particularly toxic relationship, joined the race against his own party's leader within a week. The incumbent called this "the final straw," telling Goodwin, "The thing I feared from the first day of my Presidency was actually coming true."[103]

"I DO NOT BELIEVE that I should devote an hour or a day of my time to any personal partisan causes or to any other duties other than the awesome duties of this office—the Presidency of your country," LBJ told a national audience on the evening of March 31, 1968. "Accordingly, I shall not seek, and I will not accept, the nomination of my party for another term as your President."[104] Johnson appears to have expected the party to beg him to stay. Instead, Democrats took his statement as an excuse to move on.

Despite his unintended swipe at Abraham Lincoln and Franklin Roosevelt, who both sought wartime renominations *and* reelections, Johnson garnered almost universal praise for his declared intent to deal with Vietnam at the expense of more time in power. Anti-war Democrats celebrated their apparent triumph. Student activists for the first time had helped kick a president out. Johnson admitted that night to a friend, "I'm tired of feeling rejected by the American people."[105]

His health certainly played a role in his decision. A reporter familiar with Johnson's earlier energetic visage and mannerisms recalls being "shocked" at the president's appearance when he saw him again in late March 1968: "Now he seemed exhausted. His eyes, behind the gold-rimmed eyeglasses, were not only nested in lines and wrinkles, but pouched in sockets blue with a permanent weariness."[106] Johnson saw it himself. "I frankly did not believe in 1968," he wrote in his memoirs, "that I could survive another four years of the long hours and unremitting tensions I had just gone through."[107] His prediction almost hit the mark; he died in 1973 just two days after his second full term would have ended. Although he had always pushed through physical and political struggles before, perhaps the knowledge that his male relatives often died relatively young finally got to him.[108]

His actions before and after the announcement, however, suggest that he hoped Democrats would fail to rally around any of their candidates, each of which Johnson held serious reservations about, and beg him to jump back in to save the party and the country.[109] Back in the fall of 1967, Johnson had encouraged top political advisors to strategize for the upcoming campaign.[110] Even Kennedy's candidacy announcement on March 16, two weeks before Johnson bowed out, didn't stop the president from prodding aides to rack and stack prominent Democrats in each state, organize campus groups, and keep close tabs on convention delegate counts.[111] Several weeks after Johnson's renunciation, his public approval ratings rebounded—up to 49 percent in favor versus just 40 percent against. Assessments of the president's Vietnam performance also flipped by May, with approval of his actions overcoming disapproval.[112]

Robert Kennedy's assassination in June 1968 renewed Johnson's curiosity about reentering the race.[113] Some surveys showed Vice President Hubert Humphrey, the likely Democratic nominee without LBJ in the fight, sixteen percentage points behind Nixon—a sharp contrast with Johnson's six-point *lead* over the Republican nominee in a straw poll. Humphrey increasingly drifted away from the president's Vietnam policy as the party prepared for what looked to be a contentious convention in Chicago, making Johnson even more twitchy about leaving the party in his vice president's hands. He began to schedule his public announcements more carefully and ensure that his press office disseminated two good-news stories every day, exactly what a jump-started political campaign would suggest.[114]

IF JOHNSON WANTED to save his party from imploding and get another electoral vindication from the Democrats and the American people, he would need to be ready to respond at a moment's notice to the party faithful's call for their former hero.

His special assistant Joseph Califano says that as the convention began it was apparent to those closest to the president that "LBJ hoped, and probably anticipated, that the convention delegates in Chicago would offer to draft him to be their party's candidate." Chicago mayor Richard Daley and a senior White House aide on the ground there agreed that a word from the president would spark an impressive wave for the incumbent. Johnson hesitated, wanting a clear signal from his party before committing.[115]

One senior advisor says the president imagined the delegates botching the convention so badly that "he would go in on a flying carpet and be acclaimed as the nominee."[116] In fact, Secret Service agent Clint Hill recalls Johnson bringing two speechwriters with him to his ranch in Texas, where he was watching the convention. Hill and other agents prepped an aircraft to be ready to move the president at a moment's notice. They identified its arrival point in

Chicago, selected a motorcade route there, and plotted a concealed entry into the amphitheater hosting the convention. At one point, an agent contacted Hill from the ranch to tell him Johnson, after speaking with Humphrey by phone, had immediately ordered his helicopter started. The Secret Service agents suspected the president was going to Chicago to claim the nomination; he actually went to see his daughter in Austin.[117]

The Chicago convention remains one of the ugliest in modern history, with the disagreements inside the hall paralleled by street violence outside. The Johnson draft never came. Humphrey won the nomination but lost the election to Nixon. The Democratic percentage of the popular vote dropped so much in 1968 compared to Johnson's landslide victory in 1964 that it still stands as the largest major party vote swing in American history. "I am convinced," Johnson later reflected, "that if I had run again I would have been reelected."[118] Instead, the man who had spent his whole life seeking to amass more power left his destiny in the hands of his party, which didn't want him on the ticket enough to ask him to reconsider.

Whether Johnson truly hoped to stay out of the next election or, more likely, simply miscalculated his remaining popularity within the fracturing Democratic Party may never be known. Even one of Johnson's keenest observers admits, "It is impossible to find your way through the labyrinth of Johnson's mind."[119]

Chapter Two

Undermined by Opponents
or Subordinates

While the president still had power to make appointments,
the Senate could, and frequently did, reject them. While
he was still commander in chief of the army and navy,
he had pledged himself to abide by the will of Congress.
And while he could still veto obnoxious legislation, his
vetoes were routinely overridden.[1]

—HANS TREFOUSSE
DESCRIBING ANDREW JOHNSON

THE PRESIDENT OF the United States was both a racist and a very difficult man to get along with.

He routinely called blacks inferior. He bluntly stated that no matter how much progress they made, they must remain so. He openly called critics disloyal, even treasonous. He liberally threw insults like candy during public speeches. He rudely ignored answers he didn't like. He regularly put other people into positions they didn't want to be in, then blamed them when things went sour. His own bodyguard later called him "destined to conflict," a man who "found it impossible to conciliate or temporize."[2]

But the nation's politicians simply had to interact with Andrew Johnson, for he had become the legitimate, constitutionally ordained chief executive upon Abraham Lincoln's death by assassination. Their path for managing this choleric man reveals that a president need not be kicked out of office to be removed from power.

Johnson's vice presidency remains historically unique. For his 1864 reelection bid, Lincoln had dumped his first-term vice president, Hannibal Hamlin. To appeal to non-Republicans and show he wasn't just a Northern leader, the president instead ran on a new "National Union" ticket. He picked a lifelong Democrat—the former Tennessee governor, US senator, and military governor of his home state—because he had been the *only* senator from eleven Southern states to stand with the Union in 1861 instead of walking out.

Johnson paid a price for sticking with the Union; the confederate government in Tennessee designated him an "alien enemy" of the state and confined his wife, daughters, and youngest son to the family home in Greeneville. When he'd served as the state's military governor from 1862 until his inauguration as vice president, Tennesseans escalated, forcing the family out of the house.[3]

The new vice president couldn't have started his term much worse. Feeling ill, he threw down three glasses of whiskey right before his swearing-in ceremony and inaugural speech. "I need all the strength I can get," he told Hamlin. The audience noticed, and not just because Johnson's face had turned bright red and his planned five-minute address stretched to three times longer. Shouting, gesticulating wildly, stumbling over his words, and shaking his fists, the incoming vice president went into stump-speech mode, declaring violently that he was a man of the people and that Tennessee had never left the Union. Hamlin tried to shut him up and pull him away, but failed in both. Johnson stammered and had to ask assembled officials nearby who the secretary of the navy was. During the spectacle, the attorney general leaned over and labeled it "a wretched mess" for a colleague, who in turn said, "Johnson is either drunk or crazy."

He finally stopped his meandering and allowed Hamlin to administer the oath of office. Unfortunately, he bungled that, too, stumbling through the words and adding his own commentary along the way. After putting his lips to the Bible he'd just sworn on and yelling, "I kiss this Book in the face of my nation of the United States!" officials moved him on and asked someone else, on his behalf, to perform the new vice president's traditional duty and administer oaths to the new senators.[4] Lincoln took it all in stride and vouched for Johnson, denying he was a drunkard while acknowledging his "bad slip." Johnson did the noble thing and kept himself mostly out of the public eye for the next ten days to let the scandal subside.[5] That, combined with the tradition of the times that presidents didn't consider their vice presidents part of the inner circle, meant the two men didn't interact much in the six weeks between inauguration and Lincoln's assassination on April 14.

Johnson thus started his time in office without a strong sense of exactly how Lincoln planned to ensure the final surrender of all Confederate forces in the Civil War and rebuild the war-torn nation. Although Congress had already put in place some features of the post-war period that would serve as flash points with the new administration—like the Freedmen's Bureau, charged primarily with feeding and caring for former slaves—Johnson came to the top job with a very different conception of post-war reunification. In his mind, because states shouldn't have left the Union, they never actually did. Without current representation from those states, he reckoned, the federal government had little right after the war to do much of anything in the South; they urgently needed new non-Confederate governments there.[6] His vision, of course, clashed with the so-called Radical Republicans in Congress, intent on reconstructing the South in order to guarantee the freedoms of those who had been enslaved for so long.

Johnson rankled most legislators, and the vast majority of Northerners, almost immediately. He paroled leading members of the Confederate cabinet, up to and including the former vice president.[7] He engineered constitutional changes in Southern states, appointed governors there, and allowed their legislatures to meet. Dominated by secessionists, these governments passed "black codes," allowing slavery in all but name to continue in many areas.[8]

He also made his racist views clear in statements like this one to the commissioner of public buildings: "Everyone would, and *must* admit, that the white race was superior to the black, and that while we ought to do our best to bring them . . . up to our present level, that, in doing so, we should, at the same time raise our own intellectual status so that the relative position of the two races would be the same."[9]

"Is THERE NO WAY," declared leading radical senator Thaddeus Stevens of Pennsylvania just months after Johnson's inauguration, "to arrest the insane course of the President in Washington?" He even mused that by taking actions more properly lying with Congress, the new president was setting the stage to be "crowned king."[10] Leading legislators urged the president to call Congress into a special session, or at least delay controversial moves until it was scheduled to convene in December.[11] Andrew Johnson obstinately ignored them. By the winter of 1865–1866, the president had proved himself "already more disposed to be the political partisan of the Southerners than the ally of those who had elected him," according to a confidant of General Ulysses Grant.[12]

This stubbornness and refusal to cooperate with even moderate Republicans escalated once Congress came back into session in December. Johnson vetoed both a civil rights bill, designed to fight back the dreaded black codes, and another measure to expand the functions of the Freedmen's Bureau. His message to Congress about the latter veto included condescending language, like urging legislators to take "more mature considerations."[13] The vetoes enraged Capitol Hill, especially the author of the bills, to whom Johnson had raised no objections when he'd sought the president's opinions during the drafting process.[14] The legislative branch, as a consequence, did something unprecedented in American history on a major piece of legislation. They overturned a presidential veto. Then they did it again. Ultimately, they turned back the president's rejections of bills a stunning *fifteen* times—still a record, even though Johnson served a shorter term than most presidents.[15] The Civil Rights Act's veto override in the House prompted a spontaneous outburst of applause among both representatives and spectators; the Speaker found it impossible to restore order for several minutes.[16]

Also in early 1866, a congressional Joint Committee on Reconstruction developed a constitutional amendment, which presidents have no power to either approve or deny. It sought to prohibit states from depriving citizens of fundamental rights or equal protection under the law and to rescind the constitutional formula by which states had gained the benefit of additional representation in Congress for slaves within their borders, without letting those slaves vote. Both houses of Congress passed it in June, but behind the scenes Johnson obstructed its ratification. The measure would ultimately become the Fourteenth Amendment in 1868.[17] The president also saw his judicial appointment powers curtailed. When a Supreme Court vacancy came up, Congress eliminated the seat rather than confirm Johnson's nominee. As a hedge against a potential future Johnson appointment, they went ahead and legislated in advance that the next high court vacancy, too, would not require filling.[18]

Johnson in August and September tried to rally public support around him in a multistate nineteen-day road trip, during which he gave more than one hundred speeches. Typically frosty audiences greeted the president, often drawing him into unseemly shouting matches or forcing him to cut short his visit.[19] In Bloomington, Illinois, one heckler yelled that traitors weren't welcome in the land of Lincoln; the ensuing uproar made it impossible for Johnson to complete his planned speech.[20]

"For the first time in the history of our country," wrote the New York *Independent*, "the people have been witness to the mortifying spectacle of the President going from town to town, accompanied by the prominent members of the Cabinet, on an electioneering raid, denouncing his opponents, bandying epithets with men in the crowd, and praising himself and his policies. Such a humiliating exhibition has never before been seen, nor anything even approaching to it."[21]

FROM SUMMER 1866 on, both General Grant and War Secretary Edwin Stanton were resisting—often all but openly defying—Johnson's orders from within the executive branch.

The president had declared the Southern rebellion over, seemingly ending the army's primacy over local law enforcement there. But Grant sent confidential instructions that commanders should continue martial law as needed and resist any presidential attempt to curtail the Freedmen's Bureau's actions.[22] In October, Grant twice refused Johnson's request that he join a diplomatic delegation to Mexico—the president's ploy to get the war hero out of the way. Then, in a full cabinet meeting, Johnson pretended that Grant had never objected to going to Mexico by having the secretary of state read to the general detailed instructions for the diplomatic mission. When Johnson condescendingly asked the attorney general to lecture Grant on the duty to obey presidential orders, the general stood and declared, "I am an American citizen, and eligible to any office to which any American is eligible. I am an officer of the army, and bound to obey your military orders. But this is a civil office, a purely diplomatic duty that you offer me, and I cannot be compelled to undertake it. . . . No power on earth can compel me to do it."[23]

Grant feared being away from Washington if, as he thought increasingly likely, the beleaguered president were to decide that disbanding Congress and using force to take total control of the government offered him the best way through the impasse.[24] Grant confidant Adam Badeau recorded that the general, while looking to the general public like a faithful follower of Johnson and his policies, "was in reality doing more than all the country besides to thwart Johnson's designs."[25]

Stanton, despite his steadfast opposition to the president's approach, stubbornly remained in Johnson's cabinet because he felt he could delay or even prevent some of Johnson's worst actions.[26] The secretary favored Reconstruction legislation in early 1867 that provided for military government in the South, which was passed over the president's veto.[27] He watched as successive bills from Capitol Hill received presidential vetoes, but became law anyway over Johnson's objections.[28] "The situation was unprecedented in the history of the country," wrote Badeau. "A Cabinet Minister and the General of the Army were doing their utmost to thwart the President. . . .

They then more than once discussed the means by which they too could apparently obey the directions of a superior and yet neutralize his intent and purpose."[29]

Particularly distressing to Grant, Stanton, and many others around them was the increasing violence in the South between emboldened former Confederates and former slaves asserting their rights. Already by the end of 1866, the president "became, if not treasonable in intent, yet unpatriotic in action," Badeau noted, probably representing Grant's views. "He fostered a spirit that engendered massacre, and afterward protected the evil-doers. He spoke, both with Grant in private and openly to the public, as if the Congress elected by the faithful States was an illegal body. He suggested to men's minds that he might be plotting to allow the Southerners to return to their places in spite of the North."[30]

Johnson faced a dilemma. He couldn't easily get rid of Grant, the most popular living American, who had won respect even from Southerners for his gracious treatment of Robert E. Lee after the Confederate general's surrender at Appomattox Court House in 1865. Plus, Congress wrote language into the military appropriations bill for 1867–1868 that both denied the president's right to directly control the military—all orders had to go through the general of the army (Grant)—and prevented Grant's demotion without the Senate's consent. Stanton also gained protection from Congress in the form of the Tenure of Office Act of February 1867, a constitutionally unsound measure that nevertheless prohibited presidential removal of certain executive branch officers, including Stanton, unless the Senate agreed.[31]

Johnson's veto of the Tenure of Office Act got the usual treatment from Congress: a prompt override. "He is of no account," one senator said bluntly. "We pay no attention anymore to what he says."[32] Virginia's Republican governor wrote to a prominent congressman, "I fear there will be no peace in the country as long as Johnson is in the Presidential Chair."[33] Secretary of the Navy Gideon Welles reported in June 1867 that the president was "nervous and apprehensive," all but trapped in the White House "in constant dread of impeachment."[34]

BUT JOHNSON JUST couldn't leave things well enough alone.

After suspending Stanton until Congress reconvened, the president ended up firing his war secretary outright in February 1868. Stanton refused to leave his office—literally moving in and hunkering down, day and night, for the duration of the crisis[35]—giving representatives the excuse they'd been hoping for to try to kick the president out of office. Johnson that same month became the first president to be impeached by the House.[36]

The failure of the Radical Republicans to convict him, however, didn't stop Congress from keeping Johnson boxed in. He remained something short of a full chief executive during his final ten months in office, with effective restrictions on his power locked in. General Grant, by this time a candidate for the presidential election that November, believed that "Johnson had been taught a lesson which he would not forget."[37] Johnson's leading biographer calls him a "president in limbo."[38]

During the trial itself, Congress had passed a new Reconstruction bill, which became law when Johnson didn't even bother to veto it. He did, however, issue a veto against a bill denying appeal rights in some cases, but Congress overrode that.[39] Legislators in June also rejected new presidential vetoes, on the very days they were issued, against bills readmitting several Southern states with new constitutions. The following month it happened again on bills excluding electoral votes of states that had not yet been reorganized and extending the Freedmen's Bureau another year.[40]

"Somehow I expected that there would be a change in Mr. Johnson's position after his victory over the Radicals," wrote the president's bodyguard, William Crook, who had an inside view of the whole situation. "If I had thought of it, I might have realized that the two-thirds majority was still against him. The only difference was that when they passed measures over the President's veto it was without debate. There was no longer the need for discussion."[41] Senators also turned down Johnson's nominees for lesser diplomatic posts so often that, exasperated, he announced he would only put forward a prospective nominee able to prove to him in advance that confirmation would come.[42]

One power he still held was that of the federal pardon. And pardon he did, issuing many more of them than all other presidents to that point, combined—overwhelmingly for those who participated in the rebellion against the Union. Johnson even pardoned a few of the men convicted in the conspiracy to kill President Lincoln.[43] He anticipated his old party would show some appreciation for the pain he had caused to Republicans by giving him the presidential spot on the Democratic ticket for the coming election against Grant. The party convention dashed those hopes by instead choosing Horatio Seymour, a man who didn't even want the nomination.[44]

WHY WAIT UNTIL the end of a term to remove a president? Biding time until voters can reject an unpopular or unfit president at the ballot box, or until party members can withhold a renomination, means enduring a bad situation. As seen in the Johnson case, those around the president who perceive a danger to the public—or, less nobly, to their own personal interests—can effectively remove the chief executive in place.

Enemies and allies alike use methods ranging from the deft to the downright unsavory to undermine presidents' authority. At one end of the spectrum, this is merely the centuries-old Washington game of slowing or blocking a political agenda you disagree with. When taken to the extreme, however, this rises to the level of insubordination, if within the executive branch, or constitutionally questionable infringement, if from other branches of government. You don't have to formally eject someone from the White House if you can undercut the rightful duties of the office, as several presidents have discovered the hard way.

EVEN THE FIRST chief executive fought attempts to rein in his powers. George Washington's second term stagnated as Alexander Hamilton, who exerted great influence on the president, and his followers clashed openly with Thomas Jefferson and his partisans. Washington protected the powers of the office when James Madison and others in the House of Representatives tried to force the executive branch to hand over treaty correspondence with the British. On Hamilton's advice, the president suggested the legislative request would be appropriate only in cases of impeachment—putting Congress on the defensive, because nobody wanted to pursue *that* action against the still-popular hero of the country.[45]

James Monroe moved the United States past its first party system into the so-called Era of Good Feelings, when organized opposition collapsed and politicians generally agreed about the direction of the country. Many hoped for the elimination of rancor from politics. In fact, the absence of partisan restraint led to congressional chaos and indiscipline in Monroe's own cabinet. Treasury Secretary William Crawford, trying to bolster his own chances at the presidency, lied to the president about the country's finances, telling him federal coffers held a $7 million surplus when, in fact, the government was $5 million in the red. One result: Monroe lost his remaining clout in Congress, which, to cut costs, eviscerated the commander in chief's plans to fortify military installations and reduced his cadre of major generals to *one*.[46]

Monroe thereafter lacked "the slightest influence in Congress," said Speaker of the House Henry Clay. "His career was considered as closed. There was nothing further to be expected by him or from him."[47] Another result: Crawford and Monroe nearly beat each other in the White House. The treasury secretary raised his cane to threaten the president, who grabbed fireplace tongs to swing back. No blows were landed, and both men left the room with sore feelings but without physical injuries.[48]

Monroe's successors endured various political challenges, including the formal congressional censure of Andrew Jackson, who clashed frequently with just about everyone who disagreed with him on just about anything, but nothing quite reached removal in place. In fact, no chief executive faced the full degree of emasculation Andrew Johnson did. But poor John Tyler may have come the closest.

S TARTING OUT IN the White House is hard, no matter what. It's especially tough when your predecessor has just died and, by a fluke of campaign politics, you didn't really belong as your side's vice presidential pick.

John Tyler couldn't manage to earn a nomination in the next election and his just less than full term faced stiff and, for the time, shocking resistance, all the more dramatic because it came mostly from his own party.

SIMPLE EXECUTIVE FUNCTIONS continued, and a few foreign policy successes came. But just about everything else fell flat. Seven of Tyler's twenty nominations for cabinet positions couldn't receive Senate confirmation. Eight of his nine nominations for the Supreme Court were turned down, withdrawn from consideration, or saw no action taken, giving him both a number of rejections and a ratio of failed nominations that remain unmatched more than a century and a half later.[49]

His legislative proposals didn't fare much better, with most of them dead on arrival. Even a Democratic lawmaker, more in line with Tyler's philosophy than his own Whigs were, admitted that "most of them deserved to be."[50] By delaying action, legislators hoped to put so much pressure on the federal government's ability to spend money that the president would have no reasonable choice but to agree with their policies.[51] Tyler went ahead and vetoed not one but two tariff bills, risking the federal government's main source of revenue in the process, as well as several other measures—stacking up a higher total of rejected bills than any of the country's first eight presidents, despite holding office for less time than any of them.

Tyler's message accompanying his veto of the second tariff bill offended Congress enough that it went to a special House committee. Led by the cantankerous former president John Quincy Adams, that group suggested legislators both amend the Constitution to ease congressional overrides and bring formal impeachment charges against Tyler.[52] Neither saw action at the time; even Adams and his incensed colleagues knew they didn't have the votes to see such initiatives through.[53] The House instead formally censured Tyler, as they had done to Jackson. To add a dash of salt to the wound, the House refused to record the president's subsequent protest in the official record. A resolution of impeachment that ultimately reached the floor in 1843 was easily defeated, yet reflected the legislative branch's continued determination to keep Tyler in his corner.[54]

His political enemies got downright mean, throwing epithets at him in the press that sound rough even by modern standards. One former colleague described Tyler as "absolutely inferior to many fifteen shilling lawyers, with whom you meet at every county court in Virginia."[55] The title "His Accidency" was heard in Washington as often as the traditional "His Excellency." Others called him "a man destitute of intellect and integrity."[56] One Whig newspaper just called him "Executive Ass."[57]

Lawmakers' efforts to undermine Tyler extended to his personal safety. Rocks had been thrown at the executive mansion—and, once, at Tyler himself while he was walking through the White House grounds—so he sought funding for protection. A spiteful Capitol Hill opposed the idea because it would empower Tyler to name his protective officers. One senator saw this as a slippery slope to a "standing guard, which might eventually become a formidable army" that would sow the seeds to "overshadow the liberties of the people." They settled on a smaller measure, which allowed the building to host a captain and three guards, to be selected by the city of Washington's mayor, not the president.[58] To make his life more miserable, legislators also withheld from Tyler funds to upgrade the increasingly dilapidated presidential residence, which passers-by had started mocking as the "Public Shabby House." As soon as Democrat James Polk succeeded Tyler, however, they didn't hesitate to offer almost $15,000 for White House maintenance and furnishing.[59]

No significant policies moved forward until Tyler was a post-election lame duck. He couldn't even reap the fruits of his greatest deeds in office. Congress, earlier in 1844, had rejected his treaty to annex Texas. But just hours before leaving office, the outgoing president managed to get a Congress that knew he would soon be gone to pass it, allowing him to deliver to Texas an offer to join the United States. But Polk, not Tyler, would end up as the one to welcome Texans into the Union. Even on Tyler's last full day in office, Congress couldn't resist the urge to stick it to him one last time. Legislators overrode a minor measure concerning presidential authority to build ships without specific authorization, the first time in American history Congress turned back any presidential veto.[60]

THE NEXT WHIG president, Zachary Taylor, succeeded Polk in 1849. He'd moved from the army directly into the Oval Office, where his political ignorance and inability to build ties to Congress, or even his own cabinet, spurred one of the weakest and least productive American presidencies.

At first, he simply delegated patronage choices to his cabinet, the first president to let those choices be made by others.[61] Lawmakers, upset at Taylor's unwillingness to engage in political horse trading with them on government jobs for their supporters, rejected many of his early nominations. So he waited them out. When Congress adjourned, Taylor made recess appointments—many of them.[62] Even in an administration cut short by Taylor's untimely death, the president made over four hundred such appointments, more than all eleven of his predecessors.[63]

Beyond this, Taylor generally stayed true to the principles of limited presidential leadership and deference to the legislative branch that he'd expressed in his inaugural address.[64] His presidency saw a proliferation of congressional requests for information. First, legislators wanted to know about the president's deliberations on potential statehood for California and New Mexico. He gave them what they asked for. Soon, they also demanded information about the appointments his postmaster general had made and some related decisions. He again delivered the goods. Then, they sought access to correspondence between the War Department and its military units deployed in Santa Fe. Once more, he complied. In each case, Taylor failed to question the legislative branch's authority to request the communications.[65]

NOT ALL PRESIDENTS have faced strong pushback even when expanding the executive's powers. Abraham Lincoln, for example, took truly extraordinary steps to expand presidential power during the Civil War. Rarely were efforts to limit him effective.

As the war stagnated in December 1862, a cabal of Republican senators, prodded by a scheming cabinet member, criticized the commander in chief for appointing subpar generals, pushed him to restructure his cabinet, and asserted he should obtain consent from a cabinet majority before any major decision. Lincoln resisted. Through skillful manipulation of all parties involved, he got the senators to back down and reduced his own cabinet's backstabbing. Also, in agreeing to admit West Virginia as a state by splitting it off from the rest of its rebellious commonwealth—without the input of most Virginians—the president faced charges of acting unconstitutionally, including from his own attorney general.[66] It happened anyway.

Lincoln's Emancipation Proclamation changed the status of millions of slaves in designated areas of the South but drew even greater criticism. Resistance emerged not only in the border states but among many Northern Democrats and even some Republicans, with one Cincinnati newspaper calling the proclamation "a complete overthrow of the Constitution he was sworn to protect and defend." Legal arguments against the declaration only subsided when the Constitution itself was amended to free all those formerly enslaved.[67]

And when Lincoln suspended the writ of habeas corpus during a congressional recess,[68] Supreme Court chief justice Roger Taney blasted him, claiming that only Congress had the authority to suspend this right, and later warned of the country's slide toward a "reign of terror." Lincoln simply ignored him.[69] Congress, upon reconvening, not only failed to punish the commander in chief, but it retroactively legalized all presidential deeds regarding the armed forces since the administration began, and authorized them anew under its own power. Courts later ruled Lincoln acted constitutionally under the circumstances.[70]

EARLY-TWENTIETH-CENTURY PRESIDENTS ALSO endured attempts to limit their power, which typically served less as examples of usurpation of executive power than as cases of constitutional checks and balances.

Woodrow Wilson, for example, went to extreme lengths in 1919 to try to win passage of the Treaty of Versailles and, thereby, get the United States into the League of Nations. He failed when the Senate rejected the treaty. He also inherited US intervention in Nicaragua, where US marines had been posted in 1912 and would remain (with only brief interruption) for many years.

Calvin Coolidge in 1928 used the marines to run Nicaragua's first real democratic election,[71] keeping an eye on reported machinations by the Soviet Union there.[72] Despite such national security concerns, not to mention the country's proximity to the Panama Canal, legislators got fed up with continued presidential deployments to Central America as the Great Depression hit.

Herbert Hoover used the marines to supervise a Nicaraguan election in 1930 and wanted to do the same in 1932, but Congress in June pulled funding from the navy,[73] requiring the president to use funds from other sources to do at least part of the job. The withdrawal of US forces prompted an unprecedented message to US citizens in Nicaragua, warning anyone not leaving the country or moving to coastal towns that they remained "at their own risk and must not expect American forces to be sent inland to their aid."[74]

FRANKLIN ROOSEVELT ENCOUNTERED stiffer resistance from the courts and, occasionally, Congress. Since he expanded the role of the federal government well beyond what his predecessors had left him, there was plenty to resist.

Federal commissions and administrative agencies had been around for decades—nearly five hundred commissions and similar bodies had come around between the inauguration of Theodore Roosevelt in 1901 and the end of Coolidge's term in 1929.[75] But from 1933 on, FDR's New Deal expanded them dramatically. With names like the Agricultural Adjustment Administration, National Recovery Administration, and Works Progress Administration (later the Work Projects Administration), these bodies within a few years controlled a healthy chunk of the country's relief and employment efforts. The Supreme Court in 1935 and 1936 started swatting them down like flies, judging that the government, among other errors, had interpreted too broadly the interstate commerce clause in the Constitution.[76]

Roosevelt knew he had to act to protect the institutions he thought were saving America, but ignoring the rulings or, worse, arresting justices didn't look wise. Everyone in Washington knew a historic clash was brewing. One senator watching the president converse with two justices at the White House on February 2, 1937, quipped: "That reminds me of the Roman Emperor who looked around his dinner table and began to laugh when he thought how many of those heads would be rolling on the morrow."[77]

It took three days for FDR to drop a different type of bomb. He asked Congress to pass a bill allowing him, among other things, to pack the courts—appointing as many new judges as there were sitting federal judges he deemed too "aged and infirm" to properly and efficiently do their jobs. The complicated business clogging up the courts, he asserted, was just too difficult for elderly justices to handle without assistance. Translation: older, conservative judges were on notice.[78] The proposal divided the country, spurring months of intense lobbying of the members of the House and Senate, both of which started 1937 with overwhelming Democratic majorities.[79]

Before the bill came to a vote, however, two things happened. First, Roosevelt's polling numbers dropped as his ageist arguments fell flat and the chief justice denied any significant backlog of cases. Second, the Supreme Court delivered decisions that upheld some New Deal programs, reducing the president's perceived need to spur dramatic legislative action.[80] Only a watered down version of the bill, without the court-packing provision, became law that August.

Opponents failed to rein in Roosevelt, with one small caveat, on his early World War II support to Great Britain and her allies. In the first year of the conflagration, before the United States joined the fray, much American political sentiment and public opinion wanted to keep it that way. Neutrality legislation from the 1930s prevented most forms of military aid to the countries fighting Nazi Germany and imperial Japan, but Roosevelt knew that Prime Minister Winston Churchill's government would appreciate some old American destroyers. The attorney general and other renowned lawyers assured FDR he could use his executive authority to transfer fifty much-needed destroyers in exchange for long-term leases on British bases in the Western Hemisphere, as long as military officials could certify the ships as "useless" and "obsolete." That was a bit disingenuous, because they could be made useful pretty quickly, and anti-war Republicans who knew it didn't hesitate to call it "an act of war." The "obsolete" fig leaf, however, proved enough to allow the deal to pass muster with the public during a heated presidential election.[81]

Soon after Roosevelt won his third term in November 1940, Churchill expressed to him just how dire the situation for Europe had become. "The decision for 1941," he wrote, "lies upon the seas." He asked both for warships, lots of them, and financial help.[82] Musing about the prime minister's letter while spending a few days at sea, FDR came up with a plan to provide ships, various war materiel, manufactured goods, and even food to countries fighting the Axis powers—all the goods, in theory, would be given back after the war or traded for leases throughout the Allied powers' territories. Roosevelt announced to the public that the United States must become "the great arsenal of democracy."[83] He and his cabinet officers employed denial and deception to sell "Lend-Lease," withholding specifics from a skeptical Congress and insisting publicly that the measure would keep America out of the war—when it clearly drew the country closer in.[84]

Lend-Lease legislation passed in March 1941, but not without a restriction on presidential power. Roosevelt had insisted he would hold absolute authority on Lend-Lease items, but instead the senators put into the bill that Congress would retain authority over funding and, with it, some control over the supplies going overseas.[85] That didn't serve as much of a brake on the president, who offered the Allies access to American production and, in the process, drew a venomous reaction from Nazi Germany.[86]

R ICHARD NIXON OBSTRUCTED justice during his time as president.
But his own cabinet and staff also obstructed *him*, taking the
chief executive's authority upon themselves without legal grounding.

The most frequent usurper was H. R. Haldeman, Nixon's chief of
staff for most of his presidency. Starting soon after the inauguration,
Haldeman learned that Nixon, when venting about others' inade-
quacies, would order dramatic actions. For example, after the leak
in early June of a National Security Council decision memorandum
about negotiations with the Japanese about Okinawa, the president
directed his chief of staff to tap the communications of all possible
suspects within the government.[87]

Haldeman later wrote about this type of "challenge," which he
faced often—whether or not to follow a specific ill-advised instruc-
tion from Nixon: "I sometimes decided not to, on the basis that it
was not an order that was really intended to be carried out, but rather
a letting off of steam, or that it was clearly not in [the president's]
interest that it be carried out. Usually I later informed [Nixon] that
the order had not been followed, and he usually agreed that was
the right decision. There were times, however, when he intentionally
would end-run me with an order to someone else who he felt would
do his bidding when I wouldn't."[88] Haldeman had Nixon's backing
on this, to some degree. "There may be times when you or others
may determine that the action I have requested should not be taken,"
the president had written to him before inauguration. "I will accept
such decisions but I must know about them."[89]

Haldeman seems overly confident the president "usually" approved of his self-authorized pocket vetoes. In fact, many times
Nixon came back to Haldeman within a day or two asking why he
hadn't seen follow-though on his directives, suggesting the chief of
staff took on board Nixon's approval to sit on his requests but *not* his
demand to remain informed. The Okinawa case, again, is instructive.
The night after his initial command, Nixon called his chief of staff
repeatedly—"really mad," as Haldeman noted in his diary—repeating he wanted the leaks investigated, and with extreme prejudice.[90]

Haldeman admits to nevertheless continuing to ignore some of
Nixon's orders for years.[91] In July 1971, Nixon tore into a couple of

agencies at a budget meeting, ordering 25 percent cuts in their personnel and, then, for good measure, 10 percent cuts in all other civilian agencies, too. "This is the pleasantest morning I've had in years," he quipped after issuing the command. Haldeman did not demand that the agency chiefs follow through with the cuts.[92] Although not always informed that his commands were dying by inaction, Nixon over time seemed to mind less and less, probably because he realized that Haldeman, and others, kept him out of trouble by ignoring his most egregious outbursts.

Nixon's obsession with Daniel Ellsberg, the former Department of Defense official and think tank analyst who had leaked the Pentagon Papers to the *New York Times,* led the president to order some of his famed "dirty tricks." When he heard that a friend of Ellsberg was storing a classified document at an office of the Brookings Institution, for example, Nixon told Haldeman "just to break in. Break in and take it out!"[93] When word of the effort got to White House counsel John Dean, who didn't know it was a presidential order at the time, he sprung into action to stop any actual implementation of the proposal.[94]

Nixon's unexecuted directives ranged from the harmless to acts of war. On the innocuous side, he told staffers they could no longer eat the food at congressional breakfasts. Some of them continued to do it anyway, without any penalty. And once he ordered retaliation against the Massachusetts Institute of Technology, in the form of cutting its federal contracts, after a lack of support from the school on Vietnam policy, but there's no sign such cuts came about.[95] Among the president's more momentous commands was one to his first secretary of state, William Rogers, to fire all State Department personnel in the country of Laos. The secretary, upon revisiting the issue with Nixon, was told, "Oh hell, Bill—you know me better than that." Then there was the time he ordered the bombing of the Syrian capital of Damascus. That didn't happen, either.

An aide later asserted Nixon relied on his staff to filter these "goofy ideas," to "basically let it fester for a while until he got through it and would re-think it."[96] This practice of resisting or ignoring presidential orders requires high confidence in one's ability to ascertain the president's true wishes. It also has no basis in the Constitution or federal law.

THE INCREASE IN Nixon's drinking paralleled that of the administration's troubles, leading some aides to assume some of his authority for themselves. "The tapes of his conversations sometimes show him getting increasingly drunk, especially after he gives a speech and takes supporters' calls with congratulations," says Dean, one of the few people to listen to (and help transcribe) the thousands of hours of tapes from Nixon's presidency. He says with confidence, "In some conversations, you can hear him disintegrate—by the end of the evening, he is just slurring and can barely get through the call."[97]

This dynamic contributed to National Security Advisor Henry Kissinger's expanded confidence in making national security decisions that rightfully belonged with the commander in chief. A prominent example occurred in October 1973, when the national security advisor and others managed a Middle East war while the president was in Key Biscayne, Florida, swamped by some of the darkest days of the Watergate scandal. Egypt had invaded Israel, but Kissinger, also serving by then as secretary of state, didn't talk to Nixon for hours. Instead, he communicated with Haldeman's successor, Al Haig, who was with the president in the Sunshine State.

The two men didn't bother to tell the president about the war as it erupted or seek his policy guidance; the unelected Kissinger simply dealt with the situation as he thought best. They put out a story of "constant contact" between the president and national security advisor, and Nixon later played along with that illusion of calling the shots. In fact, he focused during those days almost exclusively on how to respond to the expanding Watergate crisis.[98] When an alarming message from Soviet leader Leonid Brezhnev that escalated the crisis came in on the evening of October 24, Nixon was asleep. Kissinger asked Haig by phone, "Should I wake up the President?" Haig replied, "No."[99] Why not? Deputy National Security Advisor Brent Scowcroft, also on site in Florida, later said he couldn't rule out that Nixon was drunk at the time.[100] Kissinger ended up leading an overnight meeting in Washington to craft a reply to Brezhnev, which he sent back in Nixon's name. And the military alert level rose to DEFCON 3, a defense condition anticipating possible escalation to nuclear war. The president was not consulted about either action.[101]

From that point until the administration ended in humiliation some ten months later, Haig exceeded Haldeman's hubris and issued orders as if they came from Nixon himself. "Actually," one senior National Security Council staff member recalls, "Al Haig *was* the president of the United States."[102] He wasn't alone in keeping an unusually close eye on Nixon. Secretary of Defense James Schlesinger, concerned about his commander in chief's drinking and depression in the waning days, in summer 1974 reportedly told military commanders to check with him before responding to any direct presidential order to launch nuclear weapons.[103] And during the final hours of Nixon's presidency, Schlesinger ensured Nixon flew back to California on Air Force One without the highly protected nuclear launch codes, leaving the country without a legally valid authorizer should the need have emerged in the brief window before Gerald Ford's inauguration.[104]

Congress, too, jumped on the "let's-restrict-the-president" bandwagon. In November 1973, the War Powers Resolution, which narrowed his authority to send US forces into combat and keep them there, passed despite Nixon's veto. Any such military action now would require, within forty-eight hours, a notification to Congress, which must authorize any stay longer than sixty days. Lawmakers say it protects their sole right under the Constitution to declare war; presidents claim it restricts their constitutional role as commander in chief. The act remains the law of the land.

ON MARCH 16, 2016, Barack Obama nominated Merrick Garland, chief judge of the US Court of Appeals for the DC Circuit, to fill the Supreme Court vacancy created by the death of Antonin Scalia. On January 20, 2017, as Obama left office, Garland hadn't received even a single hearing, much less a confirmation vote.

The Senate set a new record for intransigence—no action at all on a Supreme Court nomination for 293 days.

Garland waited so long, and so unfruitfully, neither because he was a radical nor due to a lack of qualifications. Independents like former senator Joe Lieberman and Republicans like former Utah governor Jon Huntsman urged senators to hold hearings.[105] A bipartisan group of former US solicitors general called him "superbly qualified."[106] The American Bar Association awarded him a "well-qualified" rating, noting that in the hundreds of legal-profession interviews they performed during research on Garland, "not one person uttered a negative word about him."[107] What, then, was the problem?

IT HAD NOTHING to do with Garland, his qualifications, or the needs of the court. Obama, a Democrat, faced a Republican Senate looking forward to a new president some ten months later. Senators who refused to act on the nomination claimed that "standard practice" allowed them to take no action, that their chamber historically did not confirm Supreme Court nominations during election years. They either lied or didn't bother to do research before talking, because the opposite is true. More than a dozen examples show such nominations routinely *have* been acted on. The most recent case had actually occurred within the careers of some of the men claiming otherwise. In 1988, Ronald Reagan's Supreme Court nominee Anthony Kennedy received confirmation during that election year.[108] In fact, we'd have to go back to the Civil War era or earlier to find cases in which the desire to prevent a presidential prerogative trumped the tradition of giving nominees an up-or-down vote.

There's even a dramatic countercase. In late February 1841, Democrat Martin Van Buren stood ready to hand the reins of power over to the Whig president-elect, William Henry Harrison, who had defeated the incumbent in the previous election of November 1840. With less than a week left in his term, Van Buren nominated Peter Daniel to the Supreme Court. Despite congressional grumbling and partisan complaints about the "indecent haste" of the nomination,

Daniel received Senate confirmation in a land-speed record for lame-duck high court nominees.[109]

Constitutionally, the senators denying Garland his hearing in 2016 and early 2017 stood on solid ground. Article 2, section 2 states that appointments to the Supreme Court require the consent of the Senate; it remains silent on how or when that consent should come. If there had been *no* Supreme Court justices in place, Obama might have had a constitutional argument that Garland not only deserved but *required* a timely hearing. Nothing in our government's founding document, though, defines the size of the high court, much less how prompt the process for confirming its appointees must be. Thus, to the extent that the president was undermined in this case, give his political opponents credit for taking advantage of the lack of clarity in the Constitution about timely consent.

Chapter Three

Dismissed Preemptively

I am the most unfortunate man in the history of parties:
always run by my friends when sure to be defeated, and now
betrayed when I, or any one, would be sure of election.[1]

—HENRY CLAY

A FINE LINE SEPARATES fair means and foul ones in elections. Crafty politicians and, probably, most Americans view dirty tricks as part of the great game before, and sometimes after, voters go to the polls. Laws may keep the playing field reasonably level, but much of politics remains not about statutes but about norms. Where do luck and influence end and illicit activities begin?

Imagine a major party candidate, eminently qualified. He or she possesses many, even most, of the advantages that have carried other would-be presidents over the finish line to victory. Election as chief magistrate, either in the next election or further down the road, looks all but certain. Political opponents may foresee an imminent leader they don't want, followed by a long and difficult struggle to undermine, and perhaps eject, this winner after he or she gains the powers that come with incumbency. Another strategy begins to look more attractive: removing this president-in-waiting preemptively.

That's oversimplifying things, of course. But it helps to explain why some of the best-prepared candidates in history, like Henry

Clay, didn't make it to the Oval Office. It's why his name resonates with contemporary Americans less than those of even lackluster presidents like Millard Fillmore, Franklin Pierce, and Chester Arthur.

The most insidious yet nonviolent way to get rid of a president? Keep him or her out of the office altogether.

WHAT A RÉSUMÉ: elected to Kentucky's general assembly at twenty-five, and elected its speaker within a few years; appointed to the US Senate first, briefly, at just twenty-nine, ultimately serving there four separate times for a total of almost fifteen years; represented Kentucky in the House of Representatives for more than a decade, as its youngest Speaker yet and originator of many of the job's powers; helped negotiate a war-ending treaty with the world's greatest power; presented the very first *amicus curiae* ("friend of the court") brief before the Supreme Court; offered positions ranging from ambassador to Russia to secretary of war to Supreme Court justice; led foreign relations for four years as secretary of state; masterminded national compromises that, for decades, kept the country from descending into civil war. To cap it all he was called the "ideal of a statesman" by none other than Abraham Lincoln.

That's a better record than virtually anyone who's sought the presidency. It's richer, in fact, than most combinations of qualifications that two, three, or even four presidents can claim. And yet the ire of political powerhouse Andrew Jackson and the scheming of his own supposed allies across three decades squashed Henry Clay's chances to win the White House, preemptively removing the best president we never had.

HENRY CLAY'S STORY reflects that of young America. Born just a few months after the Revolutionary War battles of Trenton and Princeton, he grew up comfortably in Virginia and gained admittance to the bar there before leaving in 1797. He ventured west to make his home in Kentucky, a state admitted to the Union only five years earlier.

The arduous trip across the Appalachian Mountains planted the seeds for his lifelong goal: a federally funded system of roads, canals, bridges, and so on to ease travel, bind the country together, and bolster US manufacturers. That, to the modern ear, sounds logical and uncontroversial, perhaps even obvious. But the states dominated such infrastructure back then, and for decades wide sections of the American public saw Clay's passion for so-called internal improvements as a glaring example of unwelcome federal intrusion.

Once Clay heard the call of public service and entered the state legislature in 1803, he quickly honed his skills as a first-rate orator, and as a notorious drinker and gambler. His appreciation for late-night fun, which lubricated his relationships with the Bluegrass State's elite, gave political opponents material to hammer him for decades. Kentucky proved too small for Clay's talents and ambition, so he became a US senator from Kentucky in late 1806. No one objected that he was but twenty-nine years old, falling short of the constitutional minimum age requirement for the Senate. He remained in Washington for only two months that first time, but he used his time wisely, forging many key friendships and leaving a lasting impression of a talented man who worked hard, and played harder.

In 1810, he again filled a vacant US Senate seat from Kentucky, briefly, before shifting to the US House of Representatives. For the next four decades, with just a few absences, he made the capital's political and social scene his own. Clay's "conversation, his gesture, his very look," one future party rival admitted, "was persuasive, seductive, irresistible."[2] Few could match his wit and charm, which supplemented his leadership skills. In fact, his relative youth and scant national experience proved no obstacle as like-minded representatives elected the charismatic newcomer Speaker, a position he would hold for most of the next fourteen years. He proved nothing short of revolutionary, transforming the previously understated position to a master of directing committees and moving legislation to the floor.

Willpower, mastery of parliamentary techniques, and skillful relationship building made this thirty-four-year-old one of the most powerful men in America virtually overnight. And he basked in the limelight, engaging in floor debates more often than previous Speakers had done. Just a few decades after the colonies had gained independence, Clay used his platform to champion an energetic and expansionist foreign policy. In particular, he urged President James Madison to stand up to British transgressions, create a worthy army and navy, and, eventually, go to war with Great Britain.

When the War of 1812 began, the Speaker and his fellow "war hawks" in Congress got the conflict they wanted; and Clay got his first taste of diplomacy when Madison selected him to join the American peace delegation in Europe, led by former ambassador to Russia John Quincy Adams. The two negotiators could hardly have been more different. Adams, son of the country's second president, had a puritanical strain to his personality, a perpetually sour demeanor, and a fondness for "early to bed, early to rise" discipline. Clay, by contrast, annoyed the future president with his raucous, all-night partying, often in a room right next to Adams's own. But the delegation chief grudgingly respected Clay for his hard work, surely wondering how someone who consistently stayed up until dawn drinking and playing cards nevertheless had the energy to work all through the next day. Adams also couldn't help but notice how Clay's legendary combination of charisma and bravado proved mighty useful in negotiations. In fact, Clay stood out among the American team for recognizing—from his many nights of playing cards—that the British delegation would cave on most of its demands, convincing Adams and the others to call the British bluff. It worked, contributing to the war-ending Treaty of Ghent.[3]

The treaty negotiations thus added "statesman" to Clay's growing list of accomplishments. But the war also elevated the fortunes of another—a fateful development that would play the largest role in keeping Clay out of the White House for the next forty years.

By GIVING AMERICANS a proud finish to an otherwise unimpressive conflict, General Andrew Jackson emerged from the War of 1812 as its main hero.

Old Hickory had defeated a larger British force at New Orleans before news of the Treaty of Ghent—and, with it, the war's end—had reached Louisiana, landing him astride US popular culture like no one military leader since George Washington. He was a natural for the Monroe administration to send in 1818 to the edge of Florida, then controlled by Spain, to punch back against Seminoles who kept attacking Americans across the border. Jackson was told to avoid direct action against Spanish settlements and military posts. He did it anyway. After capturing Spain's garrison at St. Mark's, he moved on the Spanish capital of West Florida. Jackson only left the territory after compelling the Spanish provincial governor's surrender,[4] which risked a diplomatic crisis, even war, with Spain.

Monroe liked the result and didn't seem to mind the insubordination, but Clay certainly did.[5] He led a congressional attempt to censure Jackson, decrying the general's refusal to follow orders and declaring in a colorful speech that letting him go unpunished, "without a solemn expression of the disapprobation of this House," would echo Greek, Roman, and French tragedies. "A triumph of the military over the civil authority," he declared, would be "a triumph over the constitution of the land." Even one of Clay's political opponents felt it necessary to acknowledge his speech was "the most eloquent one I ever heard."[6]

Never one to let perceived slights go unnoticed, however, Jackson took offense—enough that he considered challenging his vocal critic to a duel.[7] The seeds of enmity were sown. Clay moved on to focus on how to expand the Union without upsetting the balance between slaveholding and free states. The tension exploded in 1819 as Missouri prepared to take its place among the states, with slavery intact. Eventually, lawmakers settled on a trade-off whereby (1) Missouri and Maine (formerly part of Massachusetts) would join the Union as a slaveholding state and a free state, respectively; and (2) no slavery would exist in the remaining Louisiana Territory north of $36°30'$ north, which starts westward along most of the Missouri-Arkansas border. Although Clay didn't create what became known as the Missouri Compromise of 1820, he used his parliamentary acumen and sheer determination to ensure its passage into law.[8] His work on limiting slavery's spread helped solidify his high status in the emerging "nationalist" wing of the Democratic-Republican Party, in favor of a strong federal government and internal improvements directed from Washington. By contrast, "Old Republicans," like Jackson, leaned toward strict adherence to constitutional limits on federal power.

FEW EXPRESSED SHOCK when Clay became a serious contender for the nation's top office as Monroe prepared to leave the presidency. His strong support in what was then the western United States gave him hope to win, despite being one of the youngest candidates ever for the White House.

His political instincts told him, correctly, that winning outright at the polls against John Quincy Adams (Monroe's secretary of state), Jackson (the leading candidate), and others would take a miracle. Clay also knew the Constitution well enough to see a more likely path to victory. Neither Adams nor Jackson, he calculated, would get an outright majority of electoral votes, thus throwing the vote into the House. There, as Speaker, Clay would cleverly convince enough state delegations, which each voted once, from among the top three electoral vote finishers, to select him as the seventh president.

Clay added it all up well. His logic was sound. The pieces were in place. But he failed to anticipate that former secretary of war and secretary of the treasury William Crawford—though largely disabled by a massive stroke months earlier—would nevertheless squeak out just enough electoral votes to take the third-place finish, ahead of Clay, eliminating him. He nevertheless retained the keys to the White House through his ability to manipulate several states' delegations. Jackson's plurality in most states meant little in the House, because congressmen remained free to choose—with one vote per state delegation—Adams, Jackson, or Crawford, regardless of how the citizens they represented had voted. Clay had his disagreements with Adams, to be sure. The prospect of a President Jackson, however, offended him so greatly that he engineered a win for Adams. Jackson and his supporters erupted, especially when Adams announced Clay as his most powerful cabinet officer, secretary of state.

Jackson fulminated against the perceived dirty deed. One of his political allies recalled that upon hearing the news, the general's "Jovian ire blazed forth,"[9] spurring him to later write to a colleague,

"So, you see, the Judas of the West has closed the contract and will receive the thirty pieces of silver. His end will be the same. Was there ever witnessed such a bare-faced corruption in any country before?"[10] Jackson-allied press labeled Clay "morally and politically a gambler" and even called him a "traitor" who should be tarred and feathered. The "corrupt bargain" label that foes of Adams and Clay put on the delivery of the presidency to Adams in exchange for the premier cabinet position would follow the Kentuckian through his entire political career.[11]

At first, Clay shrugged it off, hoping the ballyhoo would blow over. But as the invective directed at him grew, Clay expressed shock. "The knaves cannot comprehend how a man can be honest. They can not conceive that I should have solemnly interrogated my conscience, and asked it to tell me seriously what I ought to do!" he wrote on January 29, 1825. He made clear that he found it in the nation's best interest to avoid "the dangerous precedent of elevating, in this early state of the republic, a military chieftain merely because he has won a great victory! . . . I can not believe that killing twenty-five hundred Englishmen at New Orleans qualifies him for the various, difficult, and complicated duties of the Chief Magistracy."[12]

The perception of corruption and Clay's continued swipes at Jackson led Clay to face the closest Senate confirmation vote up to that time, with fourteen senators—Andrew Jackson among them—opposing him, unsuccessfully.[13] Clay took office in early 1825 as the ninth secretary of state and held the job for four years, succeeding in sealing commercial relations with newly independent Latin American countries, even as his efforts to improve ties to Great Britain and France fell short.

Jackson fumed and prepared his revenge. The opportunity wasn't long in coming.

THE GENERAL'S PARTISANS toiled from the time of his defeat until Election Day in 1828 to right what they saw as a colossal wrong. And when ballots and electoral votes were counted, Old Hickory had won in a landslide, kicking Adams out of office and sending Clay back to Kentucky to contemplate his political future.

While managing his estate and calculating future paths, Clay made time for a long-anticipated duel with Virginian John Randolph, a garrulous eccentric even by the standards of the time. Randolph, who habitually brought hunting dogs to the floor of the House with him, back in 1811 had beaten a fellow member of the House of Representatives with a cane for daring to complain about his canine companions.[14] Clay alone had stood up to Randolph at the time, directing the sergeant at arms to get the dogs out of the chamber.

Fifteen years later, after Randolph had loudly joined the "corrupt bargain" chorus and spewed a particularly offensive diatribe on the floor of the Senate, Clay challenged him and he accepted, prompting the men to face off with pistols across the river from the District of Columbia in northern Virginia. Each fired once. They hit neither flesh nor bone. Clay fired again, missing Randolph a second time. Both of his bullets, though, had come alarmingly close and ripped Randolph's morning gown, an odd choice to wear to a duel.[15] Instead of directing his own second shot at Clay, Randolph simply shot into the air and approached his opponent with a hand extended. Clay accepted it, prompting Randolph to declare, "You owe me a coat, Mr. Clay." Clay promptly replied, "I am glad the debt is no greater." Even Jackson ally Thomas Hart Benton had to admit Clay handled this "high-toned duel" with "generous and heroic spirit."[16]

Political battles fit Clay's style more than physical ones, however. So, true to form, he soon began planning for another confrontation with Jackson himself, this time in the 1832 presidential contest. He had little trouble being nominated to run against Old Hickory; defeating his nemesis would prove a much greater challenge.

To consolidate support going into the race, Clay had managed to get named, again, to the Senate and returned to Washington to do some legislating. As a leader of the so-called National Republican faction of the Republicans, in de facto opposition to the Jacksonian clique that was transforming into the Democratic Party, Clay followed his head and not his heart by unwisely pushing his partisans to focus on Jackson's veto of a bill to recharter the Bank of the United States. Voters were bored; although the Bank controversy mattered constitutionally and economically, it meant little to the masses. Attacks simply commanded more attention: on Clay, for his role in the "corrupt bargain" and for his partying and gambling; and on Jackson, for acting like an American king. "I'm not certain Clay could've beaten Jackson in 1832 no matter what," says era historian Mark Cheathem, "but it would have been a more effective strategy for the personal politics of the time if he hadn't focused so much on the Bank issue."[17]

Jackson stayed in office and kept Clay out of it by crushing his opponent in the balloting. Only five states went for Clay, who garnered a mere 49 electoral votes—nowhere near the victor's 219. In a sign of trouble to come both for the Union and for Clay's efforts to bind it together through internal improvements and a strong national government, Old Hickory also won a stunning 88 percent of the vote in the Deep South.[18]

"IF EVER ONE, or several States, being a minority, can, by menacing a dissolution of the Union, succeed in forcing an abandonment of great measures, deemed essential to the interests and prosperity of the whole, the Union, from that moment, is practically gone. It may linger on, in form and name, but its vital spirit has fled forever."[19]

With these words in January 1833, Henry Clay captured the crux of the crisis engulfing the nation. Right after the election, South Carolinians had declared federal tariffs null and void in their state, prodding President Jackson to proclaim that no state could nullify federal law and sparking Congress to consider authorizing the use of force to enforce the tariff acts. A civil war looked increasingly likely.

Clay jumped into the fray to build a new coalition and beat a path through the seemingly intractable mess. He found himself working with South Carolina's John Calhoun, a states' rights advocate who had just left the vice presidency out of anger at Jackson and his policies. Clay and his allies pulled it off, announcing with flair to the Senate on February 12 a middle-of-the-road tariff that would decrease over time. This satisfied Calhoun and enough South Carolinians to back down, while a partner bill authorizing force if necessary to execute federal law gave Jackson the cover he needed to sign both bills. The nullification crisis ended. The "Great Compromiser," just months after a humiliating electoral defeat, again looked like the Union's savior.[20]

Jackson grudgingly accepted the way out, but his enmity with Clay soon flared anew. The president, hell-bent on undermining what he perceived as the corrupt Second Bank of the United States, had vetoed a bill to recharter it. Now, before Congress could reauthorize the bank, he boldly withdrew federal deposits. The reaction from Congress, particularly Clay, was severe. He told the Senate:

> We are in the midst of a revolution, hitherto bloodless, but rapidly tending towards a total change of the pure republican character of the government, and to the concentration of all power in the hands of one man. The powers of Congress are paralyzed, except when exerted in conformity with his will, by frequent and an extraordinary exercise of the executive veto, not anticipated by the founders of the constitution, and not practised by any of the predecessors of the present Chief Magistrate.[21]

Such language galvanized the new Whig Party, which would rival Jackson's Democrats for the next twenty years. Clay led the Whigs in Congress to formally censure Jackson in March 1834 for what they saw as his dictatorial tendencies, the first such measure against any president.[22] While pulling Whigs together, this rebuke also rallied Clay opponents like Senator Benton, who spoke out against what he called "an empty fulmination—a mere personal censure—having no relation to any business or proceeding in the Senate . . . There was nothing to be done with it, or upon it, under it, or in relation to it."[23] Beyond demonstrating his mastery of prepositions, Benton prepared the Senate for a formal protest from Jackson—never one to let such a slight go unaddressed. The president called the censure "illegal and void" because of the lack of any constitutional foundation for it; he pointed out that only the House of Representatives, through constitutionally prescribed impeachment, could make *any* accusations against the president. Thus, he asserted, the Senate's resolution itself was "corrupt."[24]

Relations between the parties stayed tense through the remainder of the second term of the man opponents had taken to calling "King Andrew the First." Martin Van Buren, his handpicked successor, sought to ride the populist pro-Jackson wave into the White House in the 1836 election. Henry Clay looked formidable against him. "It would have been very close," says Cheathem, "and I think Clay might have won if he had run that year."[25] But he didn't, in large part because in December 1835, his beloved daughter Anne died. Upon reading the news, Clay whispered, "Every tie to life is broken," and put himself into weeks of seclusion. At the very moment when he would have needed to build his candidacy he was overwhelmed by despair and heartbreak.

The now rudderless Whig Party failed to rally around any other single candidate, ultimately fielding *three* against Van Buren. All lost handily to the Democrat. The top finisher among the Whigs was former general William Henry Harrison, whom Clay thought little of, but had endorsed anyway out of dismay at the thought of four more years of Jacksonian policies.[26]

BY 1840, EMBATTLED president Van Buren looked quite vulnerable. Clay this time envisioned his clearest path yet to the presidency, but his own party let him down.[27]

The Whigs instead rallied around Harrison. Clay surely would have defeated Van Buren if he had the chance one on one. Benton acknowledged, "The leading statesmen of [the Whigs] were again passed by to make room for a candidate more sure of being elected. The success of General Jackson had turned the attention of those who managed the presidential nominations to military men."[28] Clay steamed about his missed opportunity but the popular general took the country by storm. "The Whigs stole from the Democrats' playbook," Cheathem notes, "and they won."[29]

Harrison offered his party rival the secretary of state office for a second time, but Clay opted to try to pull the new president's strings from the Senate. Harrison had other ideas. A conflict over cabinet appointments ended with him chastising the would-be power behind the throne: "Mr. Clay, you forget that I am the President."[30]

Harrison would die just a month into his term. Former president Jackson, unaware that the two Whigs had fallen out, heard of the chief executive's passing and expressed relief that Harrison's death would prevent "the dictation of that profligate demagogue, Henry Clay."[31]

Death's removal of Harrison from the highest office in the land elevated Vice President John Tyler in his place. His relationship with Clay, tricky but manageable before, sank to depths beyond the Democrats' dreams. Disappointed that Tyler had proved no more pliable than President Harrison had during his brief tenure, Clay refused to accept Tyler's claim to his predecessor's title, only calling him "Vice President."[32] He led the party in its efforts to obstruct Tyler and successfully blocked Tyler's reelection prospects, and yet even this new window of opportunity for Clay would swing shut, this time as a result of the recurring national slavery crisis.

DEMOCRATS AND WHIGS found themselves in disarray and in high spirits, respectively, as 1844 began. The party Jackson had united now stood divided between North and South as well as by diverging policy views. Many Democrats longed for and actively supported a comeback by Van Buren; many others wanted anyone *but* the old party regular. On the other hand, Clay, finally facing neither war heroes nor personal tragedies, received the Whig nomination with both relative ease and remorse from most of his partisans for having withheld it from their titular leader four years earlier.

Representative of Whig feelings is the invitation to visit Illinois that a young Republican named Abraham Lincoln had sent to Clay, promising him "such a reception as shall be worthy of the man on whom are turned the fondest hopes of a great and suffering nation."[33] Clay's victory seemed certain. All his supporters had to do? Keep the electorate focused on economics and good governance.

That was not in the cards. Slavery, which Clay had kept compromising on to maintain the Union, reared its ugly head politically in a new way, via the proposed annexation of the newly independent Republic of Texas. Most Southerners wanted Texas to join the United States in order to expand the nation's slaveholding bloc.

Many Northerners increasingly found slavery abhorrent and became more willing to make stemming its advance a priority. Clay came out against Texas annexation and, in the process, alienated Southern Whigs. Playing coy as the election went on, however, he tried to have it both ways with winks to the South, giving abolitionists in the North strong doubts about the slave-owning Kentuckian's true stance on the issue.

Because Van Buren also opposed bringing Texas in, enough Democrats turned against him to block his path to the party nomination. "If Van Buren had been the candidate again in 1844, Clay wins," Cheathem says. "There's no question, because there's nothing Van Buren could campaign on that would have helped him defeat Clay."[34] Instead, the lesser known former Tennessee governor James Polk surprised the nation by winning the Democratic nomination and, with it, the chance to take on Clay in the general election.

On top of the Texas issue, Democrats threw in some old baggage, like that standby "corrupt bargain" charge from 1824 onward, and re-hashed stories about gambling, drinking, and dueling. An anti-Clay leaflet bearing the not too subtle title *Twenty-One Reasons Why Clay Should Not Be Elected* stated boldly that the Kentuckian whiled away his days "at the gambling table" and his nights "in a brothel."[35] Such charges carried less weight with voters than their general excitement over adding the massive Lone Star Republic to the Union, but every vote mattered in a close election.

In fact, Polk's margin of victory in the 2.7-million-strong popular balloting ended up at less than forty thousand votes. New York proved crucial. A swing of some fifty-one hundred ballots there would have handed a win in the state to Clay and, thereby, his victory in the electoral college. Instead, the growing Liberty Party, devoted to the abolitionist cause, made a strong showing in New York, taking votes that would otherwise have broken hard for Clay. Also, although John Tyler's presidency had been an abject failure, he retained enough support on his way out of the White House to swing at least a few votes to the Democrat, whom he had endorsed.[36] Yet again Clay, the indispensable man of American politics, found himself on the outside of the highest office, looking in.

His last best chance behind him, Clay resigned himself to the fact that he, the best-prepared candidate for the presidency since the republic's founding generation, would never reach it. When some Whigs urged him to run again in 1848, a quarter of a century after his first presidential bid, he pushed them off by citing "my age, the delicate state of my health, the frequency and the unsuccessful presentation of my name on former occasions." He shared his feelings of "unconquerable repugnance" to seeing his name on the ballot again.[37]

And yet declining health and the sting of repeated defeats didn't stop the Great Compromiser from doing what he did best one last time. Back in the Senate to end his career, he again saw the nation slipping toward disunion, primarily over the movement to admit California to the Union. Gathering support from allies and rivals alike, Clay spoke eloquently against secession and helped craft the Compromise of 1850, a combination of bills that averted a likely war over slavery's expansion. In so doing, of course, he just pushed the reckoning down the road a few more years, for others to ultimately resolve. But at the time, politicians of all stripes hailed it as a deft move to keep the country from imploding.

Even a longtime political foe had nothing but respect for Clay's success in 1850. Martin Van Buren asked a colleague to tell Clay that "he added a crowning grace to his public life . . . more honorable and durable than his election to the Presidency could possibly have been."[38] Clay's dramatic speech about the danger of secession would also influence Abraham Lincoln, who studied it when putting together his first inaugural address in 1861.[39]

Just over four years after delivering that masterpiece, Lincoln would lie in state at the US Capitol. He was only the second American to be accorded that honor. The first? Henry Clay, upon his death at age seventy-five in June 1852.[40]

THE SUCCESSES OF Clay reflect the tragedy of Clay. Whoever first pinned on him the Great Compromiser nickname surely meant to honor him. But being known as the man who is always willing to give something up to get others to join the deal has its downside.

For better or worse, Americans usually want clear-cut winners, not bargainers, as leaders. Clay met his ultimate goal of preserving the Union, whatever it took, during his lifetime. The very act of doing so repeatedly gave his opponents within his own party and across the aisle the ammunition they needed to keep him out of the presidency he so coveted.

And while he repeatedly forestalled Southern states' secession and likely civil war with those skillful compromises, he ended up perpetuating slavery, an institution he had grown increasingly uncomfortable with but never fully committed to eradicating. Like George Washington, he arranged that the slaves under his direct ownership would see freedom after his death. Like many supposedly enlightened slaveholders of the time, however, his imagination extended only to helping emancipated slaves move back to Africa to colonize land there for themselves.[41]

Had he not been preemptively removed from the presidency, would Clay have found a way to reach the ultimate compromise, ending slavery without enveloping the nation in a devastating war? It's unlikely. But his opponents, and even some allies, had underestimated him many times before.

WHEN ONE PARTY controls the White House for more than one term, a shift to the other party often follows. If, somehow, that first faction holds on for another four years, the pendulum swing becomes virtually certain.

In 1876, the Republican Party remarkably had held power for what would soon be a stunning *sixteen* years. But the second term of former Union general Ulysses Grant had taken shape as one of the most corrupt in American history. A weary country sought change, and Democrats were salivating at the chance to get back into the White House.

In strode a white knight, a true match for the mood of the electorate: New York's Democratic governor Samuel Tilden, who brought unprecedented anti-corruption credentials to the campaign. He also adopted the most effective campaign literature printing-and-mailing effort the nation had ever seen, putting his chosen narrative directly into tens of millions of voters' hands. All of this spurred a successful campaign against Republican Rutherford Hayes, in which Tilden convincingly won the popular vote and, most historians agree, the electoral vote if it had been counted fairly. But he failed to put the pieces in place to win the down-and-dirty contest *after* the election, which shockingly delivered the White House to Hayes in what is still considered the most corrupt election in American history. Political shenanigans preempted President Tilden's administration in the most amazing electoral story of the century, perhaps in all of American history.

MENTORED AS A young man by Martin Van Buren himself, Tilden turned his attentions to law and business, amassing a fortune via his uncanny sense of timing for the purchase and sale of assets.[42] He proved especially skillful in consolidating railroads, and doing it with more integrity than the norm for the era.[43]

Eventually public service called, but Tilden generally avoided the blatant self-promotion many other men of the era fell prey to. He instead pressed a reluctant Horatio Seymour ("Your candidate I cannot be," Seymour had declared) to accept the Democratic nomination in 1872 by telling him, "Your party has called you, and you will accept."[44] Then he managed Seymour's campaign against the wildly popular Ulysses Grant, hero of the Union war effort, earning respect for bringing Seymour a much stronger finish than most observers expected; he fell just over three hundred thousand votes short of Grant's three-million-plus total.[45]

After the election, Tilden took the reins of New York State's Democratic Party, which joined the Republican Party there in taking criticism for being under the thumb of the notorious Tweed Ring. This cabal, led by William Marcy "Boss" Tweed and his cronies, rigged contracts and jobs to build ill-gotten fortunes and to bribe greedy or vulnerable political leaders, judges, and journalists. For a while, Tilden stayed friendly to Tweed and his gang. But the flagrant corruption—just one county courthouse contract cost $12 million for work worth about $4 million, with the difference lining the pockets of unethical officials[46]—spurred Tilden to take it upon himself to "save from degradation the great party whose principles and traditions were mine by inheritance and conviction." In so doing, Tilden incurred the wrath of Tweed and his men, who tried to remove him from party management and end his political career early.[47]

Competing charters for the administration of New York City provided a new field of battle. When Tweed offered a laughable set of reforms that did little to change rotten practices, Tilden called his opponents "the most corrupt gang of political adventurers that ever ruled and robbed a helpless city."[48] In 1871, the revelation of fraudulent records exposed how the ring did business, with a prominent list of payoffs and kickbacks printed in the *New York Times*.[49] Tilden used the state party convention to go all out against the criminals: "I shall not vote for any one of Mr. Tweed's members of the legislature. And if that is to be regarded as the regular ticket, I will resign my place as a Chairman of the State Committee and help my people stem the tide of corruption. When I come to do my duty as an elector, I shall cast my vote for honest men."[50]

It worked. On Election Day in 1871, while Boss Tweed himself was reelected to the state senate, reform candidates in New York City crushed Tweed affiliates. The damage to the ring and its reputation was so severe that Tweed never actually took his seat. He ended up in jail, thanks in large part to Tilden's ongoing investigation.[51]

Now a hero of the reform movement, Tilden joined the state assembly in 1872 and became governor three years later, proceeding with prosecutions of Tweed Ring members as well as a similar Erie Canal syndicate. By also pushing for state laws to suspend public officials while under investigation, recover stolen property, and criminalize false payments, as well as lowering taxes, he made himself quite popular.[52]

A HARD-WORKING, ANTI-CORRUPTION CANDIDATE proved irresistible for the Democrats, who put Tilden atop their national ticket in 1876. Even Republicans found much to admire. "Mr. Tilden was in some respects the most striking figure in the Democratic Party since Andrew Jackson," Senator James Blaine of Maine later wrote, adding, "[He] unquestionably ranks among the greatest masters of political management that our day has seen."[53]

Tilden applied his work ethic and legendary administrative skills to his run for the White House, revolutionizing the use of campaign literature and targeted mailings under strong central supervision. He largely financed and managed the effort himself, investing in a newspaper popularity bureau and a literary bureau—full of writers, editors, artists, and other creative types—to push flattering personal portraits and anti-Hayes material out to the public via newspapers, pamphlets, and direct mail.[54] Republican nominee Rutherford Hayes, formerly a Union army officer and member of Congress and now Ohio's governor, showed no interest in an active or energetic campaign. He took a hands-off approach and made but one public appearance that fall, at the Centennial Exhibition in Philadelphia.[55]

Republicans had little to attack Tilden on. Old claims that Tilden had been slow to support Union efforts during the Civil War, neglectful on tax payments, and initially grudging in taking on New York corruption didn't really stick and appeared unlikely to sway the masses.[56] To try to match his opponent's anti-corruption credentials, Hayes pledged to step aside after one term if elected and jumped on the bandwagon by advocating civil service reform.[57] Republicans got the most traction out of repeating that Tilden surely couldn't be as honest as he seemed, and by highlighting that Tilden was just plain boring—a bookish guy who lacked personal charisma and strong speaking skills.[58] The public faced a choice, then, between the upright but understated Tilden, who made it clear he'd rather lose a million votes than that "the mechanics, the servant girls and laboring men should be robbed of their earnings," and the relatively unknown but seemingly affable Hayes.[59]

The Republican attacks kept coming, but campaign bets in New York City during the final dash for voters reportedly leaned Tilden's way at five-to-two odds.[60] Even backstabbing by bitter foes from the former Tweed Ring looked unlikely to turn the state away from Tilden.[61] This election would be close, really close, with the result ultimately relying on post-election machinations like the country had never seen.

ELECTION DAY LOOKED good for Tilden. In a record that still stands today, 82 percent of eligible voters turned out—a positive sign for the man trying to drive working Americans to the polls.

By the time polls closed on the West Coast, he already appeared to have 184 electoral votes in hand, just one short of the magic number for victory. Prominent Republicans, including future president James Garfield, thought the race over.[62] From the time initial returns from New York showed Tilden ahead, Hayes himself reportedly believed so, too: "I never supposed there was a chance for Republican success."[63] The *New York Tribune* headline read, "Tilden Elected."[64] Tilden had more than a quarter of a million votes over Hayes out of some eight million ballots cast, the apparent recipe for victory . . . if only the popular vote determined the winner.

South Carolina, Florida, and Louisiana remained close through the night. Without them, Tilden hadn't yet reached the winning electoral vote count. Republicans quickly realized they could control, or at worst buy off, the returning boards there, opening up a path to a fifth straight presidential election victory. Partisans in New York sent telegraph messages to colleagues in those three states, urging them to ensure the vote came out against Tilden.[65]

In a burst of wishful thinking and masterful expectation-setting, the Republican national chairman declared the morning after the election that Hayes had won 185 votes and would be the next commander in chief. Tilden's supporters cried foul, especially after the Republican-leaning returning boards proceeded to toss out enough Democratic votes to indeed appear to award each state's electoral votes to Hayes. In intimidation- and fraud-rampant Florida and Louisiana in particular, this strained credulity.[66] To confuse matters further, political divisions in these three key Southern states led to a farce in which each sent in two sets of returns from different elements in the state governments, all claiming to speak authoritatively. In all three states, outgoing Republican governors signed election certificates supporting Hayes. In South Carolina, the Democratic outgoing legislature sent a certificate in favor of Tilden. In Florida, the same was done by the Democratic attorney general. And in

Louisiana, a Democrat who had lost the 1872 gubernatorial election but remained the rightful governor in the eyes of many Louisianans backed a certificate for Tilden.[67] The new question was: Which certificates should Congress accept?

Eventually, the House and Senate, whose respective votes on the matter were under the control of Democrats and Republicans, settled on an electoral commission of five representatives, five senators, and four justices from the Supreme Court to decide about the disputed returns. To achieve the closest possible thing to parity, the parties agreed that the four justices should choose a fifth from their cohort as the probable swing vote on the commission. All eyes went to esteemed Illinois jurist David Davis, longtime confidant of the late Abraham Lincoln, who had appointed Davis to the high court. Originally a Republican, now a fierce independent, he'd been nominated for the presidency by a third party in 1872 and was even mentioned as a likely cabinet member under, and possible successor to, Tilden should the Democrats win this election.[68] His impartiality stood unparalleled; of his later service in the US Senate, some said, "If he voted twice in succession with the same party, he appeared to be alarmed lest he should take on the character of a partisan, and made haste [to vote] next time with the other side."[69] The political class viewed the judge as one of the most fair and balanced men in America.

But the Illinois legislature elected Davis to a vacant US Senate seat just after the electoral commission bill passed. Davis had been reluctant to join the electoral commission anyway, probably because any decision it made would alienate half the electorate and thus impede his own presidential ambitions, and the selection as a senator gave him the excuse he wanted to refuse to serve on the commission.[70] The justices in late January chose as the final member of the electoral commission Joseph Bradley, a Republican who had nonetheless voted with the court in 1876 to limit federal civil rights enforcement power in the South, making him the most acceptable option left for the Democrats.[71] The commission would have until Inauguration Day, still held in early March back then, to help Congress decide who won the election.

And when that day came, Hayes managed to take the prize. The commission and Congress had given *all* the electoral votes from the disputed states to him, leaving Tilden still one vote short, and shut out from serving as the nineteenth president of the United States. His supporters, building on their outrage since Election Day, threatened force with shouts of "Tilden or blood!"[72] and sent their cheated leader telegrams such as "If you say the word, 50,000 Louisianans will take up guns for you."[73] Members of Democratic state and county committees enrolled "minutemen" in case war broke out.[74] The final electoral vote results engendered many threatening letters to Hayes, including one containing sketches of daggers, knives, and revolvers.[75] People coast to coast mocked the rise of the man they contemptuously labeled "Rutherfraud B. Hayes."

What did Tilden, the superior planner and organizer, do with all of this? Oddly, not much.

He had spent most of December writing a long, scholarly report on the history of electoral ballot-counting, which contributed nothing to the outcome, while resisting fervent calls to take substantial action on his own behalf.[76] Far from galvanizing him, entreaties to violence only bolstered his resolve to keep calm and respect the system. He abjured violence and accepted his fate.[77] He probably would have agreed with the later reflections of Representative James Monroe, a Republican from Ohio, who wrote, "It was more important that the presidential issue should be decided effectively than that it should be decided rightly."[78]

President Grant asked Hayes to take his oath one day early in a small, private ceremony, just in case demonstrations interfered with Inauguration Day events. Hayes, however, began his term without another civil war. Tilden showed his bitterness mostly in private, playing on the new president's initials by referring to him as "Returning Board Hayes."[79]

THE DEBACLE OF 1876–1877 had several major consequences. First, it reinforced Americans' disgust with corrupt electoral politics. A committee appointed in 1878 by the House of Representatives to investigate the Hayes-Tilden election exposed to the public many unscrupulous aspects of the contest—from voter suppression before the election to ballot tampering during it to efforts by supporters of *both* candidates to bribe the three Southern swing states' election officials during the returning-board debacle.[80] Its findings suggested that while Hayes would have been the winner had African Americans felt less intimidated from voting, Tilden would have been the winner had Republicans not manipulated ballots and bribed members of returning boards.[81] Perhaps as a result of revulsion to these tactics, which appeared to exceed the dirty tricks in previous campaigns, voter turnout in future presidential election years would never again reach the level achieved in the Hayes-Tilden contest.

Second, the battle over the Southern returning boards effectively ended the post–Civil War policy of Reconstruction. President Hayes delivered what the negotiations to get him into office demanded: the withdrawal of remaining US government troops from the South. Millions of African Americans thereby lost federal protection from what would become many decades of abuses at the hands of resurgent former Confederates.[82]

Third, it reinforced the double-sided nature of presidential transitions in the United States. On one hand, the outcome of any one presidential contest, even if it looked to many like a preemptive removal of a duly elected president, remained less important to a wide swath of the public and to the ultimately defeated candidate than getting a new president in place peacefully. "It showed the deep attachment of our people to law rather than revolution as a means of settling differences," wrote Representative Monroe. "It has enabled us to feel that we could approach another dangerous crisis in our affairs with less trepidation as to the result."[83] On the other hand, the country proved willing to accept an election result widely perceived as rigged, putting in place a probably fraudulent president, in order to maintain the streak of peaceful inaugurations. At what point, if ever, would electoral injustice seem too high to tolerate?

Tilden, for his part, suffered physical decline but kept a brave public face. "Be of good cheer," he told a dinner crowd in June 1877. "The Republic will live. The institutions of our fathers are not to expire in shame. The sovereignty of the people shall be rescued from this peril and re-established."[84] He never ran again for the office he thought he'd won fair and square in 1876.

L OOKING FOR THE origins of the United States of America as a global power? You'd best include the work of James Blaine—the living, breathing bridge between the "keep the Union together" era of the man he looked up to, Abraham Lincoln, and the "America as world power" era that accelerated from the administrations of William McKinley and Theodore Roosevelt through the twentieth century.

While most political leaders in the latter third of the nineteenth century devoted their attention and effort to Reconstruction and other domestic political controversies, this crafty Republican from Maine strategized about expanding America's role in international affairs. More than his contemporaries, Blaine envisioned the global player that the United States would become. Along the way, he also stumped like few others of his time, winning rare coast-to-coast popularity.

Yet Blaine was kept out of the White House in 1884, by the thinnest of margins, due to the efforts of two very different men: a rakish party colleague whom he had mocked in a floor speech in the House of Representatives, creating a lifelong enemy, and his Democratic opponent in the election, whose willingness to tell a difficult truth won him the White House in Blaine's place.

EVEN AS A teacher and a newspaper editor in his twenties, Blaine had a keen eye for talent and a strong political sense. In 1858, he judged that Stephen Douglas would beat Abraham Lincoln for the US Senate seat from Illinois, but also assessed correctly that Lincoln would turn the tables and defeat Douglas in the 1860 presidential election.[85]

Blaine, serving in Maine's legislature when Lincoln took office, would move to the US House of Representatives during the Civil War and become Speaker of the House in 1869, all before he turned forty. Colleagues didn't always agree with him, but he usually made a strong impression. "There have been few more interesting personalities in the public life of any nation than James G. Blaine," wrote one longtime White House employee, who vividly described Blaine's "peculiar blend of temperaments in which the elemental power of a crowd goes to the head like wine, but wine which clears the brain, focuses all the faculties into the one masculine passion for domination."[86]

Usually, his strong bearing, cogent arguments, and masterful speaking style drew people to him. A Republican representative four decades his senior, Thaddeus Stevens of Pennsylvania, once blamed a losing vote on "the House, partaking of the magnetic manner of my friend from Maine."[87] Fellow lawmaker and future president James Garfield said Blaine stood out as "the readiest man with the current facts of political history I have ever known and uses them in running debate with tremendous force and effectiveness. On the whole he is the completest gladiator in debate I know of."[88]

Blaine eagerly traveled to far-flung states to campaign for fellow Republicans, developing a base of fans calling themselves "Blainiacs" who virtually worshipped him. One colleague said, "I defy anyone, Republican or Democrat, to be in his company half an hour and go away from him anything less than a personal friend."[89] "I love Blaine as much as you can possibly," an Iowa Republican wrote. "I will die unsatisfied and with lessened faith in American sense and appreciation if he is never President."[90]

Not everyone fell under Blaine's spell, however, among them the arrogant and imperious Roscoe Conkling from New York, who walked into every room as if he owned it. The two representatives clashed vividly on the floor of the House in 1866, leading Blaine to colorfully attack Conkling's "haught disdain, his grandiloquent swell, his majestic, supereminent, overpowering, turkey-gobbler strut."[91] Conkling never forgot the public insult; almost twenty years later, it would come back to haunt Blaine.

The man from Maine wanted the presidency, and he didn't like the idea of waiting for it. In only his midforties, the congressman sought the 1876 Republican nomination and it seemed like he might just get it. Then a scandal emerged. Some nine years earlier, the directors of a major railroad company had conspired to charge the government exorbitant rates for work on the transcontinental railroad and bribe government officials with the ill-gotten gains. A congressional investigation in December 1872 had found Blaine, like many others, on the receiving end of valuable railroad bonds.[92] His career took only a small hit at that time; opponents couldn't prove criminal wrongdoing.

Now that he was running for president, a clerk emerged in 1876 with letters that, he publicly claimed, showed a more active Blaine role than the congressman had let on. Blaine used a subsequent private meeting to steal from the clerk what he considered his private letters. Rejecting calls to turn them over to investigators, Blaine instead read excerpts to the House, which surprisingly seemed to stem the damage. The entire episode nevertheless exhausted the candidate, who collapsed in public, adding to Republican delegates' doubts about him and contributing to his lost nomination.[93] Even an otherwise gushing biographer had to admit the letters "put Mr. Blaine on the defensive at a most inopportune time."[94]

Something useful emerged from that election cycle. Republican orator Robert Ingersoll delivered a speech about Blaine so fulsome, even by the low standards of obsequious convention oratory, that it remains one of history's most visual descriptions of a presidential candidate: "Like an armed warrior, like a plumed knight, James G. Blaine marched down the halls of the American Congress and threw his shining lances full and fair against the brazen forehead of every defamer of his country and maligner of his honor."[95] It's hard to top that, so Blaine left the House of Representatives behind and moved on to the Senate. He wasn't there long.

Again in 1880, Blaine aimed to win the presidential nomination. Again, he lost. The party's nod and the election victory went to his friend James Garfield, who hadn't sought the nomination in the first place but took it as a way to bring together clashing party factions. The new president appointed Blaine secretary of state, a position that had already launched six men to the presidency, more than any other cabinet role.

Together, Garfield and his chief diplomat embarked upon a more assertive foreign policy in the Western Hemisphere and sought to expand the country's commercial treaties, only to see their initiatives largely cut short by an assassin's bullet.[96] Vice President Chester Arthur, who had never held elective office before, took the top spot. The upcoming election in 1884 looked like Blaine's to lose. And that's how it turned out, because of two very different men from New York.

BLAINE ENTERED THE new election year only fifty-four years old, yet he'd already been thirteen years a representative from Maine, Speaker of the House from 1869 to 1875, a five-year senator, and secretary of state. His prospects for a victory in November looked good, as the Democrats put forward Grover Cleveland, who'd never held office outside of New York State. Even former President Ulysses Grant, who had soured on Blaine when the two men fought for the Republican nomination in 1880, acknowledged four years later that "to reject such a man in all the plentitude of his knowledge, ability and will for a man of Grover Cleveland's limited experience would be beneath the good sense of the American people."[97]

Yet others disagreed, none more so than the man who had spent most of the past two decades becoming a preeminent Republican power broker and stewing over Blaine's public insult—Roscoe Conkling, now a senator from New York. The key to the contest in 1884, like other presidential elections in that era, was Conkling's state: whoever won New York was likely to take the White House. Cleveland served there as a popular governor, but the man Blaine had mocked for his "turkey-gobbler strut" still pulled many strings in the state. Conkling could carry New York for Republicans, if he wanted to. For Blaine, he didn't. When the nominee's allies reached out to Conkling to get him to speak for Blaine in the state, Conkling replied, "No, thank you, I don't engage in criminal practice."[98]

Because the parties' positions on the major issues of the day echoed each other, personal factors would play a huge role in this campaign. Conkling-leaning Republicans joined the Democratic press in consistently harping on Blaine's railroad scandal and those damned letters. Cartoonists illustrated him as a circus "tattooed man," carrying on his skin the evidence of his supposed crimes.[99] Cleveland himself refused to go low, even buying supposed evidence of Blaine's personal indiscretions, tearing the papers to shreds, and burning them. "The other side can have a monopoly on all the dirt in this campaign," he said. Other Democrats pulled few punches, however, painting Blaine's skills of persuasion as manipulative tricks to aid his schemes for power and money.[100]

Blaine's supporters over the summer found some dirt to hammer the seemingly clean Cleveland about: a reported son, born out of wedlock some ten years earlier. Cleveland put on a clinic in damage control, admitting without shame that he supported the child, even while asserting the paternity of the boy remained uncertain. To a friend who wrote to him for guidance on how the party should react, Cleveland simply responded, "Tell the truth."[101] The people loved it. His forthright approach morphed what could have been a campaign-ending scandal into evidence of his personal integrity and reliability. "After the primary offense," said a respected minister who investigated the case, Cleveland's behavior "was singularly honorable, showing no attempt to evade responsibility, and doing all he could to meet the duties involved, of which marriage was certainly not one."[102]

The election looked very close, especially in New York, as Election Day approached. Some votes in Manhattan were certainly lost to the Republican side after an elderly pastor of a church there spoke, with Blaine right on the platform beside him, about Democrats as the party of "rum, Romanism, and rebellion"—not subtle code words.[103] Blaine took days to renounce the comment, missing a chance to minimize the damage.

Conkling undermined him, too. He privately urged colleagues to vote against Blaine. He reportedly inspired many Republicans in his Oneida County stronghold to support Cleveland openly.[104] That county, which had gone for each Republican presidential candidate since the 1850s, this time turned out for the Democrat.[105] Conkling, it seemed, had gained sweet revenge on his rival.

The result? Blaine lost New York, and with it the national electoral vote majority, by merely 1,049 votes. Oneida County alone could have done it; its 2,000-plus vote margin for Garfield in 1880 oddly had flipped to a 19-vote margin for Cleveland in 1884.[106]

Blaine later served three more years as secretary of state under President Benjamin Harrison, with more success than he'd had during his brief stint doing the same for Garfield. The United States might not have the Hawaiian Islands, for one thing, without his diplomatic work in that second State Department tour. But he was never again the Republican nominee for president, much less a president.

Chapter Four

Displaced by Death

Being a forgotten president would be an improvement
for William Henry Harrison.[1]
—MICHAEL GERHARDT

O N THE COLD and windy first day of the new chief executive's term, the old man just wouldn't stop talking.

No president's inaugural address had ever exceeded forty-five hundred words. More often than not, they'd come in well under two thousand words. But William Henry Harrison insisted in March 1841 upon delivering a mind-numbing, seemingly interminable speech of around eighty-five hundred words. The crowd remained outside for two long hours in the chill, listening to him cite ancient history and devote many more words to relations between the executive and legislative branches than appeared in the Constitution's own articles on the subject. The new commander in chief made himself sick, and found himself in a coffin a month later.

That's how conventional wisdom has it. Like so many other stories about the presidency, it's a bit more complicated.

HARRISON LOOKED A bit elderly for the job back in 1836, when he ran against Andrew Jackson's handpicked successor, Vice President Martin Van Buren. At sixty-four years old, Harrison *even then* would have been, by more than two years, the oldest man elected to a first term, and when he failed he seemed ready to retire.

But the former general's image and broad appeal during that ill-fated run inspired the Whigs to put him forward as their champion again four years later. In his sixty-ninth year, Harrison in 1840 was almost as old as the aging Jackson had been when he left office in 1837, after two full terms. Harrison's renomination seemed a gift to the Democrats. Opponents slammed Harrison's physical and mental condition, including not so subtle references to him as an "old gentleman" with "feeble understanding."[2] Some Democrats even stooped to calling their opponent names like "Old Granny" and referred to his nomination as the "coffining, nailing up, and burial of the Whig party."[3]

Voters thus went to the polls with their eyes wide open about Harrison's advanced age. They elected him anyway, with a decent popular vote victory and a tidal wave in the electoral college. As he made his two-week trip from Indiana to Washington to prepare to take office, well-wishers cheered him at each stop. Superstitious types may have raised an eyebrow when he said to a crowd in Cincinnati, "Perhaps this may be the last time I may have the pleasure of speaking to you on earth or seeing you. I will bid farewell, if forever, fare thee well."[4] Another bad omen could have been the wind-driven snow accompanying his arrival in the nation's capital on February 9.[5]

A crowd estimated in the tens of thousands attended the chilly inauguration festivities on March 4. They heard their new president talk . . . and talk . . . and talk some more. Any ears that hadn't already gone numb from the blustery cold heard him declare, quite correctly, that he would not be seeking a second term as president; some of them surely felt his speech nearly lasted a full term all by itself. But what the spectators saw gave no indication trouble would soon come. "His bodily health was manifestly perfect," one newspaper reported, describing "alertness in his movement which is quite astonishing, considering his advanced age, the multiplied hardships through which his frame has passed, and the fatigues he has lately undergone."[6]

His administration began well, and quickly. Harrison made Congress happy with comments in his inauguration address that emphasized the deference he would have shown to the legislative branch.[7] While angering Whig Party heavyweight Henry Clay by passing over several of his recommendations for appointments, the president pleased many others in the party (and even some Democrats) with many of the people he chose to join his administration.[8] The Senate unanimously confirmed his cabinet right after inauguration.[9]

Harrison called for Congress to convene in late May for a special session to tackle the depleted treasury and other pressing financial concerns.[10] In his first few weeks, he made time to visit all the executive departments, an unusual move for presidents in that era. He familiarized himself with their activities and tasked them to provide detailed reports about their offices' operations. He also vowed to protect government employees who satisfactorily performed their job duties, even if they were Democrats—a rarity in those days, long before nonpartisan civil service rules would be established.[11] It was a strong, systematic beginning to the presidency.

Then he got sick.

ON MARCH 26, three weeks after that verbose, windswept day, Harrison requested the presence of his personal physician, Dr. Thomas Miller. He told Miller he'd been suffering from fatigue and anxiety, alongside a persistent abdominal discomfort and other assorted pains. Although Harrison's condition improved somewhat overnight, Miller returned to the executive mansion the following afternoon to prescribe remedies for a new symptom: a severe chill. Ailments, however, would snowball; Harrison soon suffered also from nausea, sharp thirst, and severe pains both in his right side and in his head.

His condition rose and fell in the next couple of days, but eventually turned worse as persistent coughing and shortness of breath joined his list of symptoms. By April 1, Miller saw him looking worse and acting incoherently. Lethargy and diarrhea developed until the evening of Saturday, April 3,[12] when the president said to his physician—perhaps thinking he was talking to Vice President John

Tyler—"Sir, I wish you to understand the true principles of the Government. I wish them carried out. I ask nothing more."[13] Early the following morning, Harrison died.

Historians generally say the president died of pneumonia. And he very well may have. But what caused *that*? Probably not the long-winded delivery of a dull speech that kept him out in the bitter chill and wind so long. Two doctors who recently reexamined this cold case claim Miller's own doubts about his diagnosis of pneumonia and the progression of Harrison's symptoms point elsewhere: bacteria from a nearby sewage dumping ground, which caused a gastrointestinal infection called enteric fever. This, in turn, probably triggered his lung inflammation and other aches and pains during that final week of his life.[14]

The campaign rhetoric about Harrison's age ironically hadn't prepared the elite in the nation's capital for his death. "There was no failure of health or strength to indicate such an event," wrote a senator, "or to excite apprehension that he would not go through his term with the vigor with which he commenced it."[15]

Democrats, happy about not having to face the popular general again, celebrated Harrison's departure from office. "A kind and over-ruling providence has interfered to prolong our glorious Union and happy republican system which Genl. Harrison and his cabinet was preparing to destroy," wrote former president Andrew Jackson.[16] The Democratic Party would, indeed, win the presidency in 1844.

ONE STUDY OF presidential illnesses and deaths found that American chief executives, as a group, tend to die prematurely when compared to the wider population. Sometimes death arrives during their presidencies.[17] If a political party is foolish enough to nominate someone really old or frail, it opens up an option that saves the opposition a lot of effort. It merely requires patience: remove the president by just letting him die.

Two of the country's first twelve chief executives passed away while in office; Harrison's sad story was followed, in less than a decade, by another presidential death in 1850. In each case, the opposing party took advantage of that popular leader's absence to take the White House back in the next election. Two more presidents followed suit within the century after that, but political enemies failed to similarly seize the opportunity and regain the presidency.

Although the country's first several leaders didn't come to office as young men, they generally had no life-threatening incidents while in office. George Washington during his presidency explained to Thomas Jefferson that his physical condition was declining, his bad memory was getting worse, and his mental faculties were in decay, but he lived a relatively active life for almost three years after leaving his two terms behind him.[18]

James Madison, for one, did stare death in the face while serving as chief executive. About halfway through his time in office, he arranged to have an urgent letter sent to members of Congress with whom he'd intended to meet to inform them that neither could he see them "nor can he at present fix a day when it will be in his power." It turns out he'd fallen victim to an intestinal ailment and fever that knocked him down and kept him there for the greater part of a month. Madison's illness became so severe, in fact, that he couldn't even read congressional resolutions a representative had brought to him. During the worst of it, he couldn't get out of bed at all. The spotlight rested for a couple of weeks on his older and less impressive vice president, Elbridge Gerry, who himself would die the following year. Madison eventually pulled out of it, though, and lived to be eighty-five.[19]

John Tyler, Harrison's running mate in 1840 who took the reins of power upon the elderly president's demise, faced a very different threat to his life less than two years into his only slightly abbreviated term. On February 28, 1843, Tyler joined Secretary of the Navy Thomas Gilmer, Secretary of State Abel Upshur, Senator Thomas Hart Benton, and hundreds of other A-list politicians for a very special, invitation-only trip down the Potomac River. Instead of taking a casual cruising boat, they boarded the USS *Princeton*. This state-of-the-art warship featured a cannon with a fifteen-foot iron barrel, dubbed the *Peacemaker*, which the crew fired repeatedly to demonstrate its awesome capability. The assemblage passed Mount Vernon, prompting Secretary Gilmer to ask the captain to fire the gun just one more time, to honor George Washington.[20] Tyler remained below deck, chatting with his new love interest and soon to be second wife, Julia Gardiner. Much of the capital's elite, meanwhile, assembled around the massive *Peacemaker*.

"I saw the hammer pulled back," remembered Benton, who'd taken a position next to the cannon, "heard a tap—saw a flash—felt a blast in the face, and knew that my hat was gone: and that was the last I knew of the world, or of myself, for a time, of which I can give no account." The *Peacemaker* had exploded, leaving a horrific carnage of twisted metal and mangled bodies. "The first that I knew of myself, or anything afterwards, was rising up at the breech of the gun, seeing the gun itself split open," Benton wrote. "All that were on the left had been killed, the gun bursting on that side. . . . Twenty feet of the vessel's bulwark immediately behind me was blown away." Gilmer and Upshur lay dead. So did Gardiner's father and five others. Benton was among the twenty wounded. Tyler, down under, heard the deafening boom and felt the ship shudder. But he and his lady friend, by lingering there, had escaped injury.[21] No chief executive had ever come so close to a fatal accident.

Tyler's case is the most prominent one of its type, but many American leaders have also had, or barely dodged, serious health issues or accidents during their terms. Andrew Jackson carried in his body the metallic by-products of his frequent duels as a younger man. Abraham Lincoln suffered from numerous ailments, including smallpox in 1863. James Polk deteriorated physically during his four-year term and would die, probably of cholera, just three months after it ended. Franklin Pierce, as president-elect, survived the train derailment that killed his son, who'd been sitting just behind him. Chester Arthur found out while in the White House that he had Bright's disease, a fatal kidney condition; less than two years after leaving office, it would end his life. John Kennedy's chronic back pain and Addison's disease, which caused hormone deficiencies, spurred him to take a heavy cocktail of steroids and other drugs while in office. Temporarily incapacitating medical events hit others during their presidencies, including Grover Cleveland, Woodrow Wilson, and Dwight Eisenhower.

And a few others had it worse, because they couldn't stop natural causes from taking them out of office prematurely.

A MAN WHO HAD neither run for any political office nor even voted until his own presidential election became president in 1849.

Seeing Zachary Taylor—another army general recruited by the Whig Party, popular for battlefield success instead of any governing experience—enter the White House made Democrats, and even some fellow Whigs, sick to their stomachs. In sixteen months, amid mounting political controversy, Taylor's own sick stomach would take him to the grave. Even there, he'd find no peace. Investigators dragged his body out more than a century later to test a conspiracy theory involving a dastardly mix of poison and politics.

TAYLOR HAD GROWN up modestly despite his birth on a Virginia plantation, familial ties to James Madison, and a father who'd risen to lieutenant colonel in the Revolutionary War. He moved as a boy with his family to Kentucky, where he settled on a career in the army. He'd see significant action in the War of 1812, the Black Hawk War, and the Second Seminole War. After spending some time in Louisiana as an officer, he relocated his family there and acquired a healthy chunk of property, including, under the laws at the time, slaves.

Success during the Mexican-American War made Taylor a hero. Reports spread nationwide about his leadership in battle after battle in which US troops triumphed over larger Mexican forces. Even reports of Taylor's mercy toward retreating enemy soldiers, which angered President Polk and others, who preferred a more aggressive approach toward Mexico, won him respect from many Americans. Taylor's annoyance at Polk and the other likely contestants in the presidential election of 1848 made him receptive to Whig efforts to draft him. Alongside party stalwart Millard Fillmore, Taylor defeated the lackluster Democratic ticket of Lewis Cass and William Butler with a little help from former Democrat Martin Van Buren, who garnered around 10 percent of the vote in an independent run.[22]

Taylor took office older than Harrison would have been had he won his first try at the White House. By most accounts, the man called "Old Rough and Ready" lived a healthy life. But during the second week of August 1849, not even eighteen months into his term, Taylor's travel in Pennsylvania brought him severe chills, diarrhea, vomiting, and a high fever. At one point, his doctor called in for consultations a navy surgeon stationed in nearby Erie, Pennsylvania, to whose house they moved Taylor when his fever and shaking continued. His weakness lingered, making it difficult for him to walk more than a few steps until September.[23]

Autumn back in Washington seemed to refresh Taylor. That Pennsylvania episode, however, foreshadowed worse times to come. On the political side, he largely bungled things. As historian John Hope Franklin put it, "He didn't have much of a career."[24] He delegated most appointments to his cabinet, missing opportunities to reward all those who had helped him most during his campaign. When he *did* exert influence, he used it to leave some of Polk's late selections in place to try to win over Democrats—an unpopular move among Whig loyalists—and succumbed to nepotism.[25] Early plans to boldly resolve issues in the country's western territories, from slavery's status there to the protection of Mormon communities in what became Utah, floundered. A year into the administration, Taylor had failed to present, much less enact, any significant policy.[26] Then the flawed Compromise of 1850, which held off the country's inexorable slide toward a civil war a bit longer, only succeeded because the president got out of its way.[27] "His apparent abdication of power," writes historian Michael Holt, "betrayed his campaign vows to represent the people as president."[28]

SUMMERS IN THE nation's capital are notoriously muggy, and 1851 was no different. On the Fourth of July, as the worst conditions of the season oppressed them,[29] Washingtonians attended special festivities at the emerging Washington Monument, on which construction had just begun two years earlier.

President Taylor joined the fun. He spent much of it on a shaded platform with his cabinet to watch the first president's adopted son dedicate a stone Washingtonians had donated for use in the monument's construction. The president ultimately spent hours outside in the heat and humidity, both to hear additional speakers and to take a long walk along the Potomac River. He returned in the late afternoon to the White House,[30] liberally drinking chilled milk and heartily munching on iced cherries to cool off. Not a bad idea on such a sweltering day—except authorities had just warned that such food and drink could spread the Asiatic cholera that had been making its way through the country.[31]

On top of the day's stress on his body, Taylor was already tired; he'd had trouble sleeping the night before and was under some emotional distress. So we can't necessarily blame the cherries and milk for what followed, especially in light of his gastrointestinal issues several months earlier.[32] He felt ill that night and downright awful the next day, consumed by stomach pain and diarrhea.[33] An army surgeon called it "cholera morbus," a catch-all mid-nineteenth-century term for a wide variety of intestinal ailments. Taylor in the next few days added to his symptoms a fever, extreme thirst, and vomiting. He lost his final battle on the evening of July 9, 1850.[34]

Precisely what killed Taylor remains a mystery. Benton described Taylor passing "suddenly, and unexpectedly, of violent fever, brought on by long exposure to the burning heat of a fourth of July sun—noted as the warmest of the season."[35] But why, then, didn't everyone else consuming the same things under the same conditions succumb in the same way at the same time? Others in Washington did, in fact, suffer similar symptoms that summer, but not necessarily linked to the food and drink that day. The president, like many city dwellers, that summer partook of food or water tainted by pathogens from the open city sewers of the time. The sickness just happened to hit Taylor's system hardest after that fateful celebration day.[36]

Almost a century and a half after Taylor's death, a historical novelist and former humanities professor suspected a conspiracy lurking behind these explanations. Connecting Taylor's symptoms with what she'd read about the rising political tensions and personal intrigues of his time, she wondered, Did pro-slavery political opponents poison Taylor? The suggestion seemed odd to his descendants. "Nobody ever brought it up," one of his great-great-great-great-granddaughters said. "It was not a question at all."[37] The persistent amateur sleuth went ahead and contacted a forensic anthropologist, who told her that Taylor's symptoms could indeed be explained by arsenic.

Thankfully, science could still help, all those years later. Arsenic poisoning, the expert told her, would leave ample evidence in whatever body tissue remained in Taylor's coffin.[38] The family agreed to have samples taken from his body in 1991 for examination. The results surprised few except the novelist; arsenic levels were unremarkable, hundreds to thousands of times smaller than the medical examiner would have expected to see if Taylor's foes actually had used that toxin to remove him from office.[39] Since no other known poison would explain the symptoms nearly as well, Taylor probably died of the same things many people of the era did—natural causes, such as bacteria unimpeded by antibiotics and modern-day medical treatment.[40]

SEVEN DECADES WOULD pass before another president died in office as a result of something other than an assassin's bullet. And, as with Taylor's death, Warren Harding's demise in 1923 eventually spurred rumors of foul play.

The stately Ohio senator had come in a lowly sixth place on the first round of voting at the 1920 Republican convention, but rose quickly in the deadlock above him to seize the nomination on the tenth ballot. The groundswell of enthusiastic supporters in his home state and beyond didn't include one man: Harding himself. "The only thing I really worry about," he had told a friend at the very end of 1919, "is that I might be nominated and elected. That's an awful thing to contemplate."[41] James Cox, the Democratic nominee who also hailed from Ohio, proved little competition for the charming and affable Harding. Even uninspiring campaign slogans like "Back to Normalcy" and "Let's be done with the wiggle and wobble" couldn't stop the juggernaut.[42]

Harding won by the largest popular-vote majority in a hundred years, becoming the first man to win the presidency while serving as a senator. He brought into office the advantage of relative youth: he was just fifty-four years old when elected. Few concerns about Harding's health surfaced during the campaign or early in his term. In fact, he proved lively enough to pursue not only a heavy work schedule but also plenty of wager-filled rounds of golf and cards and risky extramarital liaisons. Even a friendly biographer notes the contrast between Harding's enjoyment of the pleasures of life with his lack of historical, economic, or legal knowledge and his "relatively untrained and undisciplined mind."[43] On that basis, as one of the agents protecting him put it, perhaps "he should never have been President of the United States."[44]

He made a good show of it, at least. Popular early moves included restoring regular news conferences, which Woodrow Wilson had let fade, and opening the gates to the White House grounds, restricted since the country's entry into the First World War in 1917, so citizens could stroll right up and look in the windows.[45] Tax cuts spurred years of economic growth and signaled the start of the "Roaring Twenties." Harding nevertheless felt inadequate and overwhelmed by his duties, confiding to a friend, "I am not fit for this office and should never have been here."[46] It showed, as Harding's lax oversight over his subordinates enabled major corruption scandals that have played the largest part in landing his administration near the bottom of historical presidential rankings.

ALTHOUGH HE SHOWED a vibrant, energetic face to the world, Harding was far from a healthy man.

Nervous indigestion had presented since childhood. Before he even ran for president, his body showed the effects of more than two decades of overeating, drinking, and smoking: high blood pressure and signs of a heart problem. Exhaustion and occasional chest pains troubled him by the end of his first year in office. A nasty case of the flu soon thereafter, possibly accompanied by a small heart attack, brought sleep dysfunction and difficulty breathing while lying down.[47] A famous heart surgeon attended a dinner party with Harding in late 1922 and later informed a friend that, in his assessment, the president had advanced heart disease and "would be dead in six months."[48]

Secret Service man Edmund Starling witnessed the decline. Harding had increasingly complained to him about getting extremely tired, with heavy feet, after only eleven or twelve holes on the golf course. The president nevertheless wouldn't kick his smoking habit. Starling had also done protection duty at the White House during the previous administration, when he'd watched Woodrow Wilson's health spiral downward. Now he saw a similar deterioration in the new president.[49]

Harding and his wife, Florence, took a long trip in the summer of 1923, by train and car all the way across the country and then by ship on an unprecedented presidential visit to the Alaska Territory. His itinerary was packed with speeches, meetings with local Republicans, and other sessions. Florence could tell something was amiss before their departure. Anticipating trouble during the voyage, she had instructed the Secret Service to keep the president's doctors close by, in adjoining rooms if possible.[50] His personal doctor advised against the busy schedule his political advisors had arranged for him; one colleague from the Senate who was worried about the president's decline told Harding that he might not return to Washington alive.[51] But as soon as he hit the rails, the crowd reactions to his speeches often boosted his spirits and gave him renewed energy to punch through his various ailments. Extended stretches without any functions to attend while traveling to and in Alaska—four days at sea getting there, and several more days by rail to the interior— also helped.[52]

But not enough. While on a train from Seattle to California on July 27, the president experienced upper abdominal pains and nausea. Two of the physicians who saw him assessed that Harding's heart had malfunctioned. A couple of days later, in San Francisco, X-rays indicated pneumonia, and blood tests pointed to significant heart problems. His doctors kept the exhausted and weak president in bed for a few days, trying to prevent the damage from getting any worse.[53]

By August 2, the president seemed much improved. On that evening, as Harding's spirits were higher than they'd been in some time, Florence sat with her husband and read to him an article from the *Saturday Evening Post* titled "A Calm View of a Calm Man."[54] Without warning, his face showed a tremor, his body shuddered, and he passed away quickly in front of his wife.[55]

Controversy over Harding's death emerged. The doctors on site cited a brain hemorrhage but also mentioned a ruptured heart wall, and the totality of medical evidence suggests a heart attack was the fatal ailment.[56] But Florence's solitary presence in the room with the president as he died, her adamant refusal to allow an autopsy, and revelations about Harding's affairs—including one confirmed love child—raised suspicions that something more nefarious might have taken place. One former government official (himself involved in some of the scandals that engulfed the Harding presidency, reducing his credibility) claimed Florence admitted she poisoned her husband, declaring about the foul deed, "I have no regrets."[57] Most scholars and investigators, however, agree the evidence points to an overworked heart, rather than the hand of a jealous wife.

America's longest-serving president was also the country's most famously ill leader. Franklin Roosevelt, during President Harding's first year in office, had lost control of his legs and nearly died of what was diagnosed then as polio, but which more recent medical analysis suggests was Guillain-Barré syndrome.[58] For two decades, he dealt constantly and courageously with its effects, learning to "swing-walk" with the assistance of leg braces.

That didn't hinder his campaign in 1932 to unseat Herbert Hoover, which he did, in a landslide, to become the thirty-second president of the United States. At the Democratic Party convention in 1936 that nominated him for a second term, an acquaintance who'd been pushed forward by a well-meaning crowd knocked FDR's son off balance, pushing him into Roosevelt and breaking one of the braces. Luck smiled that day. The brace did not sever his paralyzed leg, and a nearby Secret Service agent caught the president just before he hit the platform.[59] Roosevelt took a few moments to regain his balance and had the scattered pages of his remarks gathered for him before going ahead with a rousing speech.

"Franklin D. Roosevelt was completely fearless except about one thing—fire," one of his Secret Service agents recalled. "His fear was nothing, though, compared to ours. The White House is beautiful, it's historic, and all our hearts beat a little faster when we see it. It is also the biggest firetrap in America, bar none." So in the event of a fire anywhere in the executive mansion, the agents planned to carry FDR down the stairs. They had a backup plan: canvas fire chutes, which they would drop from his room to the ground. The Secret Service took these fire chutes wherever the president went.[60]

Otherwise, the effects of Roosevelt's paralysis, which he tried to hide from public view most of the time, didn't risk his life like the medical conditions that beset him in the 1940s and ultimately killed him.

"IF THE WORLD had remained at peace," wrote Roosevelt's personal secretary, Grace Tully, "I am sure that Mr. Roosevelt should have retired in January, 1941, to the quiet Hudson River countryside which he loved so much more than the clattering Washington political scene."[61]

Some evidence backs this up. "He began the plans for the presidential library at Hyde Park in his second term," says grandson James Roosevelt, "because he believed that it was going to be the end of his time in office."[62] Instead of leaving the White House behind, however, he sensed the nation needed his continued leadership. So he sought, and won, an unprecedented third term that started in 1941. But his health would decline dramatically in the next four years, during a world war on multiple fronts.

Few people spent more time with the deteriorating president than Tully during his third term. She saw him grapple with the loss of so many Americans at Pearl Harbor and then during the years of war that followed. He hated what he saw; she, in turn, hated what she saw happening to him. "Eventually, he was a casualty of that suffering," she later wrote, "and for more than three years I watched it dragging him, slowly at first and then faster, to exhaustion and death."[63] The signs of deterioration went unnoticed by much of the public. Those close to him had no doubt he was in serious decline.

"Because my father was a combat marine in the Pacific, my mother lived in the White House during a good deal of that third term and the short fourth term," says James Roosevelt. "She was a nurse from the Mayo Clinic operating room—and she had her own observations about my grandfather's health, which she thought was clearly not good and getting worse. My mother told me it was visible to everyone around the president, but particularly to someone with medical knowledge like herself, that he was in physical distress."[64] Tully agreed. "In the latter years I observed the signs of cumulative weariness, the dark circles that never quite faded from under his eyes, the more pronounced shake in his hand as he lit his cigarette, the easy slump that developed in his shoulders as he sat at a desk that was always covered with work."[65]

FDR's journey to Tehran in November 1943 to meet with British prime minster Winston Churchill and Soviet leader Joseph Stalin required him to travel farther from the United States than any of his predecessors. It took a toll; the American delegation witnessed one particularly disturbing incident during a summit dinner. "Roosevelt was about to say something when suddenly, in the flick of an eye, he turned green and great drops of sweat began to bead off his face," recalled State Department Russia expert Charles Bohlen. "He put a shaky hand to his forehead. We were all caught by surprise." His doctor, who generally stayed close by during FDR's final two years, examined the president in his room and later reported back a diagnosis of indigestion, "to the relief of everybody," he said. It's unlikely that he had deceived anyone other than himself.[66]

By early 1944, Roosevelt could admit to a select few that he felt "rotten" or "like hell."[67] Medical examinations revealed a litany of conditions that had developed or grown worse over the years: high blood pressure, congestive heart failure, poor circulation, limited lung capacity, an enlarged heart, an intermittent slack jaw and blank stare, and reduced supply of oxygen to the brain.[68] As a result, a cardiologist was brought in to join the physician attending to his general needs. But the communication between the doctors and their very important patient was poor—in both directions. A method lay behind this madness: it allowed FDR to answer the media's questions about his condition more freely than if he had complete knowledge about his health. It also seems he did not want to hear about the full extent of his deterioration.[69]

Observers weren't fooled. "When I entered the President's office and had my first glimpse of him in several months," wrote a *New York Times* correspondent after seeing Roosevelt in the spring of 1944, "I was shocked and horrified—so much so that my impulse was to turn around and leave. . . . He had lost a great deal of weight. His shirt collar hung so loose on his neck that you could have put your hand inside it. He was sitting there with a vague, glassy-eyed expression on his face and his mouth hanging open." His concern expanded when Roosevelt spoke. "He would start talking about something, then in midsentence he would stop and his mouth would drop open and he'd sit staring at me in silence. I knew I was looking at a terribly sick man."[70]

And yet, at many other times, Roosevelt remained fully lucid, clearly the shrewd political strategist he'd been for decades. "He was a master of playing people off against each other," his grandson notes. "Whether or not he was at the top of his game on that by the end of his third term, he probably was still better at it than anybody else."[71] Paul Sparrow, director of the Roosevelt Presidential Library and Museum in Hyde Park, New York, says, "There were some periods where he was debilitated. For example, even when he was awake and cognizant, he could have trouble with names and numbers. But during his moments of clarity, which were most of the time, his judgment did not appear to be impaired."[72]

But by 1944, Roosevelt was engaged in his final campaign, attempting to stay in the White House even longer. "He felt that, as president, he was serving in the armed forces," says Sparrow. "How could he quit when he was sending millions of young men into battle? He felt he couldn't walk away; he *had* to die in the saddle."[73] Citing the war effort, he didn't campaign much at all. While speaking in August at a Navy Yard event in Bremerton, Washington, pains filled the president's chest, and the ship's rocking added sharp ones to his legs, too. He departed quickly after talking, forgoing a planned drive around the yard.[74]

His doctors increasingly deceived the press about what they knew. "The President's health is perfectly okay," his lead physician wrote in an October statement to the media. "There are absolutely no organic difficulties at all." Within a few days, when a reporter followed up, the doctor doubled down: "The stories that he is in bad health are understandable enough around election time, but they are not true." But, of course, they were true.[75]

SENATOR HARRY TRUMAN of Missouri, selected in 1944 as Roosevelt's new running mate, had also noticed the president's deteriorating health. He dined with FDR in August, after not having seen him for six months. "You know, I am concerned about the President's health," Truman told one of his aides shortly thereafter. "I had no idea he was in such a feeble condition. In pouring cream in his tea, he got more cream in the saucer than he did in the cup. His hands are shaking and he talks with considerable difficulty. . . . physically he's just going to pieces. I'm very much concerned about him."[76]

After the successful election, the two men spent virtually no time together. "My strong suspicion is that he planned to see the war to its end, then step down and run the United Nations," Sparrow speculates. "I think he picked Truman because he thought that he would be the one most likely to continue his policies."[77] To focus on war decisions and try to regain some of his lost strength, Roosevelt spent much of early 1945 away from Washington, with extensive time at his comfortable retreat in Warm Springs, Georgia.

But duty also pressed FDR into another long voyage, this time to Yalta in the Crimea in February 1945 to discuss the end of war strategy with Churchill and Stalin. Here he would add a new medical symptom to his long list of ailments: skipped heartbeats.[78] Despite such signs of growing physical and mental decline, Roosevelt skill-fully moved through the agenda during sessions he led, engaged fruitfully in discussions, and employed his traditional humor when needed.[79] Critics who try to pin the post-war balance of power in Europe on FDR's deterioration while at Yalta, claiming that FDR's weakened condition allowed Stalin the opportunity to shape the di-vision of Europe he sought, seem to minimize crucial ground truth. The Soviets were already seizing control of Eastern Europe as they advanced on Nazi Germany. Roosevelt's perfect health might have helped him gain some additional advantage on marginal issues, but dislodging the Red Army from what would become the Warsaw Pact countries would have required more than a robust lead negoti-ator at Yalta; it might have taken a ground war in Europe between former allies to push the Soviets back east.

Upon his return to the United States, the president's condition fluctuated dramatically and colleagues feared the worst. House Speaker Sam Rayburn in March saw his slack jaw and "waxy skin" at a dinner and later told friends, "This country is in for a great tragedy, and I feel it's coming very soon. I don't think the President will be with us much longer."[80] Not long after, an American diplomat who met with Roosevelt found the president "unable to discuss serious matters," meandering "aimlessly" for an hour. Some reporters a cou-ple of days later thought he was "on top" and "himself again," but on March 23 Secretary of State Cordell Hull found "he looked like death" and could communicate only in "general and vague" conver-sation, in which he repeatedly lost the thread.[81]

ON THE AFTERNOON of April 12, 1945, Vice President Truman awaited the bourbon that Speaker of the House Sam Rayburn had offered. But he wouldn't get to even sip it.

In those days, the five o'clock hour on Capitol Hill often saw leading lawmakers and others, sometimes including the vice presi-dent, gather to throw a few drinks down in the spirit of cooperation. On this day, though, an urgent phone call from President Roos-evelt's secretary preempted the festivities.

"Holy General Jackson!" Truman blurted out as he ended the call. "Boys, this is in this room. Something must have happened. I'll be back soon."[82]

Indeed it had. Roosevelt, resting at Warm Springs, had slumped in his chair and lost consciousness just after complaining of a "terrific headache," evidence of a fatal cerebral hemorrhage.[83] The only president millions of Americans could remember, in office for more than twelve years, would not wake up.

Chapter Five

Taken Out by Force

What was the practice before this in cases where the chief Magistrate rendered himself obnoxious? Why recourse was had to assassination in which he was not only deprived of his life but of the opportunity of vindicating his character.[1]

—BENJAMIN FRANKLIN

I
F EVER A president seemed likely to face threats of removal by force, it was Abraham Lincoln. Put into office by a plurality, but not a majority, of voters in a hopelessly divided country, he would see a succession of seceding states between his election in November 1860 and his inauguration in March 1861.

The same passions that ripped the United States in two also drove more frequent, more extensive, and more conspiratorial plots against Lincoln than against all of his predecessors combined. He usually shrugged them off with fatalistic nonchalance, getting through all but one of them unscathed. Retrospectively, his dismissal of even close friends' concerns for his safety looks shocking. And had his guards and aides taken a more strategic, predictive approach to protecting their president, John Wilkes Booth never would have had the opportunity to pull that trigger.

THE WORD "UNPRECEDENTED" arises often when researching Lincoln's security arrangements. Unprecedented numbers of death threats, most of them left uninvestigated, came his way after receiving the Republican nomination in May 1860. Unprecedented groups of bodyguards, most of them just standing around, attended him at campaign events.[2] And then, an unprecedented deception was used to protect the president-elect on his way to Washington.

The hate mail after the election was intense. Often it came from deranged writers, but some appeared to represent real danger. One letter had offered a warning that several people planned to travel to Washington to kill the president-elect after the inauguration.[3] Lincoln remained unperturbed, declaring about the threats soon afterward, "I never attached much importance to them—never wanted to believe such a thing. So I never would do anything about them, in the way of taking precautions and the like."[4]

That would change in February 1861. While in Baltimore, famed Chicago detective Allan Pinkerton—not part of any official government security—unearthed a dastardly plan to ensure Lincoln never made it to his own swearing-in ceremony in March. Plotters intended to cause enough trouble near the path of Lincoln's entourage, as it moved between two railroad lines there, to draw police escorts away. Then, prepositioned agitators among the public of Baltimore, a city rife with Southern sympathies, would rally a mob to overwhelm and kill their suddenly less protected target. Additionally, Lincoln's advisors had concerns about the attitude and abilities of the city's police chief.[5] Their overwhelming advice to the president-elect? Take a less conspicuous night train through Baltimore.

Briefed personally by Pinkerton, Lincoln weighed his options. On the one hand, he could follow his usual instinct and plow right through—risking his life, sure, but avoiding accusations of cowardice that surely would come if he sneaked through the city. On the other hand, he could change his schedule, rejecting his general inclination about such things—risking ridicule, yes, but avoiding becoming a corpse before his own inauguration.[6]

After reviewing reported facts from Baltimore and listening carefully to Pinkerton's assessment, Lincoln chose the safer route.

As he wrote to a congressman later, he thought it best this time "to run no risk, where no risk was necessary."[7] After the president-elect had passed Baltimore, the city's police chief admitted he would have been unable to control the rabid crowds sure to turn up if Lincoln tried to move through in the light of day, saying he "would have been grossly insulted and probably killed."[8]

Lincoln settled into Washington without incident. Inauguration Day brought out thousands of soldiers, placed at the US Capitol for the ceremony, on nearby streets for the procession, and throughout the city. The crowds didn't notice the plainclothes armed officers in their midst. But the uniformed ones, like never before, blocked most spectators' view of their new president.[9]

A S SOON AS Lincoln had completed the oath of office, attempts to expel him from the presidency violently came early and often. The White House borrowed some guards from the Washington police. Threat letters kept coming, but the few investigations that resources allowed turned up nothing actionable.[10] As insults like "imbecile" and "baboon" flew at him, claims that Lincoln was establishing a dictatorship rang far and wide.[11]

The president told his friend Ward Lamon about at least one suspicious man who had been seen skulking around the White House grounds; many more surely went undetected by the gate sentries, uniformed officers at the executive mansion's doors, and Union troops making camp on the grounds (as much for convenience as for protection of its chief resident).[12] Riding one day to Soldiers and Sailors Home, a District of Columbia site typically less hot and humid than the swampy area near the White House, Lincoln heard and felt a rifle shot that barely missed his head. The president's unknown assailant found it easy to walk or ride away in the wooded area.[13]

Only in November 1864 did the District of Columbia police chief send four officers to the White House to serve on detail as Lincoln's special personal guard. They wore civilian clothes and carried revolvers. Within the building, they asked guests to remove cloaks and wraps before seeing Lincoln, to prevent weapons from being smuggled easily into the room, but didn't conduct background checks or searches of entrants.[14] In fact, people almost universally entered and left the White House at leisure, even during cabinet meetings.[15] When Lincoln ventured outside the mansion, these guards pointedly walked beside him instead of in protective positions in front of or behind him, to appear as simple advisors or petitioners. During his excursions for entertainment—such as, say, plays performed at local theaters—one or two guards usually went along.[16] But like almost every president who took office after him, Lincoln chafed at any conspicuous protection.[17]

In March 1865, Lincoln took a bold trip to central Virginia, within sight of collapsing Confederate battle lines, just a quarter of a mile from active fighting. During a stop along the James River on the way there, a determined visitor came aboard the commander in chief's ship. One of his guards intercepted the man, who asserted he had lived near the president's home in Illinois, knew him well, and had spent large sums of money on his presidential campaign. "If what he says is true, I would know him," Lincoln said. "But I do not. The man is an imposter, and I won't see him." The man begged to be let through, even offering bribes, but failed to gain an audience with the president. Only later, after Lincoln's assassination, did the guard who stopped the man and escorted him from the ship assess that he probably was John Surratt—one of John Wilkes Booth's accomplices.[18]

That same trip held another fright for the guard. When Lincoln walked through the streets of recently captured Richmond, the blinds of a second-story window opened and what looked like a gun pointed down. Long before formal protocols had been developed, the man charged with protecting Lincoln simply stepped in front of the president to ensure his safety. No shots would be fired that evening.[19]

It would take a determined attacker to complete America's first presidential assassination. Unbeknownst to the president, just such a man had been stewing about Lincoln for years.

T HE BOOTH FAMILY name, so infamous since April 1865, would have sounded familiar to most Americans even before that fateful month.

It's hard to understand today the fame and artistic influence of the Booths. Imagine Lloyd Bridges and his sons, Jeff and Beau, but much more famous relative to their peers. Or maybe Martin Sheen and his sons, Emilio Estevez and Charlie Sheen. Junius Brutus Booth was already a leading English actor, specializing in energetic performances in Shakespearean tragedies, when he sailed to Virginia in 1821. Within a couple of years, he'd reached the pinnacle of the stage world in the United States, earning rave reviews from coast to coast. One contemporary record noted, "Booth's acting always evinced genius."[20]

One son, named for his father, focused more on theater management than acting but did appear with his father on stage in Sacramento for a production of *Othello*. Junius Jr.'s younger brother Edwin became the most popular American tragedy actor of his generation, famous worldwide and especially admired for his epic, stirring performances of *Hamlet*.[21] Another acting son, John Wilkes, lacked the dignified bearing and delivery of Edwin, probably because initially he skipped the extensive training and practice in which his father and brother had invested,[22] but he made up for much of that with daring physical performances and dashing good looks. On the night of November 25, 1864, a remarkable performance in New York featured all three Booth brothers in Shakespeare's *Julius Caesar*, the theater "crowded to suffocation, people standing in every available place."[23] The Booths were, to put it simply, a big deal.

The family also had its troubles. Junius had abandoned his wife and children in England to come to the new world with another woman, with whom he ended up having ten children. He missed many performances during his career due to bouts of heavy drinking and, apparently, mental illness. Once, when Junius couldn't be found at his boarding house after missing a performance, a search discovered him the next day, wandering through snowy woods nearby.[24] At a later date, he insisted on going out in the city of Boston for a late-night adventure after a performance; a teenage Edwin, along for the trip as his minder, boldly stopped him. Instead of physically overpowering his son, the elder Booth silently locked himself into a small, dark closet for the night. He refused to come out until Edwin, fearing for his father's life, prepared to run for help. Junius then emerged, strode across the room without a word, and went straight to bed.[25] His death in 1852 in many ways removed a burden from the family.

After finally taking acting lessons under Edwin's close watch, John Wilkes Booth (who initially went on stage as "J. Wilkes" to avoid tarnishing the family name) developed into a generally well-regarded actor. By the time Civil War battles erupted, the seeds of his discontent toward the North probably had already taken root.[26]

Also, after John Brown in October 1959 tried, and failed, to start a slave revolt by taking over the federal arsenal at Harper's Ferry (in what was then Virginia), authorities sent him to nearby Charles Town to stand trial.[27] To keep order and prevent a possible rescue at Brown's execution, the state government ordered a militia to head there from Richmond. Booth, acting in the state capital at the time, tagged along to watch the radical abolitionist die. Even though his views ran counter to Brown's, Booth reportedly expressed respect for him as "a grand character" because of how far Brown was willing to go for his beliefs.[28]

As the Southern states voted one after another in late 1860 and throughout 1861 to leave the Union, Booth spoke brazenly to fellow actors and others about his personal and political disdain for Lincoln. Soon he found himself called to something beyond the stage, especially as the Civil War continued year after year. His sympathies with the South would evolve into the nation's most successful conspiracy to date to remove a president by force.

WITH VIOLENCE IN the air across much of the nation, it would have been odd for the seeds of passion inside Booth not to grow into something extreme. "Assassination in the abstract is a horrid crime," asserted a newspaper editorial that he probably saw in

Louisville, "but to slay a tyrant is no more assassination than war is murder."[29] Despite playing the character of Brutus many times in productions of *Julius Caesar*, Booth didn't initially see his destiny as a murderer. Instead, by 1864 he had seized on the idea of kidnapping the president, delivering him to the South, and reviving the Confederacy's fortunes by enabling its leaders to exchange Lincoln's safe return for the Union's release of much needed Confederate soldiers being held as prisoners of war.

As crazy as such a plot sounds, clear thinking drove it. First, although the possibility of grabbing Lincoln had been discussed openly for some time, the president continued to ride around town with few guards, making his capture a realistic prospect even for untrained attackers. Second, a getaway looked relatively easy because the nation's capital was just a short ride from rebellious Virginia, and many District of Columbia residents and Marylanders remained friendly to the South. Third, Confederate major John Mosby had delivered a proof of concept by sneaking into the headquarters of a Union general who had been hunting *him* and kidnapping that general.[30]

Booth, recognizing Lincoln's riding patterns around town, finally gathered the accomplices he would need and mustered the courage to give the kidnap plot a go. The cabal set their trap on March 17, 1865, on the path that should have brought Lincoln back from the play he'd been slated to attend. But the president didn't go that night, and the plan collapsed.[31] And yet Booth had proven he could effectively manipulate the vulnerabilities and ignorance of like-minded individuals into a gang willing to pursue a risky but historic goal. Booth researcher and author Michael Kauffman asserts that by leaving behind a paper trail of his interactions with these coconspirators, Booth ensured he had evidence to hold over their heads—locking them in, he thought, to another attempt.[32]

Booth began to think that kidnapping wouldn't be enough, probably even before Lee's surrender to Grant on April 9, which put the war's end within sight and reduced the perceived value of capturing and trading Lincoln. If Booth wasn't focusing on shooting the president by the following morning, he certainly was later in the day after attending a spontaneous celebration at the White House.

From a window, Lincoln spoke to more than two thousand cheering citizens, infuriating Booth. First, the president said the right to vote must be given to at least some of the freed slaves.[33] Second, he finished his remarks by rubbing salt in Southerners' wounds. "I think it would be a good plan for you to play *Dixie*," he told the band. "I have always thought that it was the most beautiful of our songs. I have submitted the question of its ownership to the Attorney General, and he has given it as his legal opinion that we have fairly earned the right to have it back." The president stepped back inside, prompting the appreciative crowd to march off to the sounds of a song they'd not heard in the nation's capital in quite some time. Booth fumed.[34]

Just a few days later, as Lincoln finished the day's meetings and prepared for a night at the theater with his wife and a couple of guests, he spoke to the bodyguard who had just started a few months earlier. "Crook, do you know, I believe there are men who want to take my life?" Pausing briefly, he quietly answered his own question. "And I have no doubt they will do it."

It was the afternoon of April 14.[35]

EARLIER THAT DAY, Booth had visited Ford's Theatre and learned that Lincoln planned to bring General and Mrs. Grant with him to that evening's performance of the British play *Our American Cousin*.[36] Elated at this unexpected opportunity to end both men's lives, Booth assigned that duty to himself. He directed George Atzerodt to kill Vice President Andrew Johnson, first in the line of succession to the presidency. Their partner in crime Lewis Powell (who in early 1865 also used the names Payne and Paine) agreed to murder Secretary of State William Seward, the next most senior executive branch official. They intended their damage to the US government to be massive and memorable.

Before the play started, Booth again visited the theater, which he knew well from his many previous performances there and to which he had open access at all times.[37] He now weaponized that knowledge and freedom of movement. At the door to the president's box upstairs, he quietly and quickly cut a hole in the plaster wall to set up a simple locking mechanism he would later use to prevent the door from being opened from the outside.[38] Then he left, intending to return when all the pieces had moved into position.

Lincoln arrived during the second act, accompanied by Major Henry Rathbone and his fiancée instead of Grant and his wife, who had declined their invitation.[39] A White House guard on loan from the city police force saw Lincoln into the theater but then vacated his seat in the small hallway outside the box's outer door,[40] leaving no obstacle to Booth's access. Upon noticing the esteemed arrival in the presidential box, the actors stopped the play and the band played "Hail to the Chief" in Lincoln's honor. The audience stood and cheered.[41]

During the second scene of the third act, while watching the play below, Rathbone heard a pistol's discharge behind him, turned to see a man standing just behind Lincoln, and thought he heard "Freedom!" blurted out through the smoke. "I instantly sprang toward him and seized him," Rathbone recalled. "He wrested himself from my grasp, and made a violent thrust at my breast with a large knife. I parried the blow by striking it up, and received a wound several inches deep in my left arm, between the elbow and the shoulder." He tried to again grab Booth, who rushed forward to the front edge of the box, but the assassin jumped over the railing and Rathbone found only a bit of clothing in his hands. The president's head had now bent slightly forward, unconscious with eyes closed. As Rathbone darted to the door to yell for medical assistance, he heard beating on the door's other side and noticed a plank wedged into the wall, where Booth had placed it after entering the box silently moments earlier. No one could enter until Rathbone dislodged it.[42]

Meanwhile, audience members looking up and to their right saw a man (whom regular theatergoers recognized instantly as Booth) leaping down and landing hard on the stage. Most observers, including an attentive man sitting directly across from the president, heard Booth shout, "*Sic semper tyrannus!*," Latin for "Thus always to tyrants!" Booth certainly associated the phrase with Julius Caesar's murderer Brutus, whom he played many times on stages nationwide. Then, with an injured leg, Lincoln's assassin ran through the confused performers on stage to a door behind them, darting outside where a horse was tethered for his getaway.[43] A US Army major who'd been sitting in the front row got up on stage and almost caught up to Booth, who galloped off when the officer clutched for the reins but missed.[44]

Nearly simultaneously, Atzerodt and Powell should have taken out the vice president and secretary of state. It didn't turn out that way. Atzerodt lost his nerve, either despite or because of his robust drinking throughout the day. Instead of attacking Johnson, who enjoyed a quiet evening until shocking news about Lincoln reached him later that night, Atzerodt wandered the streets.[45] Powell, by contrast, had powered his way through Seward's home and viciously stabbed the secretary of state, who already lay in a weakened state, recovering from a devastating carriage accident nine days earlier;[46] but the new, serious injuries Powell inflicted fell short of killing Seward.[47]

Men carried the president's still-breathing but motionless body to a house across the street. Government officers there started a vigil for their leader. The family physician arrived and, after examining the president's gunshot wound, pronounced his case "hopeless."[48] Lincoln died just after seven o'clock the following morning. Twelve days later, Booth died in a Virginia barn from a gunshot wound, after refusing to surrender to a regiment of soldiers that had trapped him there.

Conspiracy theories abounded in the wake of Lincoln's murder, a natural development after assassinations. Devious purported masterminds, ranging from Vice President Andrew Johnson to Confederate president Jefferson Davis to the pope in Rome, were said to be behind the deed.[49] In this case, there truly was a conspiracy afoot, just not one involving such prominent figures. Booth built his conspiracy himself. More courageous and capable partners might have succeeded in helping him to decapitate much of the US government; instead Booth gained sickening dishonor as the first person to remove a president by force.

EJECTING THE PRESIDENT from office via electoral, political, or constitutional means seemed like too much work for occasional lunatics, radical political outcasts, and even a mentally unstable and disgruntled office seeker. For almost two hundred years, such would-be assassins have taken matters into their own hands. A few of them, unfortunately, have accomplished their evil goals. Guns, explosives, planes, and even grenades have been used to threaten the lives of many American presidents.

That this happens shouldn't shock us. Most countries around the globe, many of them with much greater frequency than the United States, have lost leaders through violence. The real surprises in this country are how relatively *seldom* such attackers have prevailed, especially recently, and how few of the plots come in the form of an attempted coup d'état against the entire government.

Despite the inevitably momentous consequences of presidential assassination, for most of the country's history getting close enough to shoot the chief executive proved easy for anyone so inclined. The fact is, relatively few Americans have wanted to murder their president. But those few have made their mark.

NOBODY SEEMS TO have wanted the first several presidents dead quite enough to do much about it.

George Washington's impressive stature, literally and symbolically, deterred potential assailants. Thomas Jefferson, the first president to move directly into the White House to start his term, opened its doors daily to let citizens in, without screening or precaution, helping highlight the change from the more patrician airs of the preceding John Adams administration. In the state rooms, the president displayed exhibits of flora and fauna from the Lewis and Clark expedition and other such eye-grabbers.[50] James Monroe considered an attack a real possibility, so he ensured the executive mansion's doorkeeper had firearms close at hand; no threats materialized.[51] And although a court-martialed army sergeant reportedly came to the White House to threaten John Quincy Adams face to face, it didn't concern the president enough to stop his habit of skinny-dipping alone in the Potomac River and walking the streets without any protection.[52]

Things would change just two months after Andrew Jackson started his second term in 1833. The first direct assault on a US president while in office came from Robert Randolph, a naval officer dismissed from service for attempting to steal thousands of dollars of government money. This disgruntled man wasn't about to go lightly. While Jackson was taking a steamboat ride to Fredericksburg, Virginia, on May 6, a stop in Alexandria allowed Randolph to slip in among other visitors boarding the ship. The sacked navy man went straight for Jackson's cabin, where the seated president had been reading newspapers.

The unexpected visitor started removing his gloves, which Jackson interpreted as a desire to shake hands.[53] Randolph had something else in mind, punching Jackson and drawing blood. Thankfully, he didn't try to shoot the president, because nothing would have stopped him from getting a shot or two off.[54] The aging general, now knowing the visitor intended to hurt him, wedged his chair against a wall, promptly kicked the table in front of him to make room to stand up, and proceeded to throttle Randolph with his upraised cane.[55] Old Hickory, like his predecessors and many of his successors, lacked anything resembling Secret Service protection. But he had friends. A group including Jackson's adopted son jumped to the president's aid and threw the attacker back.[56]

Jackson rejected one man's offer to kill Randolph on the spot in retaliation for the attack,[57] allowing the assailant to stumble off the ship, and told the authorities not to bother to chase Randolph down and charge him criminally.[58] The altercation should have prompted the powers that be to create some protection around the person of the president. But Jackson made it clear that he preferred to defend himself and would reject any "palace guard" established to stand between him and the people.[59]

Access to the chief executive would thus remain easy enough for the president to find himself face to face with just about anyone. Even a madman with *two* loaded guns.

SENATOR THOMAS HART BENTON was the Forest Gump of his time, present as background figure when a president or presidential aspirant in the first half of the nineteenth century faced danger or scandal. He was aboard the USS *Princeton* when the exploding cannon endangered the life of John Tyler; he attended Henry Clay's duels.

Benton was also at Capitol Hill on January 30, 1835. The morning had dawned like many other winter days in Washington, sunny but cold. In his second term now, President Andrew Jackson came to the Capitol building, which lacked the modern structure and majestic dome seen today, to pay his respects to the recently deceased representative Warren Davis of South Carolina. As the procession made its way to the East Portico, Jackson found himself facing almost certain death. Benton watched it all, from his vantage point at the foot of the stairs just below: "A person stepped from the crowd into the little open space in front of the President, levelled a pistol at him at the distance of about eight feet, and attempted to fire."[60]

The explosion rang through the air like a rifle shot,[61] but somehow the powder failed to fire into the barrel. Most bystanders thought the pistol had shot its bullet. The frustrated would-be assassin used the moment of confusion to drop the misfiring gun from his right hand and raise another one with his left. Again, he aimed. Again, the cap exploded. Again, no bullet emerged.[62]

Old Hickory wasn't about to grant the unemployed painter named Richard Lawrence a third try. As Benton recalls, "The President instantly rushed upon him with his uplifted cane," a sturdy weapon Jackson had employed liberally to injure others who angered him. This unluckiest of attackers narrowly escaped becoming the first man killed by a serving president; others knocked Lawrence down just before Jackson's blows fell.[63] Investigators who afterward tested the same two pistols had no trouble firing them successfully. They calculated the chance of *both* misfiring, in succession, at one in 125,000.[64]

A pair of physicians called in by a judge to examine Lawrence listened to him patiently as he rambled about his movements and motives. They discovered he had accosted the president at the White House just a week prior, demanding from Jackson money to allow Lawrence to return to his native England.[65] Eventually, the physicians got the verbose attacker to declare that he blamed the president for his lack of employment and that killing Jackson would provide "the remedy for this evil."[66]

Unfortunately for Jackson's political enemies in Congress, Lawrence also said that three senators—Henry Clay of Kentucky, Daniel Webster of Massachusetts, and John Calhoun of South Carolina—were "on his side."[67] All three opposed Jackson, who suspected a conspiracy against him. Friendly newspapers amplified his feelings, with New York's *Evening Post* opining about Lawrence being "wrought up to a frenzy by the incendiary harangues of Clay, Webster and Calhoun and their besotted fellows."[68]

Why didn't this episode then lead to a wider clash between the notoriously tempestuous president and his legislative rivals? Because Lawrence, thankfully, didn't stop at praising Jackson's political foes. He also told the investigators he considered the US president "nothing more than his clerk," because his family had been wrongly deprived of the English throne. And he said would regain it—it wasn't quite clear how to anyone other than to him, perhaps—by shooting Jackson.[69] Even Benton had to admit that Lawrence suffered from a "diseased mind."[70] A jury, after only five minutes of deliberation, found him not guilty by reason of insanity, relegating the first serious would-be presidential assassin to a lifetime in prisons and mental hospitals.[71] Benton would carry on with his dual career as senator and as diarist of presidential perils.

FOLLOWING JACKSON, WHITE HOUSE turnover ran rampant, with nine different presidents during the twenty-five years after Old Hickory. During that time, surprisingly few direct threats emerged, except for those against John Tyler, who'd grown highly unpopular as he alienated supposed political allies and foes alike.

Strolling through the executive mansion's south grounds one day, Tyler was pelted by stones hurled by an intoxicated painter. Things got dicier after he twice vetoed bills to establish the national bank. While his erstwhile Whig allies in Congress fumed, protestors descended on the White House to burn the president in effigy and fire guns into the air, all the while following the drunk painter's precedent and lobbing any rocks they could find. It was the most violent protest to occur at the president's house in the country's first fifty years. Tyler projected calm, later asking the court that tried some of the men involved to dismiss their outburst as "entirely evanescent and harmless in character."[72] Twenty years later, however, when talking to then president James Buchanan, he recalled the fright of seeing through the White House windows "these grounds illuminated by the fires."[73]

Threats to the first fifteen chief executives stopped short of killing them; protection of both the White House and the person of the president stayed light. And Lincoln's death, too, was generally seen as unique due to the extraordinary crisis of secession and Civil War, and thus it did little to spur an expanded security perimeter. Andrew Johnson thought the biggest threat to his safety came from his congressional opposition, which openly called him a blockage to be removed. "I have no doubt that the intention was to incite assassination and so get out of the way the obstacle to place and power," Johnson declared. "Are they not satisfied with the blood which has been shed? . . . If it is blood they want let them have courage enough to strike like men."[74] Sure enough, in those tense times, potential attackers with weapons made it into the room adjoining Andrew Johnson on at least one occasion, but they were turned away by his guard.[75]

Ulysses Grant, who received death threats by mail, still took long walks around the nation's capital without guards to accompany him, probably confident that his status as a war hero and broad popularity served as the best protection.[76] And president-elect Rutherford Hayes had a dinner interrupted by a bullet, which shattered a window and lodged into a wall three rooms away.[77] Still, the protective cordon around the nation's chief executive was casual, which had deadly consequences just fifteen years after Lincoln's assassination.

"PROVIDENCE AND I saved the nation, and why should not I be a hero and the equal of Washington and Lincoln and Grant?"[78]

With these words at his murder trial, Charles Guiteau defended his assassination of James Garfield. The discontented wanderer seemed incredulous that nobody else understood the inspiration for his deed: "I simply executed what I considered the Divine Will for the good of the American people, to unite the two factions of the Republican party, and prevent another war."[79] He'd already proudly declared at the scene of the crime that he'd made Vice President Chester Arthur the new chief executive.[80] Such language suggested a political motive. But the more people listened to Guiteau, the clearer it should have been that he was mad, unable to control his actions.

GUITEAU HAD BEEN a stranger neither to Garfield's aides nor to Secretary of State James Blaine as the election year of 1880 turned to the inauguration year of 1881. Appearing unrequested at the White House and the State Department over and over again, Guiteau claimed to have played a key role in getting Garfield elected. In person or by letter, he harassed officials for a government position, preferably the consulship in Paris.[81] He made himself a persistent pest for weeks on end, even stalking former president Ulysses Grant for a time before Garfield was sworn in.[82]

Finally tiring of the odd visitor's inability to take hints that he was unwanted, Blaine made the administration's view clear on May 14: "Never speak to me again about the Paris Consulship as long as you live."[83] Guiteau wrote a letter to Garfield, criticizing Blaine and prompting officials at the White House to prohibit Guiteau's entrance there.[84] He nevertheless kept appearing, right up to the evening of July 1, 1881.[85]

"It came to me one evening," Guiteau later testified, "the impression came on my mind like a flash that if the President was out of the way the difficulty would be all solved. The next morning I had the same impression. I kept reading the papers, and had my mind on the idea of the removal of the President."[86] Once the thought got into his mind, his twisted logic and perception of a divine mandate made it hard to back down: "The substance of my prayer was that, if it was the Lord's will I should not remove the President; He would in some way, by His providence, interrupt it."[87] On June 18, he went to the railroad depot with a gun. But he didn't shoot. "I intended to remove the President this morning," he wrote, "but Mrs. Garfield looked too thin and clung so tenderly to the President's arm that my heart failed me to part them, and I decided to take him alone."[88]

Just two weeks later, on the evening of July 1, Guiteau sat on a bench in Lafayette Park, just north of the White House. He had done this before, waiting and watching. This night, the president exited the mansion and began walking toward Blaine's house, unguarded. Guiteau followed him there, loaded revolver in hand, then lurked in the shadows until he came out with Blaine for a walk and a chat. He followed them back to the White House but mysteriously didn't shoot when he had an opportunity to kill both men.[89]

The following day, Blaine escorted Garfield to the railroad station to see him off on a trip through the northeast.[90] The president may have had mortality on his mind; just a couple of days before, he'd reportedly asked his secretary of war, Robert Todd Lincoln, to tell him about his father's assassination back in 1865.[91] Blaine recalled that he and the president had made their way through much of the entrance hall "when suddenly, without any premonition whatsoever, there was a very loud report of a pistol discharge, followed in a very brief interval by a second shot." The secretary of state remembered the president saying, "My God, what is this?" Guiteau had fired at point-blank range, then turned and run, but didn't even get outside the station before his capture. Blaine recognized him from his many visits to the State Department.[92] Guiteau carried a letter that said, "The President's tragic death was a sad necessity, but it will unite the Republican party, and save the Republic. . . . His death is a political necessity."[93]

One bullet had grazed Garfield's arm. The other had entered his back, near the spine, and knocked him down. Some feared he'd die quickly. But he remained conscious and went back to the White House.[94]

JAMES GARFIELD SHOULD NOT have found himself on the tragic list of dead presidents. With more competent medical help, he might have lived for decades. But the very men who tried to save his life ended up killing him.

It started at the train station. The first physician on scene, trying to locate the bullet in his back, shoved his unsterilized finger right in there. This probably caused the first of several infections that would devastate the weakened Garfield. The next doctor took an even more aggressive approach, using both his own unwashed hand and a long, unsterilized probe to poke around inside the president.[95] Once in the White House, a succession of additional medical errors compounded the problem—and the pain, as no anesthetics were used—until the president's body became so abused and infected that he had little chance.

Presidential aides did their best to make Garfield comfortable in the sweltering Washington summertime heat. They discovered that filling the cellar with crates upon crates of ice and piping the cooler air up to Garfield's room offered some relief to the suffering president, in the process creating the first White House air-conditioning system.[96] His agony nevertheless increased, and those who knew what he was enduring breathed a sigh of relief when he finally passed away on September 19. The doctor who had taken charge at the White House ended up defending his actions for the rest of his life, and an ungrateful Congress refused to pay the bills he submitted for his "care" of the president.[97]

Guiteau pleaded insanity. "The divine pressure on me to remove the President was so enormous that it destroyed my free agency," he claimed, "and therefore I am not legally responsible for my act."[98] His behavior in the courtroom, though bizarre, certainly didn't incline any jurors to like him. He talked back to the judge. He sniped at witnesses on the stand. He struggled physically with marshals. Other times, he tuned out, kicking back to read newspapers instead of paying attention. He blamed his longtime habit of leaving hotels without paying on God, who he said was responsible for board bills because of the divine service Guiteau provided.[99] Not surprisingly, jurors found him guilty as charged, and Guiteau was hanged less than a year after he'd pulled the trigger. As one analyst put it, "It is unlikely that in 1881 any jury in the country would have acquitted the President's assassin whatever his mental condition."[100]

Despite the bold murder, protection for the president barely improved. A decade or so after Garfield's death, a drunk man jumped over the White House fence, walked up to the porch (where no guards were present), and joined President Benjamin Harrison there. They chatted for a while, apparently about the unexpected visitor's desire for a government position, before the president called an usher who escorted the man off the grounds.[101] Only during the second administration of Grover Cleveland in the mid-1890s did any increase in peacetime protection come to the executive mansion. The Secret Service's assistance to the expanded cadre of policemen, however, remained small and informal.[102]

FOR THE FIRST time in more than fifty years, the US government in April 1898 declared war against a foreign adversary. The explosion of the USS *Maine* in Havana Harbor had sparked the Spanish-American War; its end three months later made the United States a world power. The hostilities also brought changes to presidential security. The Secret Service provided William McKinley 24/7 protection at the White House, scaled back to partial coverage after hostilities concluded.

MEANWHILE, A MORE shadowy threat was emerging: anarchism. During the previous two decades, an international wave of political assassinations had swept across Europe, with the killings of Russia's tsar (1881), France's president (1894), Spain's prime minister (1897), Austria's empress (1898), and Italy's king (1900). The radical propaganda that drove those murders had spread across the Atlantic before the turn of the century as European exiles fled police crackdowns there. The Secret Service quickly reestablished its White House force and insisted that McKinley always travel with an armed guard.[103]

For major events, his protection expanded to a Secret Service detail and assistance from the police and even military units. McKinley thus stood out as the best-protected president since

Lincoln's inauguration when he traveled to Buffalo, New York, for the Pan-American Exposition in 1901. Unfortunately, a motivated young anarchist also planned to attend.

Leon Czolgosz had grown up in the Midwest scraping to get by, at a time of growing labor tensions in the United States. He shined shoes and sold papers at age six; before his thirteenth birthday in 1886, he had quit school to work in a factory. Violent strikes and workplace clashes expanded in the late 1880s and 1890s, helping to drive Czolgosz toward anarchism and away from the Catholicism of his Polish parents.[104]

By 1898, he'd quit his factory job near Cleveland to spend most of his time reading radical books and newspapers. He attended political meetings in the city when he could.[105] In the summer of 1900, he liked a newspaper article about the political assassination of King Umberto I of Italy enough to cut it out, fold it, and keep it in his wallet.[106] Czolgosz in early 1901 heard anarchist activist Emma Goldman speak in Cleveland. "She set me on fire," he said later. "Miss Goldman's words went right through me, and when I left the lecture I had made up my mind that I would have to do something heroic for the cause I loved."[107]

His subsequent months spent trying to get deeper into anarchist circles largely failed, however, as his personality quirks annoyed his contacts in the movement. Many interpreted his ignorance and pedantic questioning as a sign of something more alarming, prompting a special notice about him in a Chicago paper on September 1, 1901: "The attention of the comrades is called to another spy. . . . His demeanor is of the usual sort, pretending to be greatly interested in the cause, asking for names or soliciting aid for acts of contemplated violence. If this same individual makes his appearance elsewhere, the comrades are warned in advance and can act accordingly."[108] Little did the naysayers know that Czolgosz was already on his way to Buffalo, soon to prove his devotion to the cause through lethal action.

THE PRESIDENT'S ATTENDANCE at Buffalo's Pan-American Exposition was shaping up to be a signal success for the capitalist leader, disgusting Czolgosz. "All those people bowing to the great ruler," he said later. "I made up my mind to kill that ruler." McKinley on September 5 greeted a massive crowd, including Czolgosz, but the plotter couldn't find an opportune window to use the gun he kept concealed in his pocket.[109]

On the afternoon of September 6, the president entered the large Temple of Music to greet as many people as possible. McKinley's protection that day was more extensive than that of any other president for any occasion since Lincoln's inauguration. Two National Guard regiments covered the entrances to the exposition. Open areas were patrolled by mounted soldiers and policemen. The narrow aisle leading to the stage where the president would shake hands lay under the watchful eyes of another military unit. Guards and policemen milled about the great hall.[110] Four soldiers, four local police detectives, and three Secret Service agents stood on stage with the president, two of them within arm's length.

Their presence alone would prove inadequate, for on this hot day, the assembled military, law enforcement, and presidential protective officers allowed people through to McKinley while holding handkerchiefs to dab their sweaty heads and hands. In the line of thousands waiting to approach the president, Czolgosz waited nervously. As he got close to his target, Czolgosz sneaked his pistol from his pocket into his right hand and wrapped a handkerchief around it like a bandage.[111] When Czolgosz reached the front of the line, the president reached out to shake the left one instead. At that moment, Czolgosz raised his right hand and fired twice at point-blank range, putting one bullet into McKinley's chest and another into his abdomen. An observant artilleryman and police officer tackled the shooter before he could manage a third shot, but the damage to the president was done. "This wound—it hurts greatly," he murmured.[112]

At the exposition's emergency hospital, doctors did without unnecessary probes so as not to inflict the kind of damage upon McKinley their predecessors had delivered to Garfield. Surgery removed one bullet and closed the wounds. The president seemed to be recovering over the next few days, but his condition worsened on September 13 due to then-unknown damage near the pancreas. He died in the early morning hours of September 14.[113]

Why did Czolgosz feel the need to remove this president? Well, it wasn't really about McKinley as much as about the system the president led. "I don't believe in the republican form of government and I don't believe we should have any rulers," he told interrogators. "It is right to kill them. I had that idea when I shot the President, and that is why I was there. . . . I realized that I was sacrificing my life. I am willing to take the consequences," which would indeed include his own life, taken by the electric chair forty-five days after McKinley's death.[114]

AFTER THREE MURDERED presidents, a consensus emerged that the White House and the chief executive deserved more permanent security arrangements.

IN 1902, THE Secret Service—the only real federal investigative agency at that time—took over personal protection, although it didn't receive formal congressional authorization and funding for it until four years later.[115] The scope of Secret Service duties in the next fifty years would expand to include the president-elect, the president's immediate family, and eventually the vice president.[116]

The new security regime didn't prevent potential assassins from getting through. One evening during Theodore Roosevelt's usual hour for meetings, this first president with full Secret Service protection was visited by a well-dressed man who claimed to have an appointment. Roosevelt couldn't remember if he had asked someone to come by, so he took the meeting. "It was only a few minutes before my bell rang summoning me to the Red Parlor," recalls the White House usher, "and as I entered the President walked toward me, saying quietly, 'Take this crank out of here.'" As the president slipped out, a search of the unwanted visitor revealed a large-caliber gun hidden in his rear pocket. The usher was suspended without pay for a month.[117]

While campaigning in 1912 to return to the White House after a four-year absence, Roosevelt took a bullet from a would-be assassin who claimed to have conversed with McKinley's ghost. The spirit allegedly told him not to let a murderer (presumably Roosevelt) become president. The shooter spent the rest of his life in mental hospitals.[118]

WOODROW WILSON, WHO beat both Roosevelt and incumbent William Taft in that same election, led the country into World War I. Security tightened accordingly. His Secret Service men took extraordinary means to protect the president, from examining every inch of railroad tracks he would be taken over to virtually occupying any golf course Wilson played on.[119]

A unique challenge came when the commander in chief decided to attend post-war negotiations in Europe, requiring ocean travel and an extended stay in France. A battleship and set of destroyers accompanied the president's ship in case any mines or residual German U-boats popped up. Cavalry and bicycle-mounted French security guarded the president's procession in Paris, sparking much anxiety for the Secret Service agents stuck in a carriage well behind Wilson.[120]

"All during the War, he never once showed a sign of fear," head usher Ike Hoover recalled. "On the contrary, he many times annoyed those assigned to protect him by unnecessarily laying himself open to attack." For example, Wilson agreed *once* to avoid his usual seat in a conspicuous corner of a theater's presidential box in favor of a position less visible to the audience. From that point on, he insisted on sitting up front as before, saying, "I felt guilty hiding behind women's skirts, sitting in the back seat."[121]

More than a decade later, soon after his own inauguration, Herbert Hoover experienced a true White House oddity. A doorman, police officer, Secret Service man, and experienced usher all allowed a stranger to enter the president's dining room as he was entertaining guests. Hoover saw him and asked, "What do you want?" The man replied, simply, "I want to see you," but the president told him he had no appointment. This agitated the interloper, who moved toward Hoover while exclaiming, "You better have an appointment with me!" Only then did a butler bolt over and push the unwanted guest back out the door through which he had entered. Thankfully, the man had just been sightseeing and presented no mortal danger.[122]

WITH THE POSSIBLE exception of Abraham Lincoln, no president faced such a diverse and elaborate set of threats to remove him by force as Franklin Roosevelt. Much of it grew out of opposition to his big-government New Deal plan for tackling the Great Depression or to his support for the Allies in Europe in 1940 and 1941. It was also a function of his tenure; plotters simply had more time to take shots at him because he was in office longer than any other president.

His first challenge, like Lincoln's, arrived before his inauguration. Giuseppe Zangara, an unemployed Italian immigrant inspired by anarchist ideas, attended a rally for the president-elect in Miami in February 1933. FDR gave a short speech, then shots rang out. Security men collapsed around Roosevelt and got his car moving away[123] while others apprehended Zangara, who proudly exclaimed, "I have the gun in my hand. I kill kings and presidents first and next all capitalists!"[124] Roosevelt avoided injury, but four people were struck by bullets in the attack and two of them, Chicago mayor Anton Cermak and a bystander, later lost their lives as a result.

Zangara would also die, put to the electric chair for murder. But before he did, he bragged about having come close to killing Italian king Victor Emmanuel III a decade earlier.[125] "I want to kill all presidents," he asserted in his thick accent. "I see Mr. Hoover, I kill him first. Make no difference. President just the same bunch. All the same. Run by big money."[126] A Secret Service agent who interviewed Zangara called him a "crafty, crazy, deluded character who had a hate for all rulers and all governments."[127]

Zangara also suffered from severe, nearly constant stomach pain, probably related to a chronically infected gall bladder discovered during his autopsy.[128] On the stand at his trial, he connected it to his assassination attempt: "I want to make it fifty-fifty since my stomach hurt I get even with capitalists by kill the President. My stomach hurt long time."[129] One of the doctors who judged Zangara to be sane enough for trial eventually regretted it. "Medically, he was *not* sane," he admitted twenty years later. "Legally, he was considered sane in that he could recite the rules of behavior and knew when he was acting contrary to those rules. I am sure if he were alive today and we had the modern facilities for examining him psychiatrically, he would be adjudicated as a very insane person and probably hopelessly insane."[130]

Security tightened around the president-elect, reaching a new extreme when more than a thousand officers met him in Jersey City after the assassination attempt, and fourteen carloads of law enforcement officers escorted his vehicle into New York City.[131]

ONCE HE'D TAKEN the oath of office, Roosevelt's position and life continued to be at risk. The president received five thousand threatening letters each month, and so the Secret Service expanded its operations: scanning food for poisons, putting packages through X-rays, and investigating employees at locations hosting banquets for the president.[132]

"President Roosevelt was realistically aware of the 'sitting duck' target he presented, immobilized in his wheelchair," one of his Secret Service chiefs noted. "He was as concerned as I with the fact that he could not fight off an assailant nor run out of firing range. His physical safety completely depended on the agents around him."[133] Those agents had a couple of close calls in FDR's first term that reinforced their need to remain vigilant.

While scanning a crowd as the president drove through Boston, one agent saw a man get past some police officers, who were watching the president instead of the people around him—a mistake you'll rarely see Secret Service agents make. When the man bolted for Roosevelt's car with his fist clenched, yelling, "You dirty son of a bitch," the agent took him down with a flying tackle. At another event in Erie, Pennsylvania, the president stood on the back of a train, waving to a throng of supporters after a speech, when some kind of knife flew into the arm of a man standing next to him, bouncing off without injury. Agents fell into a circle around FDR while one of their colleagues grabbed the weapon, which turned out to be a rubber dagger.[134]

One purported plot, with a scope and depth remaining unclear almost a century later, stands out as potentially the most complicated threat to remove a president by force in US history. A whistleblowing retired marine general revealed in 1933 that a cabal of anti-FDR conservative businessmen had sought the general's assistance in taking over the government. The powerful group of anonymous bankers and industrialists supposedly feared Roosevelt's New Deal programs would spur a pure socialist state in America. A man claiming to represent them tried to convince the respected officer to lead hundreds of thousands of veterans into the nation's capital to seize the White House and reduce the new president to a mere figurehead, the public face of a fascist government. Legislators held hearings about the whole affair but many in Congress, the press, and the public dismissed it as too outlandish to have presented a realistic threat.[135]

THE JAPANESE ATTACK on Pearl Harbor in December 1941 brought both war to America and upgrades to Roosevelt's security.

At the first report of the surprise assault, his protective detail called in all off-duty Secret Service men and told Washington's chief of police to send a team of uniformed police officers to the executive mansion. The service's detail at the White House grew quickly from sixteen agents to more than three dozen.[136] They expanded their protective measures on site, even confiscating German, Italian, and Japanese reporters' White House press credentials.[137] A special detachment of military police set up sentry boxes around the White House grounds while blackout curtains in the building's windows prevented unwanted observers from seeing the Roosevelts' exact whereabouts.[138] Not all defenses worked as planned; an electronic signal system added to the heightened iron fence around the executive mansion was too sensitive, allowing birds and small animals to drive agents mad with false alarms.[139]

The president's home in Hyde Park, New York, also saw enhanced security during the war, including guard towers on the property and the establishment of a new military police brigade to protect him when there.[140] To address unconventional threats, those agents ensured a gas mask always remained within their reach. Later in the war, they took a Geiger counter everywhere FDR went, to detect potentially damaging radiation and evacuate the president as needed.[141]

Two separate wartime plots caused particular concern. Frank Wilson, the Secret Service chief at the White House in 1943, examined a disturbing report from his colleagues in New York claiming a military deserter named Christopher Cull planned to kill Roosevelt with a powerful nitroglycerin bomb. Wilson put Secret Service officers in New York and Washington on special alert after the suspect's former shipmates on the SS *Florida* told investigators he'd annoyed them by praising Hitler and talking openly about conducting sabotage attacks on airplanes or ships. Arrested in New York, Cull declared, "My purpose was to kill that son-of-a-bitch Roosevelt" and proudly wrote a statement laying out his antipathy for the president and detailing his plan for assassinating him. He landed himself in a hospital for the criminally insane.[142]

The Germans also plotted to kill FDR, most notably when he traveled to Tehran in late 1943 for meetings with Winston Churchill and Joseph Stalin. The Soviets told their American allies that on the eve of the summit, they had arrested dozens of specially trained soldiers who had planned to use grenades and various other weaponry to attack the leaders. The Soviets worried that other Germans remained at large with guns and bombs.[143] Roosevelt put on his best nonchalant airs when telling the press about the reported threat a few weeks later: "I suppose it would make a pretty good haul if they could get all three of us going through the streets."[144] Six months later, the Russians told US officials they had captured and executed the missing Germans, but US officials remained unclear about the true threat from the plot given that all the crucial information about it came from the manipulative Soviets.[145]

HARRY TRUMAN POSED quite a challenge to the Secret Service when he succeeded Roosevelt. Unlike the man they'd protected for twelve long years, Truman walked—often, and quickly. He did it primarily to keep healthy. It didn't hurt that it made him seem a man of the people, less like the more distant, patrician Roosevelt.

He received more smiles and waves than potential threats, but Truman's brisk excursions annoyed the personal detail guarding him, which numbered some thirty agents when he took office.[146] One Saturday early in his presidency, for example, Truman saw no official business on his calendar and decided upon a brisk stroll. He didn't bother, of course, to tell anyone responsible for his protection. Darting out alone from the north entrance of the White House. Security officers who ran to catch up with him saw military men on the sidewalks recognizing and formally greeting their commander in chief but feared that other passers-by might raise something more dangerous than a salute.[147]

A couple of months later, a boisterous mob spontaneously descended on the White House. The loud, openly drinking mass of humanity grew larger by the minute, enveloping the mansion and blocking potential exit routes for the president should evacuation from the site become necessary. But those guarding the chief executive worried little on this night in August 1945, for the crowd of nearly a hundred thousand people assembling at the White House had gathered to cheer their accidental president and celebrate the unconditional surrender of the Japanese empire—and, with it, the end of World War II.[148]

TRUMAN WAS NAPPING, not walking, when the greatest threat to him materialized.

The First Family had vacated the White House in November 1948, after Truman's election to a full term of his own, after engineers and architects declared the building's structure unsound, with parts of the second-floor residence capable of dropping into the main level at almost any time. Truman, no fool, moved across the street to the US government property traditionally used to board visiting dignitaries, Blair House.[149] On the unseasonably hot afternoon of November 1, 1950, the president was relaxing before attending a statue dedication ceremony across the Potomac River at Arlington Cemetery.[150]

A pair of Puerto Rican militants who opposed American control of their Caribbean island hoped to catch Truman's protective detail snoozing, too. They plotted a simple assault on Blair House, whereby they would approach the building from opposite directions, shoot the three guards out front before they knew what hit them, and combine to overpower any security detail inside. They needed at least one of them to penetrate the inner rooms to find and kill the president, whom they wanted to murder in order to raise awareness of Puerto Rico's independence movement.[151]

To protect Truman and his family at Blair House, Secret Service agents had set up what they called their "defense in depth" plan. An outer ring of armed White House policemen and Secret Service agents stood guard at all entrances and watched the public sidewalk. The middle ring consisted of agents with larger, more diverse weapons just inside each entrance and near stairways. An armed agent, always right outside the president's door, stood as the last line of defense.[152] The gunmen could see that outer ring, and they probably suspected other officers were inside. But they knew nothing about either the layout of the deceptively large property—technically, at that point, one unified residence inside two building fronts—or the whereabouts of the president.

They would need to employ shock and awe tactics to reach their target. They failed. One of the attackers shot well, killing a White House policeman and injuring others before taking a bullet to the head and dying on the spot. His less skilled partner had forfeited their surprise by bungling his shots. He allowed the officers outside ample chance to fire back and gave the agents inside time to take precautions in the event one of the attackers got through. The second attacker would live, but he carried injuries with him into his imprisonment of almost thirty years.[153]

The whole thing ended in less than one minute. As the bullets flew, the president looked out his window to see what the commotion was all about, putting himself at great risk. But Truman didn't see it that way, treating it all in his usual direct, folksy manner. "There's no story so far as I am concerned," he told the inquisitive press the next day. "I was never in danger."[154] Indeed, he had insisted on departing on schedule for that statue dedication in Arlington. "A President has to expect these things," he said.[155]

Nevertheless, the Secret Service cracked down. The police guards doubled; protective agents restricted the public's access to the front of Blair House. Most disturbing of all for Truman? He grudgingly gave up his practice of walking freely, when and where he chose, through the streets of Washington.[156]

DESPITE THE COLD WAR that he inherited from Truman, Dwight Eisenhower had it relatively easy on the personal protection front. Not that the menace had faded entirely—in fact, thousands of threats came to the Secret Service's attention during his administration—but the largest challenge became guarding the president during his many golf outings.

"If the killer is an expert marksman the high ground at most courses gives him an excellent shot at objects below," wrote U. E. Baughman, Ike's Secret Service chief. "Also, the trees and limbs that bound fairways afford perfect concealment. Then on a golf course one knows the exact route the potential victim will take. And the fact that one's putative target plays a course regularly or even fairly regularly gives plenty of opportunity to work out the details of the plan . . . These considerations chilled my blood."[157] As a result, Eisenhower's golfing entourages always included a doctor as well as a swarm of protective agents, spread out across that course's many acres. Unlike the other golfers they were disguised as, these players had rifles and submachine guns in their golf bags.[158] On the links, though, the biggest threat to the president came from . . . himself.

At Augusta National one spring day, Ike's cart wouldn't stop and rushed headlong toward a creek. The president leapt off, but the cart circled around and came at him. The few nongovernment golfers on the course must have marveled at the sight of Eisenhower sprinting for his life from a runaway golf cart, with a nervous squad of Secret Service agents in hot pursuit. Ike escaped unharmed, but the same can't be said for his cart. Agents gang-tackled it to end the day's unexpected excitement.[159]

JOHN KENNEDY WON the presidential election in 1960. The contest had been one of the closest in US history. Kennedy's age, relative inexperience, and Catholicism made him a divisive figure, exacerbated by perceived irregularities in places like Chicago. It's little surprise, then, that the Secret Service received dramatically more threats during Kennedy's first year than during Eisenhower's final one.[160]

In an attempt to pull off what Zangara could not against FDR, one deranged man almost prevented JFK from taking office at all. On December 11, 1960, when the president-elect attended services at a church near his family's beachfront compound in Palm Beach, Florida, a protective agent spotted a suspicious, disheveled man approaching the president's pew. After escorting him out of the building, the agent dutifully watched him drive away and told the Palm Beach Police Department to remain on the alert for that car.[161]

The agent's diligence paid off four days later. Police officers near the Kennedy property spotted the same man, Richard Pavlick, in his vehicle—loaded with what the Secret Service chief later called "enough dynamite to blow up a small mountain," as well as the means to detonate it. He readily admitted his intent to kill Kennedy, who he thought had won the presidency only because his father had bought it for him. Pavlick's interrogation revealed he intended to crash into Kennedy's limousine as it left the family compound and explode the dynamite upon impact, but he lost the nerve upon seeing Jackie Kennedy and her children nearby.[162]

Kennedy, as president, was quite aware he was a target. On the morning of November 22, 1963, for example, he told his aide Ken O'Donnell, "If anybody really wanted to shoot the President of the United States, it was not a very difficult job—all one had to do was get [on] a high building someday with a telescopic rifle, and there was nothing anybody could do to defend against such an attempt."[163]

LEE HARVEY OSWALD had been looking for purpose, for meaning, since his teenage years, and that quest took him down the dark path to murder.[164]

Dropping out of school at age fifteen, Oswald tried to join the marines but was too young. Before enlisting just after his seventeenth birthday, he'd already written a letter to the Socialist Party of America claiming, "I am a Marxist."[165] His troubles in the marines ranged from accidentally shooting himself in the elbow to saying "provoking words" to a noncommissioned officer while drunk, and it didn't take long before he lost his desire to remain in military service. In September 1959, after Oswald claimed he needed to go care for his mother, the marines released him from active duty. A year later, he received an "undesirable discharge."[166]

By then, it had become clear that he'd left the marines to move to the Soviet Union in October 1959 and renounce his US citizenship. His life in the supposed communist paradise quickly disappointed him. "The work is drab," he wrote in January 1961 in his diary, later obtained by the Warren Commission. "The money I get has nowhere to be spent. No nightclubs or bowling alleys, no places of recreation except the trade union dances. I have had enough." By June 1962, he'd returned to the United States with a wife and young daughter and moved to the Dallas–Fort Worth area.[167]

Oswald's next seventeen months are a portrait in failure and self-radicalization. In April 1963, he fired a rifle into the Dallas home of an outspoken conservative, retired major general Edwin Walker. "I was sitting down behind a desk," Walker remembered, "I heard a blast and a crack right over my head." The bullet came within an inch of its target.[168] Dismayed by his missed opportunity there, but emboldened that the police didn't identify him as the shooter, Oswald went to New Orleans for the spring and summer, distributing pro-Castro leaflets and appearing on local television and radio to promote communist Cuba's cause. He didn't recruit a single other person to assist his efforts.[169] Then he traveled to Mexico to try to get visas from skeptical Cuban and Soviet officials. He failed there, too.[170]

Throughout his time back in the United States, Oswald took on a string of jobs when he bothered to find work. In October 1963, he landed a position at the Texas School Book Depository, whose south-facing windows had a beautiful view down onto Dealey Plaza and Elm Street.

LOCAL MEDIA FOR several days had publicized JFK's visit to Dallas and even his planned movements on Friday, November 22. At twelve thirty in the afternoon local time, Kennedy's limousine turned onto Elm Street. Within six seconds, Oswald fired three times from his position at one of the Texas School Book Depository's sixth-floor windows. Two of the bullets, including a devastating head shot, struck JFK; Texas governor John Connally was also injured. As trailing Secret Service officer Clint Hill jumped onto Kennedy's limo to shield Mrs. Kennedy, the driver accelerated and raced to Parkland Memorial Hospital, but nothing could be done to save the president's life.[171] Oswald would be captured and, later, shot while in police custody.

There's no shortage of fascination about nearly every aspect of the events before, on, and after that fateful day. Vincent Bugliosi's *Reclaiming History* is an exhaustive and majisterial account, including systematic debunking of various conspiracy theories. On the assassin, Bugliosi is clear: "Oswald, an emotionally unhinged political malcontent who hated America, was guilty as sin. Based on the Himalayan mountain of uncontroverted evidence against Oswald, anyone who could believe he was innocent would probably also believe someone claiming to have heard a cow speaking the Spanish language." Of course, not all the naysayers claim the killer was innocent; many claim he was either set up or part of a wider conspiracy. To that, Bugliosi says (his emphasis), "There was not one speck of *credible* evidence that Oswald was framed or that he was a hit man for others in a conspiracy to murder the president."[172]

So why, then, did Oswald remove the president? No evidence indicates that he was driven by a desire to elevate Lyndon Johnson to Kennedy's place. Nor does anything credible suggest that he aimed to take down the US government. The truth is underwhelming to most of us, because it violates our natural expectation that big, important causes must be behind events bringing big, important consequences. Oswald was probably driven by a particularly toxic combination of factors similar to that of all too many other murderers: insecurity, frustration, restlessness, aversion to authority, and a desire to be recognized. The means and opportunity that landed in his lap on November 22, 1963, combined with that mix of motives, aren't as thrilling as so many imaginary plots, especially when accompanied by gruesome video of the shocking event, but they do explain the tragedy of that day.

A T THE COST of distancing elected leaders from those they govern, the dramatic expansion of the security cordon around the White House and the president since the Kennedy assassination has helped prevent another removal by force. The risk, however, has remained high and diverse.

Lyndon Johnson came to appreciate the Secret Service during his final minutes as vice president. Riding directly behind the president's car, he barely had time to hear Oswald's gunshots before his Secret Service agent jumped from his seat in the front to cover his protectee. "A great big husky roughneck from Georgia threw 185 pounds of human weight on me and said, 'down,'" Johnson recalled. "And there wasn't any place for me to go but down, because he was on top of me. His life was being offered to protect mine."[173] For more than five years afterward, the men and women of the Secret Service would continue to defend him. One historical LBJ what-if involves a man named Sirhan Sirhan, whose attention Johnson drew. "Must begin to work on . . . solving the problems and difficulties of assassinating the 36th president of the glorious United States," Sirhan had written in his diary.[174] But instead of trying to murder Johnson, he set his sights on Robert Kennedy, a presidential hopeful, whom he shot and killed in June 1968 at a campaign rally in California.

Richard Nixon, who succeeded LBJ in January 1969, was no stranger to the personal risks that come with leading the country. While serving as vice president in July 1958, Nixon escaped injury and possible death at the hands of an angry mob in Caracas. A truck had blocked Nixon's motorcade, allowing a crowd angered by US policy toward Venezuela to swamp the vice president's car. Wielding guns and clubs and hurling bricks, bottles, and rocks,[175] they pushed the Secret Service back into a tight circle around the car, which the mob rocked and seemed ready to overturn. Fearing the worst, the agents had drawn their weapons, and steeled their reserve to start shooting, when Venezuelan forces finally arrived and helped the motorcade to safety.[176]

By Nixon's first year in office, the Secret Service had expanded to more than 750 agents.[177] He would be targeted by at least six different would-be assassins. The most prominent was Arthur Bremer. In April 1972, he narrowly missed his window to shoot Nixon in Canada before turning his attention the following month on presidential candidate George Wallace, whom he shot and paralyzed from the waist down.[178]

The most common problem with Nixon was his desire to stop his car to allow him to shake hands with people in the crowd. "So we learned to work out with him and his staff, ahead of time, where they were going to stop," says one of his former Secret Service agents. "It wasn't impromptu; that's just the way it was presented. We'd have a couple of agents in the crowd there, and we'd have someone there an hour ahead of time who could look for the wackos. I can tell you, as a guy who protected Richard Nixon for six years by myself, you could see those wackos a block away. It's like they're painted with a sign that says, 'STOP ME.'"[179]

"IT WAS KIND of an ultimate protest against the system," explained Sara Jane Moore about her attempt to kill Gerald Ford.[180] Before September 1975, when she pulled the trigger on the president in San Francisco and missed, no woman had attempted a presidential assassination. And yet she wasn't the first woman to try to shoot Ford in California that very month.

Back on the morning of September 5 in Sacramento, Ford walked from his hotel across the state capitol grounds for a meeting with Governor Jerry Brown. He remembers a clear, sunny day, the crowd so friendly that he started shaking hands. A woman two or three rows back caught his eye because her bright-red dress seemed out of place. So did the gun she raised at him.[181] While Ford pulled back and ducked, a Secret Service agent pushed the weapon down and twisted the woman's arm, leading her away from the president as she said repeatedly, "It didn't go off!"[182] The investigation showed there hadn't even been a bullet in the chamber. Lyn "Squeaky" Fromme, it turns out, sought to use her arrest and trial to draw attention to her idol, cult leader Charles Manson. Nevertheless, a jury found her guilty of trying to kill Ford and sent her off to prison.[183]

Moore's turn came seventeen days later. As Ford left his San Francisco hotel for his ride to the airport, this time without shaking hands, he waved to the crowd and heard a shot.[184] A bullet came within a few feet of hitting him. As Moore had fired from forty feet away, a bystander pushed her arm, which sent the bullet off course into the hotel wall. The investigation discovered that she hoped, by killing Ford, to prove her commitment to members of radical movements in the Bay Area, with whom she'd burned her bridges by becoming an FBI informant.[185] She had alerted police just two days before Ford's visit that she had a gun and was considering testing presidential security. The police took her gun and informed the Secret Service, who interviewed her but found no grounds for arrest. She quickly bought another gun and proceeded to do what she'd previewed for them.[186]

The Secret Service went through some serious self-reflection afterward, and it managed better during a 1979 incident before one of President Jimmy Carter's scheduled speeches in Los Angeles. The nervous and evasive behavior they saw from a man in the crowd, only fifty feet from where the president would stand, spurred them to pull the man aside. He had a starter pistol with blank rounds, and claimed to be part of a larger plot in which his harmless shots would distract everyone while other, real assassins (never located) did the dirty deed.[187] He also went to jail.

BUT FOR THE gut instinct of quick-thinking Secret Service agent Jerry Parr on the afternoon of March 30, 1981, Ronald Reagan would have joined Lincoln, Garfield, McKinley, and Kennedy on a short but tragic list.

John Hinckley had just shot six bullets toward Reagan as he left the Washington Hilton hotel. The protective detail's training kicked in instantly. One agent grabbed the president and got him roughly into the backseat of the waiting limousine, while his colleague filled the space between Reagan and the crowd, shielding Reagan with his body. Their shift leader shut the limo door; the agent driving the armored vehicle promptly hit the gas. Yet another agent took Hinckley to the ground, disarming and handcuffing him. His duty then shifted to protecting the vulnerable assailant from the angry crowd.[188]

As the car sped away, Parr asked the president if he'd been hit. He replied that he didn't think so, but said his chest hurt. That made sense: after half carrying, half throwing Reagan onto the limo's floor, Parr had put his full weight down on the president. His quick exam found frothy blood in Reagan's mouth, a sign the blood came from his lungs, and the president told him it was hard to breathe. Parr made the quick decision to change their destination from the White House to George Washington University Hospital. With that choice, he saved Reagan's life.[189]

The president, though struggling to breathe, managed to walk into the emergency room under his own power. Then, with little warning, he crumpled. He, and his protective detail, had suspected only that he'd broken a rib and didn't yet know that a bullet had collapsed his lung and filled his chest cavity with blood. Without immediate attention, he would die.[190] Thankfully, because Parr had directed the limo to the hospital, the president was in good hands and would eventually recover. Later, recording his memories for his diary, Reagan would note, "Getting shot hurts."[191]

The machinery of many bureaucracies kicked into hyperdrive to determine the motive and any possible accomplices of the attempted assassin. What investigators found both relieved and shocked them. Hinckley hadn't shot Reagan to bring down the system of government. He didn't seek to advance the vice president or any other officials. He wasn't making any political or social statement at all. He sadly, simply, desperately wanted to get the attention of actress Jodie Foster.[192]

After his two terms ended, Reagan shared what had crossed his mind when first going into the operating room. "I remembered the trip I had made just the week before to Ford's Theater and the thoughts I'd had while looking up at the flag-draped box where Lincoln had died," he wrote. "Even with all the protection in the world, I'd thought, it was probably impossible to guarantee completely the safety of the president."[193]

REAGAN'S VICE PRESIDENT and successor, George H. W. Bush, faced no major threats of removal by force. But *his* successors—Bill Clinton, George W. Bush, and Barack Obama—each did.

In the wee hours of September 12, 1994, pilot Frank Corder tried to fly a stolen Cessna into the White House. He crashed into the South Lawn, killing himself but nobody else. It remains unclear if Corder intended to harm Clinton, who wasn't even in the executive mansion at the time.[194] The treasury secretary, who oversaw the Secret Service, ordered a security review, but it had barely begun when another incident occurred. Francisco Duran stood outside the White House fence the very next month and fired twenty-nine rounds through it into the building's north facade. One bullet penetrated a window in the West Wing, but the president was in a room on the other side of the mansion. Bystanders subdued Duran, and no one was injured. The Secret Service found a letter in which he'd written, "Can you imagine a higher moral calling than to destroy someone's dreams with one bullet?"[195]

George W. Bush's greatest danger came while he traveled overseas. At an outdoor event in Tbilisi, Georgia, on May 10, 2005, a man in a huge crowd waited for the president to start speaking, then pulled the pin from a hand grenade and hurled it toward the president. It landed sixty-one feet away but failed to explode because the attacker had wrapped it so tightly in a red handkerchief that the firing pin couldn't deploy.[196]

For Barack Obama, the most disturbing threats came via attacks at the White House itself while he was away. On a Friday night in November 2011, when the president and his wife were traveling but his mother-in-law and one of his daughters sat inside, bullets came at the executive mansion from a car parked hundreds of feet away. Secret Service agents heard the shots; one at ground level even thought she saw falling debris from the southern face of the building. A supervisor, however, assumed the gunfire came from a nearby construction vehicle's backfire and ordered agents to stand down.[197]

Four days later, a maid saw a broken window and concrete chunk on the floor of the south-facing Truman Balcony. The search that followed found a bullet in a window frame, another bullet hole, and some metal fragments. By that time, the First Lady had returned, and was livid when she heard about what had happened without immediate action or any communication with her and the president.[198] The man who took the shots had been venting back home in Idaho weeks earlier about the federal government and declaring that Obama "had to be stopped." Conveniently, he wrecked his car after the incident and left his gun inside; police quickly arrested him in Pennsylvania.[199]

In September 2014, a man with a knife—taking advantage of protective officers' attention on the South Lawn, where the president had just boarded a helicopter to take him to Camp David[200]—jumped the north fence and sprinted to the north portico of the White House. An off-duty Secret Service agent stopped him only after he'd pushed past one officer and gotten into the building.[201] These incidents during the Obama administration, like the other attacks in the one hundred–plus years before them, drove those protecting the president to examine existing procedures and update their methods for ensuring that Lincoln, Garfield, McKinley, and Kennedy remain the only presidents removed by force.

"All of the growth around the protection of the president, all of the policies and procedures," says former Secret Service agent Jonathan Wackrow, "is borne out of blood."[202]

Chapter Six

Declared Unable to Serve

I did not fear death so much as I feared disability. Whenever I walked by the Red Room and saw the portrait of Woodrow Wilson hanging there, I thought of him stretched out upstairs in the White House, unable to move, with the machinery of the American government in disarray all around him.[1]

—LYNDON JOHNSON

"THE PRESIDENT IS a very sick man," the doctor's bulletin announced, and "absolute rest is essential for some time."[2] This statement from Woodrow Wilson's physician on October 3, 1919, told the world two truths about the president: his illness was serious, and he would be out of contact for a while. It withheld much, much more. Nothing substantial was revealed that day, nor during the next couple of months, about the cause, Wilson's prognosis, or courses of treatment.[3]

The information-starved public wanted more. So did senators, about to debate the treaty that could bring the United States into the League of Nations, a cause the president championed above all others. Wilson's own cabinet lacked guidance on an ever-growing stack of executive actions. Even the man who could at any moment be called upon to take Wilson's position, the vice president of the United States, was kept in the dark.

The presidency, for months, ground to a halt.

WILSON, ONLY THE second Democrat to win a presidential election since the Civil War, had benefited in 1912 from a split in the Republican Party. Incumbent William Taft and former president Theodore Roosevelt essentially knocked each other out of the race that year, letting Wilson slip into the White House with less than 42 percent of the popular vote.

Wilson for a time kept the United States out of the catastrophic conflict raging in Europe, but ultimately he led the country into and through the First World War. Ike Hoover, chief usher at the White House, thought him in relatively good physical and mental health during that time, up until Wilson left for Europe in December 1918 for the first of two extended trips to negotiate the war-ending treaty.[4] While he stayed in Paris in early 1919 to lay the foundation for the post-war peace, Hoover noticed a flurry of odd presidential decisions. Wilson suddenly changed the American delegation's automobile use policy with no apparent cause. He ranted to anyone in his entourage who would listen that every member of the local hospitality staff was listening in on his conversations. He abruptly took an obsessive interest in the location and condition of each piece of furniture in his suite. "These were very funny things," Hoover later wrote, "and we could but surmise that something queer was happening in his mind."[5]

Returning home from Europe in July, Wilson looked forward to a more stable time. He didn't get it. The campaign on behalf of the treaty, filled by long days of tense meetings with senators, was stressful and exhausting. "Day after day, week after week, those conferences continued, but nothing seemed to result except increased fatigue for the President," recalled his second wife, Edith. "The increasing demands on my husband's brain and body exacted a toll which pyramided, while I looked on with an anxious heart."[6] Stalled by calls in the Senate for revisions to the treaty, which would prove difficult for the treaty's other parties to sign on to, Wilson decided to take the treaty case directly to the American people, via a weeks-long train trip through the Midwest to the western states. Republicans skeptical about the treaty and its collective defense provision, he felt, would buckle under the wave of popular support he could generate on the tour.[7]

His doctor and wife, concerned about his health, tried to persuade the president to cancel, but he insisted.[8] Wilson's private secretary recalled the president saying, "Even though, in my condition it might mean giving up my life, I will gladly make the sacrifice to save the treaty."[9] Energized by the opportunity to advocate for the peace plan he'd helped craft, Wilson departed Washington, DC, on September 3. He'd stop in a dozen states, give three dozen major speeches, make many more short presentations from the back of the train, attend parades, shake thousands of hands, and attend various political meetings in just three weeks. The exertion strained him nearly from the start of the trip, in the form of serious headaches.[10] Later in the tour, Edith suggested canceling a few days' events to rest. He turned her down flat. "No, I have caught the imagination of the people," he said. "This will soon be over, and when we get back to Washington I promise you I will take a holiday."[11]

Heading into an event on September 25 in Pueblo, Colorado, Wilson seemed off balance, stumbling on the single step from the car to the entrance. Once inside, he mumbled during his speech and failed to project as well as usual. His Secret Service man noticed later that night that the president seemed to be walking oddly.[12] Overnight on the train, Edith was surprised by a knock on the door between her husband's room and her own. She opened it to find him in obvious physical distress, complaining about a crushing headache. She called for Dr. Cary Grayson, the president's physician, but he could give Wilson no relief. By morning, it was clear that something serious had happened.[13] The left side of Wilson's face looked fallen and didn't move; saliva dribbled out of the left corner of his mouth as he slurred his words. He had trouble moving his left arm and leg.[14]

As Edith and Grayson agreed to head back to Washington, the deception of the public began. Grayson told the press that Wilson's simple "nervous exhaustion" demanded that the party return to the

White House without making any remaining scheduled appearances.[15] Nothing specific was said about the incident the night before or the president's dramatic symptoms. Stops along the way for passengers and supplies brought onlookers to the tracks to try to get a glimpse at the sick president, so Edith pulled down the shades, making the car seem "like a funeral."[16]

The worst, sadly, was yet to come.

EARLY ONE DREADFUL morning a week later, Edith found the president on the floor of his bathroom. She rushed to get her husband a blanket and pillow for his head—the doctor was already on his way to the room.

Several hours earlier, on the evening of October 2, she'd felt optimistic for the first time in weeks. Although the day of their return to Washington had been rough—the president had paced the White House halls in agony from his persistent headache—the next couple of days brought improvement and Wilson even read a Bible chapter to his wife before retiring early. She checked on him frequently in his separate room during the night, and all looked well until her visit there just after eight o'clock in the morning. He sat on his bed, unable to reach a water bottle. "I have no feeling in my hand," he told her. "Will you rub it? But first help me to the bathroom." The short walk proved quite difficult and painful for him, even with her assistance, so she stepped out to call Grayson. The faint noise she heard within seconds was the president hitting the bathroom floor, unconscious.[17]

Grayson, discovering that Wilson couldn't move his left side or communicate clearly, immediately suspected that a blood clot had caused a massive stroke. A neurologist already planning to see the president the next day came to the White House earlier than expected and concurred. That type of stroke, in the right hemisphere of the brain, rarely kills the patient and has little effect on cognitive functions, but it was likely that some physical impairment would remain, and psychological and emotional damage is common.[18] "He just lay helpless," the usher recalled. "All his natural functions had to be artificially assisted and he appeared just as helpless as one could possibly be and live." It took more than a month until the president could be carried from his bed to a chair nearby, but even then he remained "a shadow of his former self."[19]

Grayson and Mrs. Wilson knew the duties of the presidency lay beyond his abilities for now. At the same time, his resignation would crush his incentive to recover and thereby see to completion the one task he cared about more than any other: getting the United States into the League of Nations.[20] Without consulting with the vice president, the cabinet, or Congress, they decided Wilson's progress depended on him remaining president but forgoing any engagement on official business for as long as possible.

Because seeing and interacting with most people, in their minds, would bring him too much stress, they severely restricted access to the president to themselves, a handful of doctors and nurses, essential White House staff members, and Wilson's daughters from his first marriage.[21] That was it. For months. Outside that circle, only a trusted few—including the president's private secretary, the secretary of state, and a handful of others—even heard the truth about his paralysis and disability in those early weeks. Most of the cabinet, everyone in Congress, and the general public could only listen to the rumor mill to guess his actual condition, given the bland and information-bereft statements from the White House.[22]

The vice president, whom the Constitution decreed should discharge the powers and duties of the presidency during any presidential disability, remained in the dark. Thomas Marshall, though, felt relief and not anger at his exclusion: "I hoped that he might acquire his wonted health. I was afraid to ask about it, for fear some censorious soul would accuse me of longing for his place."[23] Eventually, Wilson's private secretary decided Marshall had to know the extent of the president's deterioration. Refusing to tell him directly, he sent a trusted emissary to brief the vice president, who couldn't even speak upon hearing the news.[24] When senators urged Marshall to assert some leadership and push for a declaration of disability, he flatly refused any action at all unless Congress officially declared a presidential vacancy *and* Mrs. Wilson and Dr. Grayson provided written agreement. So nothing changed.[25]

THE SECRETARY OF STATE presided over a cabinet meeting a few days after Wilson's collapse during which the men present discussed the Constitution's inability clause. Grayson joined them and made it hard for the cabinet to do much but wait. Asserting that the president's mind remained clear, Grayson said he'd had a nervous breakdown, suffered from indigestion, and was dealing with a depleted system. The doctor refused to answer appeals for more specifics on his condition.[26] Instead of relief, annoyance at the tight circle around the president prevailed.

Key papers requiring presidential action went through Grayson to Mrs. Wilson, who took it upon herself to decide which ones her husband needed to hear about. Most of them never received replies, because she saw her primary duty as keeping from him anything less than absolutely crucial. This, of course, caused cabinet members and Wilson's private secretary no small frustration; the president's signature was needed for an ever-growing stack of appointments and other actions. A few decisions did come down from the residence in the president's name, but nobody could be sure if the decisions or the signatures on them were truly his or Edith's. Available evidence strongly suggests that the First Lady took great liberties with her new role. She acted on things her previous discussions with the president gave her some insight into, and pushed them as presidential choices.[27]

Most decisions were stalled. Future president Herbert Hoover, leading the post-war American Relief Administration (through which the United States provided crucial provisions to devastated Europe), sent Wilson his resignation from this and other offices but never received a reply or even an acknowledgment of receipt.[28] As the months went by, most executive officers simply stopped asking anything of the president. Government operations just muddled through as best they could.[29]

The secretary of state, in Wilson's absence, continued to lead cabinet meetings to conduct as much executive business as possible. But that stopped in February 1920 when the president sent a startling letter to him expressing surprise that such meetings were occurring and demanding an explanation. The secretary defended his actions—by letter of course, because he still couldn't see his boss—quite reasonably claiming that somebody had to coordinate ongoing actions. But an irritated Wilson asked for his resignation anyway. The exchange of letters made Wilson look ungrateful, and when they went public congressional and press reactions reflected disdain for the president's haughty tone. Outsiders still had no specific health information from the White House; whispers about Wilson's insanity became louder. Some on Capitol Hill sought new laws for declaring presidential disabilities.[30] In March, the Senate rejected Wilson's beloved Treaty of Versailles, with its provisions for a League of Nations. The cabinet meetings he finally started hosting again in April were tense and awkward.

Those around the president painted a dark picture of his remaining days in the White House. Ike Hoover, the chief usher, said Wilson had changed "from a giant to a pygmy . . . he could articulate but indistinctly and think but feebly."[31] Secret Service agent Edmund Starling lamented, "Even when conscious, he was unreasonable, unnatural, simply impossible. His suspicions were intensified, his perspective distorted."[32] Starling also admitted that Edith Wilson and Dr. Grayson "stood between the President and the rest of the world while he was ill. How much they kept from him will never be known."[33] More information has come to light since Starling said that in the 1940s, pushing author William Hazelgrove to go further. "Edith Wilson was never nominated, she was never on any ballot, she never took the oath of office," he writes, "but she did carry the burden of presidential power from 1919 to 1921."[34]

DECLARING A PRESIDENTIAL disability is one of the ways to separate a person from the chief executive's office, on top of voting them out and waiting for them to die, that receives mention in the Constitution. As the case of Woodrow Wilson exposes, its application under the founders' original design was fraught with practical difficulties.

ONLY IN THE final weeks of the Constitutional Convention in 1787 did the delegates tackle the issue of presidential succession and, with it, what to do if a chief executive became unable to do the job. A committee that had been created in July to draft a working document from discussions up to that point inserted placeholder text naming the president of the Senate as a temporary fill-in if a president developed a disability. James Madison and others on August 27 quibbled over the details, challenging in particular who should act for the president; suggestions ranged from the chief justice to a presidential council.

Then John Dickinson of Pennsylvania voiced two fundamental issues, asking, "What is the extent of the term 'disability'?" and "Who is to be the judge of it?" His questions must have been too hard to handle, because delegates quickly threw the issue to *another* committee tasked to address postponed topics.[35] That group, in turn, came back in early September with text describing a new position, the vice president—who, upon the president's "inability to discharge the powers and duties of his office," would "exercise those powers and duties until another President be chosen, or until the inability of the President be removed." Subsequent attention focused more on the means of selecting this backup leader than the barely discussed clause on "disability" (a term the delegates usually used interchangeably with "inability").[36]

The final text related to disability eventually read, in the Constitution's article 2, section 1: "In the case of the Removal of the President from Office, or of his Death, Resignation, or Inability to discharge the Powers and Duties of the said Office, the Same shall devolve on the Vice President." It allowed Congress to pass laws providing for who should act as president if *both* the president and vice president were removed, adding "such Officer shall act accordingly, until the Disability be removed, or a President be selected."

That sounds straightforward. But a few problems quickly emerged. First, as the country in 1841 had been forced to confront, the section's phrasing was ambiguous. Did the delegates want the vice president to take on the powers and duties of the office but not actually *be* the president? (This is most constitutional scholars' interpretation of the founders' intent.) Or did they think the vice president should become a fully loaded president, as John Tyler convinced them to accept? Second, the words "In the case of . . . Inability to discharge the Powers and Duties of the said Office" remain painfully unhelpful on Dickinson's key questions: What constitutes a disability—and who decides?

In the early years of the republic, the issue was moot. Citizens and especially rival partisans questioned some presidents' suitability for office, but they didn't try to remove them due to a disability. Over the course of more than two centuries, however, we've managed to get through the incapacitation of Woodrow Wilson, which probably warranted removal, and other situations that came close to the same.

THE FIRST PRESIDENTIAL brush with a potentially disabling event, more than a century before Wilson's tragedy, remains the only one involving the chief executive fleeing a foreign army on US soil. In 1814, James Madison almost lost the ability to fulfill his oath not due to physical injury or mental illness, but capture.

The War of 1812 hadn't gone well. The war fever that pushed US leaders into a conflict with the world's greatest power proved a bad idea, because the British forces generally defeated the Americans in two years of confrontations across the continent. Secretary of State James Monroe worried that the hostile navy might sail right up the Potomac River from Chesapeake Bay and raid Washington. He urged the new secretary of war to fortify defenses around the nation's capital but was told such an enemy move would be impossible.[37] The British, in fact, *were* coming. Earlier sessions of Congress had withheld funding to build a credible army. And the secretary of the navy had requested reinforcements from Philadelphia, but neglected to expedite their transmission. Instead of seeking to inflict damage on the approaching British fleet, the commander of a flotilla of American gunboats followed orders to destroy his own ships so they would not fall into British hands.[38]

A British force of around forty-five hundred men disembarked and moved on land to Bladensburg, Maryland, a few miles east of the District of Columbia. There on August 24 they met a ragtag collection of American fighters, joined by President Madison, just behind the lines. After an initial burst of spirited firepower at the British, the Americans made a hasty retreat back toward the capital.[39] Madison raced his horse there, too, arriving to find the executive mansion virtually abandoned and many of the city's residents scattering westward into northern Virginia and Maryland. His wife and most of the household staff had bolted just half an hour earlier. The president sat down long enough to cool off and enjoy a glass of wine before mounting his horse again to avoid becoming a prisoner of the approaching British army.[40]

That night, the light from the fires British soldiers set at the White House, the US Capitol, and most other public buildings in the city could be seen from forty miles away.[41] They had sacked and burned the seat of government, humiliating the president.[42] But it could have been worse; he could have been abducted.

WHAT WOULD HAVE happened? It's hard to imagine that Madison's imprisonment by a foreign power could be considered anything but an inability to carry out the duties of the presidency. The vice president, by the Constitution, should pick up the reins in such a case, but who would have declared it so? The Capitol building itself, which in those days housed the House of Representatives, the Senate, and the Supreme Court, was a hollowed-out ruin. Regardless, Congress stood in recess, with its members scattered across the country until September.

If Vice President Elbridge Gerry had taken over due to Madison's kidnapping, would he have handed the reins back to the elected president upon his eventual release? That's how it's supposed to work; but, as we saw with John Tyler's rise in 1841, constitutional meanings are influenced by practice. Gerry wouldn't have exercised the powers and duties of the office long, because he died just over a year later, on November 23, 1814.

The next in the line of succession was the president pro tempore of the Senate. Two days after Gerry's death, senators put into that position John Gaillard, later described by a colleague as "urbane in his manners, amiable in temper, scrupulously impartial . . . as much the favorite of one side of the house as of the other."[43] But at the time of Gerry's death, Gaillard's election to the temporary presidency of the Senate hadn't yet happened. The body, briefly, didn't have a president pro tempore. So the next in line would have been Speaker of the House Langdon Cheves, a South Carolinian who would end up urging Southern states to secede and form a Confederacy earlier than most Southerners gave up on the Union.[44] History would have looked quite different with a Cheves presidency.

Several presidents have endured a silent disability: depression. Operating effectively in the White House is difficult no matter what, but trying to do so with deep despair can be debilitating. According to a 2006 study, more than a quarter of all presidents during their time in office met established criteria for one or more psychiatric disorders—with depression, by far, standing out as the most common.[45]

During the Civil War, Abraham Lincoln seemed surrounded by sadness. The widest circle of it was that of the nation itself, ripped apart by a bloody conflict that left behind more than six hundred thousand deaths and widespread devastation. Closer in was that of his family; his wife probably suffering from mental illness and the tragedy of her lost sons. And Lincoln himself carried a shadow with him much of his life.

Events in childhood and early adulthood started Lincoln down a melancholic path. He grew up in near squalor; the first four places he lived in each had but one room and only a dirt floor. He turned inward—even writing of himself in the third person, "He studied with no one"—especially after the death of his beloved mother when he was barely nine years old.[46] The slightly older sister who often took care of him when they were young also passed away, during childbirth, when Lincoln was eighteen.

When Lincoln's fiancée, Ann Rutledge, succumbed to what was probably typhoid fever and died in August 1835, by which time

Lincoln had become a state representative, he had a breakdown. It went beyond grief; one local man indicates that Lincoln was so depressed he "had to lock him up and keep guard over him for some two weeks . . . For fear he might Commit Suicide."[47] A fellow legislator said, "He told me that he was so overcome with mental depression, that he never dare carry a knife in his pocket."[48] Lincoln directed his energy into studying law, an early example of the pattern that would serve him well later in life: immersion in a new task to help pull him out of the darkest times.[49]

A second episode in early 1841 may have been even worse. A set of political disappointments for Lincoln, his decision to break an engagement with eventual wife Mary Todd, and his friend Joshua Speed's announcement that he was moving out of town sent Lincoln into a downward spiral. For a few weeks, he avoided most social contact and presented a danger to himself. "Lincoln went crazy," Speed would write, "had to remove razors from his room—take away all knives and other such dangerous things, etc., it was terrible."[50] Lincoln wrote to John Stuart, his law partner and friend, "I am now the most miserable man living. If what I feel were equally distributed to the whole human family, there would not be one cheerful face on the earth. Whether I shall ever be better I cannot tell; I awfully forebode I shall not. To remain as I am is impossible; I must die or be better, it appears to me." Only after he missed six full days of legislative business and most of at least one other, friends and colleagues started to notice improvement.[51] At the same time, his doctor started prescribing "blue mass pills," which Lincoln would take for years. Unfortunately, they contained mercury, along with honey and licorice, probably causing long-term neurological damage instead of helping ease his melancholia.[52]

Mutual friends helped Lincoln resume his relationship with Mary that summer, and they would wed before the end of the year.[53] Her family connections bested his and they often got along quite well. She bore four sons, only two of whom survived through his presidency. But she also had myriad troubles, including frequent panic and anxiety attacks, a persistent storm phobia, and lifelong struggles managing the anger she took out liberally on both her husband and their household help.[54] He told at least two confidants, including his law partner William Herndon, that Mary was insane.[55]

Both of them took very hard the loss in early 1850 of their second son, Eddie, to tuberculosis. Mary secluded herself and stopped eating for a time. Even the birth of Willie late that same year didn't get her over the sadness of Eddie's passing. As for Lincoln, "He was a sad-looking man," wrote Herndon, "his melancholy dripped from him as he walked."[56]

TAKING OVER AS the sixteenth president of the United States while Southerners seceded and war loomed large didn't exactly cheer Lincoln up. The early events of the Civil War made it worse.

After less than a year in office, he wrote, "It is extremely discouraging. As everywhere else, nothing can be done."[57] A few months later, in July 1862, he admitted to sleep problems and a weak appetite. Asked about his emaciated look, he replied, "I cannot take my vittles regular."[58] A senator who expressed fear for Lincoln's health didn't get the answer from the president he expected: "I must die sometime."[59] Perhaps most telling was Lincoln's commentary after the devastating Union loss at Fredericksburg, Virginia, in December that same year. More than a thousand soldiers had died, with nearly ten thousand injured, in just a few days. "I wonder if the damned in hell suffer less than I do," the president said. "If there is a worse place than hell I am in it." A governor overheard him, over and over, asking, "What has God put me in this place for?" His depression lasted through the winter.[60]

He deeply missed one thing that seemed to have given him joy even in the dark early days of his presidency; his eleven-year-old son Willie caught a serious fever and died in February 1862. The president's grief became so intense that he stopped attending to government business and spent day after day crying over the loss of the son with whom he was so close that he seemed able to read his mind.[61] The absence of Willie during the post-Fredericksburg crash certainly lengthened and deepened it. Lincoln poured his affection into his youngest son, Tad, letting him interrupt war councils and other meetings anytime he liked. "I don't know but I may succeed in governing the nation," he told guests one night after being pulled away by Tad, "but I do believe I shall fail in ruling my own household."[62]

Despite the anguish Lincoln endured, one of his best biographers finds no evidence that his private pain rendered him unable to function as president. On his dying day, in fact, with Lee's surrender behind him and the end of the horrible conflict within reach, Lincoln seemed to have turned a corner. "We must both be more cheerful in the future," he told his wife, "between the war and the loss of our darling Willie, we have been very miserable."[63] In fact, the president's tragedies may have spurred some of his greatest attributes. Lincoln silently suffered, yes, but that torment powered his legendary persistence and compassion.

SOME SIX DECADES LATER, another president would suffer significant depression in the White House. The loss of a beloved son would serve as the precipitating event for a downward spiral that affected the country's governance.

Did it meet the definition of "disability"? Probably not. But the reserved demeanor, even disengagement, during much of Calvin Coolidge's time in the White House probably had its roots in deep depression. If it occurred today, his condition would raise questions, rightly or wrongly, about his fitness for office.

IF AMERICANS IN the twenty-first century can recall Coolidge at all, it's usually his mix of snarky wit and brevity that comes to mind. When a reporter asked the president if he would give a speech at the fair he planned to attend the next day, Coolidge snapped back, "No, I am going as an exhibit."[64] In another story, probably apocryphal, but almost too "peak Coolidge" not to be true, a guest at a large dinner party announced she had made a bet that she could get the president to say three words. His reported reply? "You lose."

As a mayor, Massachusetts state senator, president of that senate, and lieutenant governor, Coolidge had established himself as a diligent politician. While governor of Massachusetts in 1919, he brokered an agreement between the management and striking workers of the Boston elevated railway system, raising their wages and getting them back to work.[65] That same year, he ordered the state militia to keep the peace in Boston after the city's police officers went on strike. When they were fired, Coolidge wouldn't reinstate them, saying, "There is no right to strike against the public safety by anybody, anywhere, anytime."[66] His strong work ethic seemed to continue after taking the vice presidency in 1921. Unlike most of his predecessors, Coolidge worked full days, attended cabinet meetings, and seemed to enjoy his role as president of the Senate.[67]

Warren Harding's death in August 1923 elevated Coolidge to the presidency. For most of the next twelve months, his immersive work habits continued. He interacted extensively with the press. He hosted cabinet meetings. He courted congressional allies. Secret Service agent Edmund Starling noted how ably he performed a range of job tasks.[68] One biographer labels him "hyperactive" in seeking the Republican nomination for the 1924 election.[69] And he got it, on his way to joining only Theodore Roosevelt as an "accidental president" who went on to win a term as chief executive in his own right.

Then disaster struck. It started small. His youngest son, Calvin Jr., got a blister on one of his toes while playing tennis on the White House lawn, but the injury stubbornly wouldn't heal. Blood poisoning soon spread throughout the boy's body, and the president became increasingly beside himself. He stepped up his own efforts as the doctors' efforts failed. Once he ventured away from his son's bedside for a while, but only to the White House grounds to capture a wild rabbit. He raced inside, cradling the animal, in a touching attempt to give the dying boy a brief moment of joy. Less than a week later, Calvin Jr. died.[70] Antibiotics would have killed the culpable *Staphylococcus aureus* bacteria, but penicillin's discovery was still four years away.[71]

COOLIDGE REELED. And he blamed himself. "If I had not been President," he wrote later, "he would not have raised a blister on his toe, which resulted in blood poisoning, playing lawn tennis in the South Grounds. In his suffering he was asking me to make him well. I could not. When he went the power and the glory of the Presidency went with him."[72]

The first family left Washington to bury their son back home in Vermont. But the deep sadness stayed with them at the White House. The reelection campaign slowed to a standstill. Coolidge did little to further his own cause, making only a few speeches between July and November.[73] The president almost always left the opposition's campaign barbs unanswered, seemingly no longer interested.[74] Not that it mattered; the nation's prosperity and a weak opponent, little-known Democrat John W. Davis, handed Coolidge an overwhelming win.

Coolidge had changed, henceforth alternating between inaction in many areas of life and enthusiastic, almost manic concentration on details of fiscal policy. Coolidge slept as many as eleven hours overnight, on top of regular afternoon naps.[75] Never much of an exerciser to begin with, he exerted himself even less. "All his physical tendencies," his Secret Service agent said of the post-election period, "were toward inertia." Eventually, that agent's efforts to get Coolidge into motion succeeded, but only by riding an electric horse that had been sent to the White House.[76] That, along with an occasional theater show or fishing trip, provided the little joy Coolidge appeared to still have, apart from putting his head down to focus on nuances of tax rates and debt reduction. One suspects Coolidge wasn't joking when he telegraphed word in late 1924 that "at times I dream of balance sheets and sinking funds, and deficits, and tax rates, and all the rest!"[77]

Such dreams must have offered relief from the other visions he endured daily. Simply walking through the executive mansion, he admitted, brought constant reminders of what had been. "When I look out that window," Coolidge said, "I always see my son playing tennis out there."[78] He still did his job, but it clearly mattered less to him than it had before. "I do not know," he wrote, "why such a price was exacted for occupying the White House."[79]

There were political effects, too. Losing his son and then his father, who died in March 1926, may have pushed Coolidge toward the ineffective Kellogg-Briand Pact that aimed to make war obsolete by declaring it illegal.[80] Dealing with Congress largely fell by the way-side.[81] When his choice for attorney general in March 1925 faced an uphill climb for Senate confirmation, Coolidge failed to fight with vigor for the nomination. The result? For the first time since Recon-struction, the Senate rejected a cabinet post nominee.[82] Previously affable with the press, by the summer of 1927 the president snapped at reporters that their recent dispatches had been garbage, and that they should compile their stories into a work titled "Faking with the President."[83]

Good economic times, however, continued to roll. Most Repu-blicans, ignorant of the pain in Coolidge's heart, wanted him to run again. "After I had considered the reasons for my being a candidate on the one side and the other," a spiritless Coolidge later wrote, "I could not say that any of them moved me with compelling force."[84] One biographer said he served his final years in office "as a mere shadow of his former self."[85] And his Secret Service chief bluntly named the cause: "The novelty of being President had worn off; the glory of it had gone with Calvin's death."[86]

P HYSICAL DETERIORATION WHILE in office didn't happen only to Wilson. And more often than not, our chief executives and ad-visors have taken the same route those around Wilson did, trying to hide major medical issues from the public, the political opposi-tion, and even their own allies and aides. The shootings of Garfield, Lincoln, and McKinley impaired each president before his death, ranging from Lincoln's few hours to Garfield's many weeks. Never did the country have the full truth quickly, if at all.

But it doesn't take a bullet to incapacitate a president. Another prominent case involved a president and his doctors withholding from virtually everyone that he had a dreaded disease and, to protect that secret, arranging life-threatening surgery on a moving ship at sea, with him tied to a chair lashed to a mast. Sometimes in presi-dential history, truth truly is stranger than fiction.

"WERE IT IN my mouth I would have it removed at once."

With these words in late June 1893, Dr. Joseph Bryant told Grover Cleveland, the twenty-fourth president (who had also served as the twenty-second, due to a four-year interruption by Republican Benjamin Harrison), that the one-inch growth on the roof of his mouth looked dangerous. Dr. Bryant concurred with the surgeon general's assessment that it must be malignant and needed quick attention.[87] Cleveland understood and assented.

The president's decision about how to handle the surgery raised two interrelated problems. Late–nineteenth century society treated the blunt mention of the word "cancer" as a horror. All but the most gauche instead referred to "the disease," or simply denied its existence.[88] Almost a decade earlier, when a doctor had traced Ulysses Grant's throat pain to an advanced malignancy, he'd avoided using the word with his esteemed patient. "Is it cancer?" the former president had asked. "General, the disease is serious," the doctor had replied, "and sometimes capable of being cured."[89] To the public, Grant's doctor usually wouldn't even go that far: "The difficulty is in his mouth, and it is of an epithelial character. The irritation has now been greatly relieved."[90] He'd died less than a year later. Cleveland, having seen the reaction when it became known that Grant had cancer, was not about to admit he had "that which must not be named," especially just as he was starting his second term.

While the timing for this discovery would never be good, the spring of 1893 was particularly awful. The economy had crashed during what became known as the Panic of 1893. Stock prices dropped, banks and other businesses closed, unemployment soared, and government gold reserves fell to dangerously low levels. It would stand as the worst economic downturn in the United States until the Great Depression some four decades later. And in 1893, the American people looked to the president like never before to stabilize markets and the economy. "Mr. Cleveland is about all that stands between this country and absolute disaster," the editorial board of the *Commercial and Financial Chronicle* wrote, "and his death would be a great calamity."[91]

To avoid public knowledge of the cancer and its removal, Cleveland approved a clever but risky plan of denial and deception. His doctor arranged to meet accomplished surgeon William Keen on a boat in New York to stage a most unusual operation, the riskiest in presidential history.[92] Because no hospital visit could be kept private, the cabal had decided to perform the necessary surgery below deck on a yacht owned by a friend of the president, while Cleveland was en route to vacation in the Northeast. The bare minimum of doctors surreptitiously made their way to the *Oneida*;[93] its small saloon already had been cleared of most furnishings, disinfected, and prepared for the president's surgery with an oversized chair tethered to one of the ship's two masts and a single battery-powered lightbulb in place.[94] Even by operating room standards of the time, it was rudimentary.

The president's life, at risk from the cancer, would on July 1 be exposed to new dangers: the administration of anesthesia under less than ideal conditions, waves that would make delicate surgery even more challenging, and the inability of the doctors to deal with any major complications. Cleveland, though only fifty-six at the time, was overweight and worn out physically and mentally from the immense stress since taking the oath a second time in March. His doctors worried that the ether usually used for surgeries of this scope would cause respiratory, cardiac, or renal issues. So they planned to use the less risky, but less powerful, nitrous oxide as long as possible during what they expected to be an operation longer than an hour.[95]

The ship sailed into Long Island Sound and, thankfully, the waters remained calm. To protect against extraneous movement, the president was strapped into the chair.[96] The need for secrecy severely restricted contingency planning for the unprecedented operation. Only doctors deemed absolutely necessary participated, and even these were instructed to inform their families simply that they would be absent a few days for an important out-of-town operation.[97] The captain and minimal crew merely heard that the president needed two badly ulcerated teeth removed, eliminating their ability to help plan for any emergency.[98]

The doctors did indeed take out two teeth, but they didn't stop there. Going through his mouth without cutting his face, they removed Cleveland's entire left upper jaw and part of his soft palate,[99] after discovering that the tumor had actually grown through it[100]—all, miraculously, without complications.[101] A second, shorter operation to ensure the absence of all malignant tissue followed and, again, went smoothly.[102] The president had a prosthetic jaw installed to allow him to look no different than before.

THE ONEIDA ARRIVED at the president's announced destination, the western edge of Cape Cod, after five long days. That trip from New York normally took less than sixteen hours, sending the press into a frenzy about the president's whereabouts. The deceivers had been gifted a heavy fog, which allowed them to pretend it was the weather that had delayed their disembarkation.[103]

When they finally docked, Cleveland walked off under his own power, as reporters watched from a distance, unable to see evidence of the incredible surgery that had occurred during his voyage.[104] Over the next couple of days, the doctors and the president's private secretary would lie to cover their tracks and excuse his unwillingness to entertain visitors. "He is suffering from rheumatism," they said. "No operation has been performed, except that a bad tooth was extracted," they said. "The thing that had occasioned the prolonged journey on Mr. Benedict's yacht was only a bad case of dentistry," they said. The press remained skeptical, especially when the loose lips of the dentist who had participated in the operation put them on the trail of a bigger scoop.[105] Something major must have happened, they knew, because guests who started seeing Cleveland in the next couple of weeks described his weight loss and irritability.[106] But the president's men vilified one bold journalist who correctly reported the bulk of the story; he only received vindication in the new century, after Cleveland had died.[107]

By the time the president returned to the nation's capital in August, he'd adjusted to his prosthetic jaw and could talk without most anyone seeing or hearing differences from his previous speech patterns.[108] The deception, it seemed, had worked.

A FTER LEARNING ABOUT the in-office health crises of Grover Cleveland and Woodrow Wilson—and Franklin Roosevelt during his final months (perhaps years)—the country's leaders should have clarified the legal structure for declaring a presidential disability. They did not.

Thus, when Dwight Eisenhower had a heart attack while playing golf in Denver in September 1955, putting him in an oxygen tent at a nearby army hospital, the government's response seemed mostly stuck on repeat. But unlike the other presidents who had faced disabling events, Ike eventually did something about it.[109]

EISENHOWER'S CHIEF OF STAFF had no presidential directive to follow in such a contingency, no plan to guide him.[110] His vice president, Richard Nixon, similarly wondered what to do, absent clear constitutional or legal guidance.[111] Of one thing he was quite aware: "Any move on my part which could be interpreted, even incorrectly, as an attempt to usurp the powers of the presidency would disrupt the Eisenhower team, cause dissension in the nation, and disturb the President and his family. Certainly I had no desire or intention to seize an iota of presidential power. I was the Vice President and could be nothing more."[112]

In the coming weeks, Nixon would sign ceremonial papers on behalf of Eisenhower and preside over meetings of the National Security Council and cabinet to keep routine business running, with the president's assent. Thankfully, Congress was not in session and the international scene remained calm.[113] At least, in this case, the president's staff moved past initial speed bumps and soon forthrightly released frank reports about Eisenhower's progress. He remained hospitalized until November, waiting an extra week there to ensure he could be seen walking out to his car instead of needing a wheelchair.[114]

Nixon later said, "There had never been any reason to worry about the President's health." He would have thought differently had he known Eisenhower's medical history.[115] Dating back to the 1930s, Ike had a range of conditions from high blood pressure and arthritis to stomach pains—and, possibly, a heart attack in 1949.[116] He certainly exacerbated things with an unhealthy diet and persistent chain smoking, which had grown to a four pack a day habit before his presidency.[117] His ailments continued after the 1955 heart attack, with a partially blocked intestine in June 1956 that required surgery. Although he resumed some duties within a few days, he didn't return to full presidential activity for more than a month.[118]

One afternoon just a year into his second term, Eisenhower prepared to sign a stack of documents in his private office at the White House. "I experienced a strange although not alarming feeling of dizziness," he recalled. He grew frustrated when he couldn't seem to grip the paper in front of him; when he finally did, he said, "The words on it seemed literally to run off the top of the page." The president dropped his pen and couldn't pick it up, then had trouble standing up. Worse still, when his secretary responded to his call, he found it impossible to put his thoughts into words.[119] He went to bed, doctors came, and they assessed he'd had a stroke. They could not tell with certainty how seriously it affected his nervous system, or whether a series of other, more damaging strokes would follow.

Ignorant of the extent of the damage and still unable to form sentences, Ike decided to host the scheduled state dinner with the visiting king of Morocco that evening anyway. Not only his speech but his judgment had been impaired. His advisors reasoned with him, only to hear him scream, just clearly enough to be understood, "There is nothing the matter with me! I am perfectly all right!" Then he struggled to get out additional words, or even syllables, to explain just how well he was. His wife told the president's advisors, "We can't let him go down there in this condition."[120] And they didn't. His stubbornness faded for a moment, allowing them to convince him to lie down and rest while Nixon hosted in his place. As word got out about the stroke, calls for Eisenhower to hand over more than dinner duty to the vice president rolled in,[121] and Ike's chief of staff told Nixon he might be president within twenty-four hours.[122]

The danger of having a president self-assess his fitness for office became all too clear. While acknowledging the effects of a stroke could endanger the problem solving and decision making needed to perform presidential duties, Eisenhower decided upon a test. He insisted on attending a NATO conference, three weeks hence. "If I could carry out this program successfully and without noticeable damage to myself, then I would continue in my duties. If I felt the results to be less than satisfactory, then I would resign."[123] The high-stakes meetings with the country's most important allies, during an exceptionally tense time in the Cold War, seemed an unusual place to wing it and see what happened. But no mechanism existed at that time to do anything but trust the president's self-assessment, and hope for the best.

"THREE ILLNESSES IN three successive years," wrote Eisenhower, "any one of which could have been completely disabling if not fatal, convinced me that I should make some specific arrangements for the Vice President to succeed to my office if I should incur a disability that precluded proper performance of duty over any period of significant length."[124]

Thus inspired, the president drafted a letter spelling out exactly what he wanted done, and how, should the need arise. He summoned Nixon and Attorney General William Rogers, asked them to read his letter, and sought their reactions. As Nixon recalled, Ike incorporated a few minor suggestions, but only a few, for the letter handled the situation so well that the attorney general said Eisenhower "would have made an excellent lawyer."[125] The language seemed consistent with the relevant language in the Constitution, so Eisenhower made slight revisions only and sent a final copy to Nixon, the attorney general, and the secretary of state (the most senior cabinet officer).[126]

Part of the letter was made public the following month, which read, "In the event of inability, the President would—if possible—so inform the Vice President, and the Vice President would serve as Acting President, exercising the powers and duties of the office until the inability had ended." This language added something the original constitutional formulation lacked: naming the president as the person responsible for identifying the inability and declaring it. The letter went on: "In the event of an inability which would prevent the President from so communicating with the Vice President, the Vice

President, after such consultation as seems to him appropriate under the circumstances, would decide upon the devolution of the powers and duties of the Office and would serve as Acting President until the inability had ended."[127]

This contingency shifted the burden to the vice president, whom the Constitution had neither identified nor prohibited for such a role. But the letter left it entirely up to the vice president as to whom, if anyone, he would consult before deeming the president unable to do his job. By giving his attorney general and secretary of state a final copy of the letter, Eisenhower made one or both of those natural choices—but what about the rest of the cabinet? The chief of staff? The president's physician? His spouse? The Secret Service detail? Congressional or judicial leaders? All of those choices would fall into Nixon's lap if another crisis made the president unable to communicate his wishes to the vice president.

Finally, the public part of the letter revealed that Eisenhower would reserve one particular right to himself. "The President, in either event, would determine when the inability had ended and at that time would resume the full exercise of the powers and duties of the Office."[128] The president seems to have overlooked his post-stroke experience, when he felt confident enough in his abilities to host a state dinner despite his inability even to speak coherently.

Some agreement was better than none at all. The idea made enough sense, in fact, that Eisenhower's successor, John Kennedy, used it with his vice president, Lyndon Johnson.[129] Johnson had no vice president when he took office after Kennedy's assassination, so he made an agreement with John McCormack—the Speaker of the House, and thus the next person in the line of succession—along the same lines.[130] After new vice president Hubert Humphrey took his oath of office in January 1965, LBJ had the same chat with him.[131] Johnson even consulted with Eisenhower in late 1965 as he prepared for surgery on his gall bladder using anesthesia, ultimately conveying instructions to Humphrey just in case major decisions were required while the president remained unconscious.[132] He would go under anesthesia again the following year to remove a throat polyp and repair a hernia.[133]

Not long afterward, a new development made all such arrangements obsolete.

C HANGING THE CONSTITUTION of the United States of America was not intended to be easy. Getting an amendment ratified is one of the most difficult things for the government to do. It requires two-thirds votes in the House of Representatives and in the Senate, followed by approval from three-fourths of the states or a Constitutional convention called for by two-thirds of state legislatures. Maybe that's why it has happened only twenty-seven times so far in more than 225 years.

One thing the process does not require: any input or assent, in any manner, from the president of the United States.

Something as momentous as a formal change to the Constitution seems worthy of some presidential attention, though, especially when the amendment in question affects his responsibilities. So in February 1967, President Lyndon Johnson hosted a ceremony in the East Room of the White House, where the General Services Administration chief signed the proclamation that the requisite number of states on February 10 had indeed ratified the Twenty-fifth Amendment, making it law. Johnson added his signature to the document, too, as a witness, thus acknowledging the procedures he would be bound to follow if he were to become disabled.

EISENHOWER'S HEALTH CRISES had raised awareness of the dire need for updated presidential disability processes in the nuclear era. The immediate push for the constitutional amendment that ultimately addressed the issue, however, came in November 1963, when Lee Harvey Oswald's bullets killed Kennedy. What if, many in Washington wondered, instead of killing the president, the attack had left him in a degraded mental state, or comatose?

"There was a sinking feeling in the pit of my stomach," Indiana senator Birch Bayh remembered about that day, "as I recalled that only a month before a series of unusual circumstances had resulted in my being appointed Chairman of the Senate Judiciary

Committee on Constitutional Amendments—the subcommittee whose direct responsibility it was to recommend a solution to the problems of Presidential disability and vacancies in the office of Vice President."[134]

It took much effort, much testimony, and much patience, but Bayh used his position to lead the way toward clarifying several outstanding issues related to the presidency. Two of them—vice presidential succession to the full presidency in the case of a vacancy in the top job, and procedures for getting a new vice president when *that* position goes vacant—received less attention than the issue of disability, which senators and representatives debated in depth. They discussed whether this should be limited to mental disability (it was not). They talked about whether this should be limited to only either long or short periods of disability (it was not). They even mentioned its applicability to that old situation that James Madison had nearly faced, falling into the hands of an enemy (nothing rules out its application in such circumstances).[135]

What they came up with followed Eisenhower's letter to Nixon fairly closely. But it added potentially crucial elements, like specificity about the vice president's consultations in the event of a disability, a process by which the president can challenge an involuntary declaration of his disability, and a mechanism by which he can stay so declared anyway.

Section 3 of the amendment packs a lot into one sentence: "Whenever the President transmits to the President pro tempore of the Senate and the Speaker of the House of Representatives his written declaration that he is unable to discharge the powers and duties of his office, and until he transmits to them a written declaration to the contrary, such powers and duties shall be discharged by the Vice President as Acting President." That's straightforward. One of the few issues open to interpretation has involved the transmittal—do the two congressional leaders need to have the written declaration in hand before the transfer of powers takes effect? Those involved have judged that the act of sending it alone meets the requirement.

Section 4, addressing how others can declare the chief executive unable, gets more complicated. Like Eisenhower's formulation, it puts the vice president up front in the decision, and transfers power to the vice president temporarily for the duration of the disability. Who should decide the president can't adequately function in the job? That engendered much debate; everyone from Congress and the Supreme Court to White House staff and independent physicians came up. But in the end, the person that made the most sense for political and separation of powers reasons was the vice president, in conjunction with "a majority of either the principal officers of the executive departments or of such other body as Congress may by law provide." (The drafters chose the "executive departments" phrase over "the cabinet" to match similar usage in the Constitution itself, which contains no reference to the cabinet.) That "other body" that Congress can designate could be just about anything, from a panel of doctors to all of Congress itself. If the vice president and the majority of whatever such group agree, and a written declaration of that is transmitted to the Senate's president pro tempore and the House's Speaker, the vice president becomes acting president.

IN A SMOOTHLY operating disability scenario, the president will recover, send a written declaration to the same two congressional leaders that no disability exists, and resume the powers and duties of the office. But what if those who prompted the transfer of power disagree with the president's timing for transferring them back?

The drafters of the amendment thought of that, and they developed a mechanism: within four days, the vice president (and, again, a majority of either the principal officers of the executive departments or of such other body as Congress may by law provide) can send those two congressional leaders another written declaration to state that the president remains unable to discharge the powers and duties of the office.

Congress, assembling within forty-eight hours if not in session, has twenty-one days after receiving this new declaration to decide the matter. If two-thirds in both the House and Senate vote that the president is still unable to do the job, the vice president remains the chief executive until the cycle repeats—in theory, forever. But if one or both houses of Congress fail to clear the two-thirds hurdle, the president is restored.

Although the language of section 4 as written *seems* to make clear that the vice president maintains the powers and duties of the office during the four-day challenge period—and the intention of the drafters certainly points that way—the amendment doesn't explicitly say it. Thus, as explored by law professor Brian Kalt, an aggrieved but still disabled president could claim to be back in power immediately and thereby create two competing centers of executive authority while Congress and courts either try to decide the matter or let the opponents fight it out.[136] That would produce an unprecedented constitutional crisis.

"The Twenty-fifth Amendment raises more questions than it answers," says Julie Silverbrook, executive director of the Constitutional Sources Project. "It essentially codifies into our Constitution something that feels like a coup. If the members of your cabinet think that you are unfit to serve as president, they can vote to throw you out of office? That's very dangerous."[137] Because of such perceptions of a coup, it's unlikely that section 4 will ever see action outside of clear cases of disability. "It's really best designed for the comatose or missing president," Kalt says. "If you think about the incentives that vice presidents have for *not* stepping in and saying, 'The president needs to go,' the Twenty-fifth Amendment doesn't take away the big one: the problem that the action would look like a coup, with a disloyal vice president in the role of usurper."[138]

During the Senate's deliberations over the amendment, Everett Dirksen seemed to anticipate that such problems could arise, but declared, "We must assume that, when confronted with a monumental national crisis, when subjected to the white heat of political scrutiny, those charged with responsibility will do what is in the public interest."[139] Let's hope he's right.

SINCE THE ADOPTION of the Twenty-fifth Amendment, that fourth section of the amendment may have been worth considering but has remained unused. Several chief executives, on the other hand, have found themselves in circumstances where invoking section 3 made great sense. They've chosen to do so three times—so far.

THE FIRST PRESIDENT to serve a full term under the amendment's provisions, Richard Nixon, faced no life-or-death physical crises like Eisenhower.

He'd had problems with depression dating back to at least his vice presidency, probably to childhood.[140] Henry Kissinger, Nixon's national security advisor throughout his time in office, would privately call him a "madman."[141] But the most alarming potential incapacity for sound decision making that often approached a disability was largely self-inflicted, through self-medication—especially heavy drinking when times got toughest. As commander in chief, Nixon overindulged often enough that Kissinger, when out of Nixon's earshot, would refer to him as "our drunken friend."[142] Even officers on the National Security Council staff who lacked daily interactions with the boss noticed, and labeled it a problem.[143]

After one dinner at the White House in December 1973, Senator Barry Goldwater of Arizona had to ask a Nixon aide if the president was mentally unstable. "No," came the reply. "He was drunk."[144] Another associate claimed that Nixon "got really paranoid" when moving past two drinks; the effect worsened when he combined liquor with his sleeping pills and an anti-seizure drug he took to counter depression.[145] As his presidency spiraled under the Watergate investigation, he seemed to mix these even more. "The president," Nixon's son-in-law told a senator in August 1974, "was up walking the halls last night, talking to pictures of former presidents—giving speeches and talking to the pictures on the wall." He blamed a combination of alcohol and sleep deprivation.[146] But even these anecdotes show him short of being categorically unable to perform his duties as president.[147]

Did anyone see this mix of chemicals, lack of sleep, and increasing depression as enough of a threat to raise his frequent incapacitation with the White House counsel? "Never," says John Dean, who held the job for most of the Nixon presidency. Dean would have been a natural source to sound out about the Twenty-fifth Amendment, not only by dint of his position but because he'd served on the House Judiciary Committee staff during its crafting. "Not a single person asked me about that," he recalls. "I think everyone understood it was a last resort, not something designed to remove a functioning president."[148] Historians still debate whether the combination of drinking, pills, and depression left Nixon, at all times, fully functioning.

WHEN JOHN HINCKLEY shot and very nearly killed Ronald Reagan on the afternoon of March 30, 1981, just over two months after his inauguration, the near chaos at the White House that day showed that better procedures were needed to ensure future administrations were prepared for such contingencies on day one.

In the hours immediately after the attack, the president of the United States could barely breathe, and underwent surgery. Reagan clearly could not make any decisions during much of this time. The obvious thing to do would be to invoke section 4 of the Twenty-fifth Amendment, which had been added specifically to deal with situations when the president "is unable to discharge the powers and duties of his office" by letting the vice president and the majority of the executive departments' principal officers transfer power, at least temporarily.

The responsible officials on that day did not do so. Getting the vice president and a majority of cabinet chiefs together on a moment's notice would have been nearly impossible, and the logistical pieces weren't fully loaded for them to execute an action had they seen fit to do so. First of all, George H. W. Bush was in Texas at the time, and even talking to him presented an unexpected challenge. When Secretary of State Al Haig finally got a line through to the plane that Bush was on in the skies above the Lone Star State, they couldn't hear each other clearly. It took a teletype machine on board to give Bush the recommendation to return to Washington as soon as possible.[149] He wouldn't have consistently clear communications until he landed near the nation's capital in around four more hours. And only later that evening did Fred Fielding, the White House counsel, sit down with the vice president in his office to get him up to speed on legal options, including the Twenty-fifth Amendment.[150]

Second, how would all of the cabinet chiefs get together on a moment's notice to weigh in on a potential declaration of disability? Solid working relationships hadn't yet been built among just the few top officials who gathered at the White House, much less among the wider group of department heads. "They were strangers in the Situation Room," says Fielding. "Everybody was still trying to develop their own job and their own staffs."[151] The uncertainty that dominated even the Sit Room several hours after the incident would have presented huge obstacles to decisive cabinet action, even if those officials had already been fully briefed on Twenty-fifth Amendment scenarios, which it appears they had not. Fielding recalls that upon mentioning the amendment that day to some of the cabinet officials at the White House, "I could see eyes glazing over . . . They didn't even know about the twenty-fifth amendment."[152]

Chief of Staff Jim Baker, counselor Edwin Meese, and political liaison office chief Lyn Nofziger—all at the hospital with Reagan—were aware that the president could temporarily relinquish presidential authority. They discussed the possibility quietly in a supply closet, down the hall from the operating room, and quickly rejected it.[153] The attorney general, before heading to the White House from the Department of Justice, had directed a top legal advisor to learn more about how the transfer of power mechanism would work, and do it quickly.[154] And he tasked another lawyer at Justice to draft two memos for possible use: one by which Reagan could invoke section 3 of the Twenty-fifth Amendment, and another by which Vice President Bush and the cabinet could invoke section 4.[155] But one person had started the logistics for something like this weeks earlier. "At the time of the assassination attempt," Fielding remembers, "I was drafting a contingency book. It had sample letters to invoke the Twenty-fifth Amendment—everything. But I was still working on it!"[156]

After his surgery ended close to seven o'clock, Reagan bounced back and forth between consciousness and unconsciousness from the anesthesia and shock to his body, and he remained on heavy pain-killers.[157] He wasn't reasonably capable of making any substantive decision until at least late that evening. Even though the immediate crisis had passed, the president would do little heavy work for several weeks.[158]

"What would we have done had we really known how seriously the president was hurt? I don't know the answer," admits Fielding. "Had we known that the problem was more severe than initial reports indicated, it might have impacted on that decision. But we didn't know."[159] Reagan's White House physician said the Twenty-fifth Amendment never occurred to him at the time, but in retrospect it "should have been invoked, no doubt about it." For the doctor, Reagan's inability to communicate effectively for "at least a day or two," meant that a transfer of power to the vice president was in order. "If ever there was a time to use it, that was it."[160]

Officials in the Reagan administration took the entire experience as a kick in the pants to ensure better preparedness in the future. Within days, the Office of Legal Counsel at the Department of Justice had a memorandum about the Twenty-fifth Amendment ready in case quick study was needed again. And Fielding quickly completed his contingency book full of procedures, draft letters, and supporting documents.[161]

FOUR YEARS AFTER the assassination attempt, doctors removed a polyp from Reagan's colon. During the procedure, they saw a larger growth, raising cancer concerns. The president the next day underwent a nearly three-hour surgery to remove it.[162]

For the first time since the passage of the Twenty-fifth Amendment, the powers and duties of the chief executive were transferred to the vice president—even as the president claimed the amendment didn't really apply.

When it had become clear that doctors would put Reagan under for the surgery, Fielding showed the president his options for transferring power. "One letter had nothing extra—straight, full Twenty-fifth Amendment," he says. "The one he picked was explicit about not tying other presidents' hands."[163] That language, as transmitted to the Speaker of the House and president pro tempore of the Senate, per the requirements of the amendment, included this explanation and caveat:

After my consultation with my Counsel and the Attorney
General, I am mindful of the provisions of Section 3 of the 25th
Amendment to the Constitution and the uncertainties of its
application to such brief and temporary periods of incapacity.
I do not believe that the drafters of the Amendment intended
its application to situations such as the instant one. Nevertheless, consistent with my long-standing arrangement with Vice
President George Bush, and not intending to set a precedent
binding anyone privileged to hold this Office in the future, I
have determined and it is my intention that Vice President
George Bush shall discharge those powers and duties in my
stead commencing with the administration of anesthesia to me
in this instance.[164]

The president's typical sense of humor appeared even as he put
pen to paper and made history by invoking the amendment's temporary transfer of power for the first time. "Once he signed it," Fielding
says, "he handed it to me and he jokingly directed that I should tell
Vice President Bush that Nancy did not go along with the transfer
deal."[165]

Reagan completed the long procedure, woke up, and took a couple of hours in post-op to shake off the anesthesia. Fielding joined
the White House chief of staff to test the president.

"We had light conversation with him about what was going on
in the world," Fielding recalls, "He seemed lucid." So they turned to
the real reason they were there—the transfer of power—and handed
him the two-sentence letter they'd drafted to inform the congressional leaders he was taking back the powers and duties of the office.
They assessed that Reagan's ability to process the letter would be
enough to show he was capable of resuming the powers and duties
of the presidency.

"He held it up and his eyes started twitching and rolling around
and blinking. The Chief of Staff and I looked at each other and pretty
much decided instantly that it was a little premature for us to discuss this with him." Thankfully, Reagan saw their looks of concern.
Laughing, he reminded them that he remained without his usual

contacts or glasses, saying "I just can't read the darn thing." With glasses on, he quickly read the letter, chatted briefly about it, and stated clearly, "I want to sign it now."[166] He did, and George H. W. Bush's acting presidency of almost eight hours ended.

"President Reagan didn't want to invoke the Twenty-fifth Amendment," says Fielding, "but I told him he should. He did, in fact, invoke it with that letter, even while saying he doesn't want to tie the hands of those who come after him. He broke the ice without breaking the ice."[167]

Perhaps that period of declared disability should have gone on a bit longer. One of the crucial moments in what became the Iran-Contra scandal occurred when Reagan met with his national security advisor and chief of staff in the hospital as he recovered. Israeli arms sales to Iran to help obtain the release of American hostages being held in Lebanon allegedly came up, but memories differ on whether, and if so exactly how, Reagan approved the action.[168] Post-surgery medications could still have been impairing his memory, if not his judgment. Reagan himself said in 1987 about the allegation of his approval in that hospital room, "I'm having some trouble remembering that, but then I want to tell you that there were so many things going on and so many reports, and some of this was during the time that I was laid up in the hospital and so forth."[169]

WHILE TAKING A jog at Camp David on May 4, 1991, about halfway through his presidency, George H. W. Bush found it hard to get a full breath and was overcome by extreme fatigue. The atrial fibrillation (an irregular heartbeat) didn't knock him unconscious but placed him in Bethesda Naval Hospital for tests, leading doctors to diagnose the overactive-thyroid Graves' disease.[170]

No transfer of power occurred because of his heart incident or the subsequent medical tests. But if the doctors had recommended a procedure requiring anesthesia, a distinct possibility at one point, all the players were prepared. Several weeks after inauguration, the president had met with his wife, her chief of staff, the vice president, the White House chief of staff, the White House counsel, the

White House physician, and a Secret Service representative. In the Oval Office, they discussed the procedures and consultations that would need to occur should a potential disability arise. And all the necessary documents had been gathered and readied for it.[171]

They came just shy of being put to use early the next year, when Bush visited East Asia. While in Tokyo on January 8, he teamed up with the US ambassador in a tennis match against the Japanese emperor and crown prince. Later that day, though, the president began feeling ill; his doctor blamed the intestinal flu.[172] The state dinner hosted by Japanese prime minister Kiichi Miyazawa didn't go as planned. After eating his salmon and caviar, but before getting to the grilled beef with peppery sauce, Bush slumped down, vomited on both Miyazawa and himself, and passed out.[173] Leaping to action, a Secret Service agent got to the president and protected him on the floor while his doctor checked him out. Bush woke up and left, going to bed with plenty of embarrassment but no apparent injuries, and no need to consider the Twenty-fifth Amendment.[174] Barbara Bush couldn't help but put her unique spin on it, saying the uncomfortable incident must've resulted from his tennis defeat earlier in the day.[175]

Heavy attention to Reagan's use of the disability provisions of the Twenty-fifth Amendment and Bush 41's readiness to do the same if needed meant fewer people got worked up when the latter's son invoked it, twice, during his term. In June 2002, George W. Bush's colonoscopy procedure used anesthesia, so he handed the powers and duties of the presidency to Vice President Dick Cheney for just over two hours.[176] "It went perfectly," Fred Fielding, White House counsel for Bush as he had been for Reagan, says. "Because Reagan had broken the ice, there was no hesitation."[177] In fact, Fielding says, Bush didn't question the need for the invocation before signing the formal letter to trigger it; he merely displayed his interest in presidential history, "very curious about the incident before with Ronald Reagan and why it had been handled the way it had been."[178]

Cheney would take the reins once again for a little over two hours in July 2007 for another anesthesia-assisted Bush colonoscopy.[179]

That second occasion sparked an idea for Cheney: to write a letter to his grandchildren during the acting presidency, to give them a souvenir of the special moment.[180]

Chapter Seven

Impeached and Removed

A well-constituted court for the trial of impeachment is an object not more to be desired than difficult to be obtained in a government wholly elective. The subjects of its jurisdiction . . . are of a nature which may with peculiar propriety be denominated POLITICAL, as they relate chiefly to injuries done immediately to the society itself. The prosecution of them, for this reason, will seldom fail to agitate the passions of the whole community, and to divide it into parties more or less friendly or inimical to the accused.[1]

—ALEXANDER HAMILTON

RICHARD NIXON ACCOMPLISHED some great things as president from 1969 through 1974, particularly in foreign and environmental policy. He was also an insecure, disloyal, self-destructive, dishonest manipulator who obstructed justice and abused the powers of the presidency. He left office on August 9, 1974, as a result of impeachment.

History tells us that he resigned and handed power to his vice president, and that is technically what he did. But step back a bit from the letter of resignation, and it's clear that Nixon was ejected by the impeachment process and the prospect of his certain removal from office that a few more weeks or months would have brought. He would not have resigned but for the sword of impeachment hanging over his head. The system ultimately worked: it got rid of the man who had proven himself unfit.

"In his conduct of the office of President of the United States, Richard M. Nixon . . . has prevented, obstructed, and impeded the administration of justice."

These words, and many others offering details of Nixon's obstruction of justice, made up the first article of impeachment the House Judiciary Committee passed on July 30, 1974. A second article passed the same day charged that the president had "repeatedly engaged in conduct violating the constitutional rights of citizens, impairing the due and proper administration of justice and the conduct of lawful inquiries, or contravening the laws governing agencies of the executive branch and the purposes of these agencies." In other words, he abused his power. One other article, focusing on Nixon's refusal to cooperate with congressional subpoenas, also made it out of the committee, though by a narrower margin.[2]

Nixon's troubles that led to this drama generally shelter under the umbrella of "Watergate," the name of the Washington, DC, complex Nixon reelection campaign underlings broke into in 1972. But it really started at least a year earlier when the president ordered aides to shut down leaks, and they went after information to discredit the source of the Pentagon Papers, Daniel Ellsberg, by breaking into his psychiatrist's office. The unit involved, linked to officials in Nixon's campaign committee, included Howard Hunt and G. Gordon Liddy, who were also involved in an operation placing listening devices inside the Democratic National Committee offices in the Watergate. The night of June 17, 1972, five burglars working with Hunt and Liddy, including the security coordinator for Nixon's reelection committee, got caught in the act, launching the most famous political scandal of modern American history.

The Watergate break-in didn't involve Nixon directly. There's no evidence he ordered or even knew about that particular action. His troubles instead came from these burglars' connections and with the cover-up. Within days, the news of the break-in gained high interest among his aides because the FBI investigation into the affair looked increasingly likely to reveal ties to senior officials in the campaign and even to the White House itself—and to lead law enforcement to many other "dirty tricks" Nixon and his aides had directed over the years.

"The problem is that there are all kinds of other involvements," chief of staff H. R. Haldeman said to the president on June 21, "and if they started a fishing thing on this, they're going to start picking up threads."[3] Nixon eventually took on board Haldeman's meaning. He tacitly approved White House aides' efforts to shut down the FBI's work on the case.[4] The next day, Haldeman told the president that investigators had made significant inroads and that "it goes in some directions we don't want it to go." Because of Hunt's previous employment and sophisticated equipment found at the scene, some FBI agents suspected CIA involvement in the Watergate incident. Haldeman suggested they get CIA leaders to contact the FBI director and imply that because investigating the break-in would get into national security issues, the Bureau should stand down. "Alright, fine. Right," Nixon said, later suggesting how Haldeman should phrase it with the FBI director.[5] "And that destroys the case," the president declared. "Play it tough," he added. "That's the way they play it, and that's the way we're going to play it."[6]

Then, on August 1, the president and his chief of staff talked about the efforts taken so far to keep the Watergate burglars quiet. "Hunt's happy," Haldeman said. "At considerable cost, I guess?" Nixon replied. After Haldeman agreed, the president said, "It's worth it," later adding, "That's what the money's for. . . . they have taken all the risk and they have to be paid."[7]

The Watergate burglars were convicted in January 1973 and sentenced to jail time. The hush money didn't prevent connections with Nixon's reelection campaign from emerging. Prosecutors kept discovering evidence of meetings about and approvals for the reelection committee's "dirty tricks" efforts, taking them higher up the ladder, implicating, among others, John Mitchell—Nixon's reelection campaign chief and former attorney general.

White House Counsel John Dean, worried about the tightening noose around the president, had a frank discussion with Nixon on March 21, 1973. He suspected, incorrectly, that the president remained unaware of many aspects of the White House denial and deception effort on Watergate and hoped that making it all clear to Nixon would prompt him to order the cover-up to stop. "We have a cancer, within, close to the presidency that's growing," Dean said. "It's growing daily. It's compounding, it grows geometrically now, because it compounds itself."

To ensure the president understood, he declared, "We're being blackmailed. . . . People are going to start perjuring themselves very quickly that have not had to perjure themselves already to protect other people and the like." As the remarkable conversation progressed, Nixon said, "I would certainly keep that—that cover for whatever it's worth." Dean told the president doing so would implicate Haldeman, Mitchell, domestic affairs advisor John Erlichman, and Dean himself in witness tampering. "And that's an obstruction of justice."[8] Nixon didn't seem overly concerned, soon asking Dean how much money would be needed to keep people quiet. "I would say these people are going to cost a million dollars over the next two years." The president seemed unfazed. "We could get that. You, on the money, if you need the money, I mean, you could get the money. . . . I know where it could be gotten. I mean, it's not easy, but it could be done."[9]

The blunt talk not only failed to take Nixon off course, it seemed to ratchet up his commitment to covering things up. "I tried to put him in an impossible situation," Dean told me. "I thought he'd have to act. He didn't."[10]

Nixon was still playing puppet master, trying to control things, which would hurt him later, because he was recording the office discussions. The tapes of these conversations would accelerate the president's fall.

IMPEACHMENT HAD ALREADY crossed Richard Nixon's radar before Watergate. In his first term, two representatives had introduced three separate resolutions in the House to take that historic step against the president, but they did not cite Watergate. One cited his "high crimes and misdemeanors" but gave no specifics; the other two related to his conduct of the war in Southeast Asia. All of them went to the Judiciary Committee, which took no action.

Impeachment was explicitly addressed in Nixon's presence on April 15, 1973. Recalling that it took "considerable fortitude" to say it, Dean informed Nixon he was worried that if the president failed to correctly address the downward spiral, the result could be his impeachment. The president—according to the White House counsel's notes, because the tape covering much of this day's conversations went missing—assured Dean he would handle it.[11]

He didn't. The cover-up of the cover-up continued. To deflect mounting criticism, on April 30, the president announced the resignations of Haldeman, Erlichman, and the attorney general, as well as the firing of Dean, who was cooperating with investigators. On May 18, the acting attorney general appointed Archibald Cox as special prosecutor and gave his guarantee that Cox would operate without executive branch control.[12] All summer, Dean and other White House aides testified to both prosecutors and a special Senate Watergate Committee; at hearings of the latter, the existence of a White House taping system was revealed in July.

The house of cards had begun to tumble. And new resolutions to impeach the president started rolling out. First came a generic one, lacking actual articles, on July 31.[13] The first one listing specific articles of impeachment came on October 23.[14] Between July 1973 and January 1974, seventeen measures to impeach Nixon came up from various representatives; all went to the Judiciary Committee. Twenty other resolutions sought to spur a dedicated House investigation of whether the time for impeachment proceedings had come.[15]

In the meantime, both the special prosecutor and the Senate's special committee demanded that the White House release the tapes related to discussions of Watergate. Nixon wouldn't share them. So both parties issued subpoenas to the president demanding he turn them over. He and his legal team dithered and delayed, all the while refusing to hand over the tapes. The subpoenas, however, had raised the temperature several degrees; getting rid of the tapes now would constitute destruction of evidence and could contribute to growing public perceptions of the president's guilt and his efforts to obstruct justice. Why hadn't Nixon already followed the advice of his Watergate counsel and ensured the tapes disappeared before the subpoena came?[16] "He thought the tapes could be used selectively," Dean says. "Some people told him to do it, but he wasn't thinking like a lawyer."[17]

Despite all those impeachment resolutions, the president retained significant support among Republicans in Congress and, as a result, viewed the special prosecutor as more of a threat than anything coming from Capitol Hill. When Cox refused to drop the subpoena, Nixon ordered the acting attorney general to fire him. Because he had promised that Cox would remain independent and unimpeded, the attorney general refused and resigned. Nixon then asked the deputy to fire Cox. He, too, wouldn't do it and resigned. The act fell to the solicitor general, third in command at the Department of Justice. He also considered resigning, but the two men who had just quit urged him to stay in place to maintain some semblance of department morale and senior management continuity. So he fired Cox, completing what became known as the "Saturday Night Massacre."[18]

A new special prosecutor was named in November; Congress went on recess just a few weeks later. But as all of this sank in, impeachment was no longer just a word, a concept, a theory. It was looking certain to become a direct threat to the president when legislators returned in January 1974.

PETER RODINO, REPRESENTATIVE from New Jersey and chairman of the House Judiciary Committee, had read a book on the history of the 1868 impeachment of Andrew Johnson, the only successful impeachment of a president up to that point in American history.[19] Members of his committee staff began digging through dusty congressional records to find out how that case had been investigated, but found nothing useful.[20] They had no clear path ahead and would have to break new ground once the full House authorized them to proceed.

That spark came on February 6, when a stunning 410-4 vote directed the committee to investigate whether grounds existed to impeach the president, to report back to the full House, and to recommend articles of impeachment, if it saw fit. The committee quickly ruled that it would use all legal means available to get testimony—and that any presidential refusal to furnish relevant materials would itself be grounds for impeachment.[21] Tensions rose, even in hallways on Capitol Hill. Within a few months, Rodino would need two bodyguards after receiving threats.[22]

Committee staff expanded to process all the information from the special prosecutor's office, as well as previous testimony from the Senate Watergate Committee and its own hearings. As stories kept emerging about the cover-up, momentum shifted away from the president. By April, a Harris poll showed for the first time that a majority of Americans favored Nixon's impeachment.[23] The White House announced in May that the president would supply no further material to the Judiciary Committee, prompting even the formerly pro-Nixon *Chicago Tribune* to call for his resignation.[24]

July 24 brought two big developments. The televised hearings of the committee ended, beginning the report stage.[25] And the Supreme Court ruled 8-0 that Nixon had to turn over the tapes. The solicitor general told him defying the high court's ruling would lead to "instant impeachment."[26] The damning audio of Nixon's cover-up conversations would now be made public.

Three days later, the committee voted on five articles of impeachment. The first three—covering obstruction of justice, abuse of power, and refusal to obey congressional subpoenas—made it through the committee, each with some Republican support. The final two—one addressing Nixon's actions in Cambodia, the other his inappropriate use of federal funds on his two homes and unauthorized tax deductions—failed to pass because even Democratic committee members wanted to focus on the main charges. In the committee's offices after the vote, Rodino wept. "I pray we did the right thing," he told his wife on the phone a few minutes later. "I hoped it didn't have to be this way."[27]

It probably did have to be that way. "If the impeachment hand-writing hadn't been on the wall, Nixon wouldn't have resigned," says law professor Brian Kalt. "It was essentially a plea bargain. Once the possibility of impeachment became imminent, it made him resign."[28]

The chairman and committee exercised restraint by *not* passing other impeachment articles describing presidential actions that, while bad, seemed less likely to clear the constitutional hurdle of "high crimes and misdemeanors." "The Democrats chose what they saw as the safer route, the less controversial route—they laid aside the questions that would lead to more disagreement," says constitutional expert Keith Whittington. "It reinforced the notion that the impeachment power is better used for a relatively narrow set of circumstances than for checking presidents more generically."[29]

The committee sent the three articles to the full House, along with a report of more than five hundred pages that lay out its case. Within a draft circulated to representatives was this blunt summary: "For more than two years, the President engaged in a course of conduct which involved deliberate, repeated and continued deception of the American people."[30] Each of the Republican members who'd voted no in the committee soon defected, allowing the committee's impeachment vote to be announced as unanimous to the full House.[31] On August 20, the House accepted the impeachment report by a vote of 412-3.[32]

By then, Nixon had already given up, resigning from the office on August 9. The inevitability of his impeachment and conviction drove his choice. After all, even the president's Republican defenders on the committee came out and declared, "Our gratitude for his having by his resignation spared the nation additional agony should not obscure for history our judgment that Richard Nixon, as President, committed certain acts for which he should have been impeached and removed from office."[33]

"IF HE BE not impeachable whilst in office," North Carolina's William Davie said about the position of president, "he will spare no efforts or means whatever to get himself re-elected."[34]

Davie was reacting on July 20, 1787, to the delegates at the Constitutional Convention who wanted to get presidential impeachment out of the draft text. He got help from George Mason, who wanted "malpractice or neglect of duty" to remain as a cause for impeachment, and said, "No point is of more importance than that the right of impeachment should be continued. Shall any man be above Justice? Above all shall that man be above it, who can commit the most extensive injustice?"[35]

In a session a couple of weeks later, the esteemed Benjamin Franklin piled on, declaring that critics would have to turn to assassination if impeachment proved unavailable.[36] Elbridge Gerry added his view of impeachments: "A good magistrate will not fear them. A bad one ought to be kept in fear of them."[37]

Some constitutional method for getting rid of an unfit president before the end of his term was gaining favor among the delegates. How to gain the benefits of such a mechanism without causing more harm would challenge them all.

EVEN BY THE end of July, the men assembled in Philadelphia realized they'd reached dead ends on so many issues that they needed a reset. So they formed a Committee of Detail to try to work those kinks out.

The draft text handed to this committee contained four fundamental provisions for the executive: the presidency would consist of a single person, be chosen by the legislature, serve a term of seven years, and be ineligible to serve a second term. All but one of those points would change during the crucial weeks that followed; the single-person president became the sole survivor.[38] The committee members kept two of the causes for impeachment they'd inherited—treason and bribery, which each seemed relatively straightforward—but replaced the phrase they didn't like, "malpractice or neglect of duty," with a new idea, "corruption."[39] But they still couldn't agree about what body should try an impeached president. In early September, another committee revised the relevant language. Its members ditched corruption, leaving treason and bribery as the only impeachable offenses, and shifted trials of impeached presidents to the Senate.[40]

Finally, on September 8, the full group of delegates discussed the new language. "Why is the provision restrained to Treason & bribery only?" asked Mason. "Treason as defined in the Constitution will not reach many great and dangerous offences." He suggested adding "maladministration" as a third reason to impeach.[41] James Madison expressed concern that "so vague a term will be equivalent to a tenure during pleasure of the Senate." Mason, less excited about his own idea now, withdrew it and suggested "other high crimes and misdemeanors."[42] No one seems to have objected, and they moved on.

Madison spoke out against the Senate trying presidential impeachments, worrying that the combination of a House empowered to impeach and a Senate empowered to convict and remove would make the executive branch too dependent on the legislative one. The prescient Hugh Williamson chimed in to tell Madison not to worry, suggesting that the Senate's many interactions with the president meant "there was more danger of too much lenity than of too much rigor towards the President."[43] The delegates soundly defeated Madison's motion to remove the Senate's role, so it stayed that way, with the stipulation that "no person shall be convicted without the concurrence of two thirds of the Members present: and every Member shall be on oath."[44]

With that, and a few revisions by an editing committee, the delegates settled—out of exhaustion, if nothing else, given the many months of debate that had already taken place—on the language we see in the Constitution now. To remove an unfit chief executive, a majority vote in the House of Representatives impeaches (basically, indicts) for "Treason, Bribery, or High Crimes and Misdemeanors," and a guilty verdict from at least two-thirds of senators present, in a trial with the chief justice presiding, removes a president. The Constitution's article 3, section 3 even helpfully defines what treason means in impeachment cases: "Treason against the United States, shall consist only in levying War against them, or in adhering to their Enemies, giving them Aid and Comfort. No Person shall be convicted of Treason unless on the Testimony of two Witnesses to the same overt Act, or on Confession in open Court." Bribery, then and now, seems clear enough not to need a definition in the text.

But what were "high crimes and misdemeanors"?

Clearly the phrase is not synonymous with or broader than "maladministration," which Madison objected to, or else he would have protested the new term, too. But why on that day, in that room, with that assemblage of great minds available, did they settle for that clunky phrase, which wasn't used in common conversation even then, without agreeing on its definition or even, it appears, discussing it at all?

The delegates probably thought defining impeachment too broadly (with something like "maladministration") could make the chief executive dependent upon the legislative branch. They also were clear that leaving presidential power unrestricted wouldn't end well, hence their combination of four-year terms, veto overrides, the need for confirmations and treaty approvals—and, yes, the prospect of impeachment and removal for something other than just treason and bribery.

We can infer a few things from what they *didn't* do. First, they held off on requiring that the potentially impeachable act be a crime. Treason and bribery are crimes, and it would take one hell of a lawyer to argue that "high crimes" aren't crimes, as well. But adding "misdemeanors" meant that transgressions falling short of criminality could result in impeachment.

Second, because they were silent about specific impeachable offenses beyond treason and bribery, the use of "high crimes and misdemeanors" looks like an attempt to grant the country's future representatives flexibility instead of binding their hands with a restrictive list. Madison, after all, had said of the president during the convention debates, "He might pervert his administration into a scheme of peculation or oppression."[45] The delegates had covered peculation (embezzlement) with "bribery." Oppression, however, comes in many forms, some of which would presumably fall under the vague "high crimes and misdemeanors."

Third, the delegates and their immediate political heirs clearly didn't see that they'd gotten impeachment so wrong at the convention that they needed to amend the Constitution. With twelve amendments during the country's first thirteen years, the founding generation proved that amendments were a valid part of the system. Yet they chose not to amend "high crimes and misdemeanors."

Legal historian Raoul Berger in the early 1970s did impressive research on the use of "high crimes and misdemeanors," tracing it back to fourteenth-century English practice. While finding no precise definition, he did reveal that the phrase consistently referred to acts harming the state or its institutions.[46] As Charles Black has pointed out, nothing rules out a presidential act being both a "high crime" or "misdemeanor" *and* an example of poor administration,[47] so at least some degree of bad execution of the laws could rise to the level of impeachment. Black offers an admirable working definition. "High crimes and misdemeanors," he says, "ought to be held to those offenses which are rather obviously wrong, whether or not 'criminal,' and which so seriously threaten the order of the political society as to make pestilent and dangerous the continuance in power of their perpetrator."[48]

Presidential impeachment and removal is supposed to be an event with participation across the government. "Impeachment was by the people's House, with the trial by senators—who, before the Seventeenth Amendment, were chosen by state legislatures," says Julie Silverbrook, executive director of the Constitutional Sources Project. "So their design included not only a horizontal check and balance between the branches of the federal government, but also a vertical check and balance between the states and the federal government."[49]

It was hard to deny that the delegates wanted the other branches of government to have some stake in the impeachment and removal process. This involvement across the entire political landscape—the House as the impeaching body, the Senate as the trial body, and the chief justice as the presiding official in the latter—suggests that dumping an unfit president should be a big deal, a step not taken lightly. Not all of those who have sought to impeach presidents during the past two hundred–plus years kept this in mind.

POLITICAL DISAGREEMENTS IN the United States started early, and explicit criticism of presidents followed closely in their wake. But even with the vitriol between John Adams's Federalists and Thomas Jefferson's Democratic-Republicans, for example, no serious efforts emerged to impeach either one of them or the other early chief executives.

Starting in the 1820s, though, impeachment talk caught on. The Tennessee legislature considered a resolution instructing its congressional representative to pursue impeachment against the sixth president, John Quincy Adams, for his supposed conspiracy with Henry Clay to win the White House after losing the popular vote to Andrew Jackson. Even Jackson's supporters, however, thought better of it, fearing such a move would only reinforce the opposition's narrative about Jackson's bitterness and intolerance. The resolution went nowhere.[50]

Jackson subsequently used his popular mandate to extend the powers of the presidency, infuriating members of the emerging Whig Party in the process. Unlike the president, Whigs in Congress considered the best government to be one in which the legislature led and the chief executive merely enacted its policies as directed. So it's little surprise that Congressman Edward Everett of Massachusetts in June 1831 raised with party leader Clay the possibility of Jackson's impeachment in the House.[51] Even though Clay had called Jackson's election the greatest calamity to strike the United States since its independence,[52] he knew how to calculate political odds. The president simply remained too popular for the measure to succeed.

"On the question of impeachment, suggested by you," Clay replied to Everett, "I entertain no doubt of the President's liability to it. But, at present . . . from the composition of the Senate, there is not the least prospect of such a prosecution being effectual." He warned his colleague that any effort to impeach and remove Jackson would, instead, make him even more beloved by the masses, so the initiative died.[53] That realization about the importance of a president's personal popularity on impeachment and removal prospects would be lost on Clay's congressional successors more than 160 years later, during the presidency of Bill Clinton.

JOHN TYLER WAS the first president to come to office upon the death of his predecessor, and the first president rejected by his own party and not renominated.

Tyler holds yet another distinction: the Whig outcast also became the first president who faced an impeachment vote in the House of Representatives. His greatest sin to those who opposed him was his boldness in doing something we take for granted now, and which the Constitution explicitly empowered him to do: veto legislation. The Whigs who had nominated him as vice president and now controlled Congress, however, didn't like presidential vetoes except to turn back clearly unconstitutional measures. Using them to negate bills for policy reasons was unseemly, in their philosophy. Tyler, upon taking the president's chair, didn't see it that way, so he started vetoing things. Several things. In fact, despite having the shortest term yet for any chief executive, he issued six regular vetoes. That's a higher total than any president before him and the most among the first sixteen presidents.[54]

Particularly annoying were his successive vetoes of national bank bills in August and September 1841. The first one bothered Whigs on its merits (or lack thereof, in their minds). The second one did that *and* offended them, because legislators had specifically addressed Tyler's particular objections to the first bill in the text of the new one.[55] This was a bridge too far for party members, who almost universally quit from Tyler's cabinet and then cast their own president out.

And yet Tyler kept using that veto. In the summer of 1842, he killed a couple of tariff bills, necessary for bringing revenue into the government. House leaders sent Tyler's veto message on that second tariff bill to a select committee—chaired by John Quincy Adams, who had joined the House of Representatives two years after his presidency ended—to consider options. The Adams-drafted majority report said, in part, "The power of the present Congress to enact laws essential to the welfare of the people has been struck with apoplexy by the Executive hand. Submission to his will, is the only condition upon which he will permit them to act. . . . In this state of things, he has assumed, as the committee fully believe, the exercise of the whole legislative power to himself."[56]

As a result, Adams continued, "The majority of the committee believe that the case has occurred . . . to impeach the President of the United States." This broke new ground; no Congressional committee had before found that events had met the criteria of article 2, section 4. Adams, however, had learned a lot of politics in his seven decades, and he could envision what would happen if they pushed forward with impeachment: "The resort to that expedient might, in the present condition of public affairs, prove abortive."[57] In other words, he told his colleagues, Tyler deserves impeachment, but we don't have the votes to pull it off.

The House voted its approval and adoption of the committee's report without formally impeaching the president. Tyler sent a rebuke to the representatives, claiming they had no constitutional right to criticize him *except* through formal impeachment charges.[58] The House gave Tyler the legislative version of the middle finger by not even officially recording his protest.[59] Whigs also pointed out the rich irony: eight years earlier, President Jackson had sent a similar rejoinder to the Senate upon its passage of a censure motion. Who joined the senators in not recording that protest? Then-senator John Tyler.

One persistent representative in January 1843 insisted that his colleagues weigh in formally on whether a new committee should investigate nine specific charges against the president that, he said, were impeachable. This led to the first-ever floor vote on de facto impeachment charges. The measure, however, lost by a wide margin.[60] From that point on, legislators realized that having a weakened Tyler in place proved more politically useful than struggling to remove him.

T HE RELATIONSHIP BETWEEN Tyler and the Congress was terrible. The one between Andrew Johnson and Congress proved that things can always get worse.

Johnson, succeeding the assassinated Abraham Lincoln, provoked Congress repeatedly. He paroled leading Confederate officials. He appointed governors for unreconstructed Southern states. He treated such states as if they'd never rebelled against the Union, supporting their right to institute discriminatory "black codes." He vetoed civil rights and other bills. Congress, to apply pressure on

Johnson or to pay him back for such measures, did everything from overturn presidential vetoes to direct the process through which he must issue military orders. One representative described "an open political hostility, but one which rapidly advanced to a condition in which violent epithet and mutual denunciation indicated the deplorable relations of the two great departments of the Government."[61]

Applying pressure on Johnson through usual means wasn't enough for the so-called Radical Republicans on Capitol Hill. Whether motivated by constitutional concerns about the fault lines between executive and legislative powers (which influenced some lawmakers), or personal dislike of the president (which plenty felt), disagreement with his policies toward the South (which dominated Capitol Hill), they wanted him out of office.

They had a unique setup to do so. For the first time in American history, the president's opposition held not only a majority in the House of Representatives but also a two-thirds majority in the Senate, sufficient for impeaching and removing the president.

THE FIRST MOVE toward ousting Johnson through congressional voting came on January 7, 1867. A representative proposed that the president had violated the law through various corrupt uses of power—in his appointments, pardons, vetoes, disposal of public property, and election interference—and sought a referral to the Committee on the Judiciary. That measure passed the House overwhelmingly and the committee investigated the claims until the end of the congressional session in early March; a resolution to continue the effort passed quickly in the next Congress and the investigation went on until November.[62]

Meanwhile, the two branches of government kept clashing. In March came the first of several Reconstruction acts that became law when Congress overrode presidential vetos. Two follow-on acts in March and July were both made law over Johnson's vetoes.[63] Across many months, the president tried to sabotage the ratification of the Fourteenth Amendment, which provided federal equal-protection guarantees, and grew frustrated as the Senate refused his nominees for multiple federal offices.[64] By November, the Judiciary

Committee had examined ninety-five witnesses, produced twelve hundred pages of their testimony, and reported to the full House its recommendation that events warranted impeachment.[65] But representatives soundly defeated a resolution to impeach Johnson on December 7, 1867.[66] Most everyone disliked Johnson; that wasn't the obstacle. They just couldn't identify the "treason, bribery, or high crimes and misdemeanors" the Constitution required for an impeachment vote.

But lawmakers had already laid a trap. Back in February 1867, they had overridden Johnson's veto of the Tenure of Office Act, which denied the president's power to fire and replace identified executive branch officers—including the secretary of war, at that time Edwin Stanton, a strong advocate of military occupation in the South—without Senate consent. The law was extreme, saying not only that such officials couldn't be removed until senators had confirmed a replacement but also that presidential violations of the act would be "high misdemeanors."[67] It passed the Congress and Senate easily, though not without some later regrets. Moderate Republicans like James Blaine, although supporting it at the time, later considered it "against the early decision of the founders of the government . . . against the repeatedly expressed judgment of ex-President Madison, against the equally emphatic judgment of Chief Justice Marshall, and, above all, against the unbroken practice of the Government for seventy-eight years."[68] Nevertheless, at the time, most members of Congress thought they'd simply need to wait for Johnson to commit another unforced error.

The act did keep the president from firing the secretary of war through most of the year, but the two men still clashed over policy and different interpretations of executive- and legislative-branch authorities. On August 5, Johnson wrote to Stanton: "Public considerations of a high character constrain me to say that your resignation as Secretary of War will be accepted." The war secretary's response the next morning remains a Washington classic: "In reply I have the honor to say that public considerations of a high character, which alone have induced me to continue at the head of this department, constrain me not to resign the office of Secretary of War before the next meeting of Congress."[69] Johnson—again, trying not to trigger the Tenure of Office Act—merely suspended Stanton and appointed General Ulysses Grant his acting successor.[70]

Upon their return on January 13, 1868, the Senate denied the president's suspension of Stanton, spurring Grant to return the secretary of war's office to him.[71] Johnson thought Grant deceived him by implying he'd stay in the position until courts ruled on the matter.[72] Grant thought Johnson tried to make him violate the law by asking him to stay, even enticing him to do so by offering to pay Grant's fine and serve his jail sentence.[73] One representative considered the president's effort to induce Grant to break the law itself a "high official misdemeanor."[74]

A few weeks later, Johnson couldn't take it anymore. He removed Stanton on February 21, announcing Lorenzo Thomas as his replacement. Stanton stood pat, however, leading to an uncomfortable face-to-face confrontation with Thomas as the supposedly removed Stanton camped out in what he still felt was his office, refusing to leave even to go home or to cabinet meetings.[75] Grant supported Stanton's decision to hold on.[76]

Capitol Hill erupted in fury at the president's blatant disregard for the Tenure of Office Act. A prominent congressman, feeling his worst assumptions about Johnson vindicated, asked colleagues, "Didn't I tell you so? What good did your moderation do you? If you don't kill the beast, it will kill you."[77] Another representative said, "I am in favor of the official death of Andrew Johnson without debate. I am not surprised that one who began his Presidential career in drunkenness should end it in crime."[78]

JOHNSON'S DETRACTORS IN Congress, now holding the excuse they wanted to initiate formal impeachment charges, held a quick vote on February 24 and impeached the president, without debating specific articles detailing how he'd committed treason, bribery, or high crimes and misdemeanors.

"Certainly the Radical Republicans in Congress had a much more expansive view of what the impeachment power was to be used for—in this case, how the president used his powers in ways that damaged the future of the Republic," says constitutional expert Keith Whittington. "And the impeachment power is the correct mechanism for addressing that."[79] The committee they appointed to draft a set of precise articles returned them quickly to the House, which in turn forwarded them to the Senate on March 3.[80]

The eleven articles of impeachment were both detailed and repetitive. Eight of them referred in one way or another to Johnson's replacement of Stanton with Thomas, one dealt with presidential instructions contrary to the law requiring military orders to go through Grant, one addressed Johnson's public screeds against members of Congress, and the eleventh and final one was a combination of the other articles. The weakest of them by far—which still passed, but received twenty-one fewer votes than the next closest article—was the tenth, which chastised the president for making "with a loud voice, certain intemperate, inflammatory, and scandalous harangues" and uttering "loud threats and bitter menaces."[81] Although moderate Republicans later regretted the impeachment effort based on these articles, the Radical leaders were amping up the rhetoric, comparing the president's "acts of usurpation, lawlessness and tyranny" to those that drove the revolutionary generation to separate their colonies from King George.[82]

The Senate now took over. Following the procedures in the Constitution, the Supreme Court's chief justice presided as seven House managers and the president's defense team made their case to the senators, most of whom had already made up their minds. For almost two months, the trial went on, and on, and on. Most days, spectators in the galleries who sought sensational moments left disappointed because of the dry speeches and testimony.[83]

On May 16, the full Senate of fifty-four members voted on the catch-all article, which the managers had judged most likely to succeed because it had a little bit of something for everyone who might be inclined to boot the president out of office. Some thought the president was doomed; the secretary of state had already drafted a resignation letter to submit immediately after the conviction he expected to come.[84] The majority of his cabinet, however, felt confident of an acquittal.[85]

As the alphabetical role call prompted votes from each senator, all eyes turned to the few senators whose decisions hadn't yet become obvious. William Fessenden of Maine, an opponent of Johnson who nevertheless had concerns about his removal, said, "Not guilty." Joseph Fowler of Tennessee added a few seconds of drama when his quiet answer sounded to some like "Guilty." He followed up quickly with a loud and clear "Not guilty!" One by one, each senator on or near the fence shied away from conviction. Soon the only remaining unknown was Edmund Ross of Kansas, whom both the president's allies and the Radicals had pressured hard. Quietly ripping pieces of paper into strips that fell at his feet while the others voted, knowing that he might be about to end his political career, Ross also decided to vote against removal.[86] The seven Republicans who voted against impeachment would in fact never again win election to the Senate; Ross endured physical assault upon his return to Kansas.[87]

The president had thus escaped conviction by squeezing out exactly the number of votes he needed to prevent the two-thirds majority. After similar results in the balloting on two other articles two weeks later, the Senate stopped voting and the impeachment trial ended.[88]

As soon as the first article had fallen one vote short, Radicals screamed foul and began an investigation into the treachery they assumed bought the acquittal votes from undecided senators. At the same time, celebrations across the South featured fireworks and guns fired into the air.[89] When the president heard of his Senate acquittal, he briefly teared up, then ordered whiskey from the White House cellar. A group of his closest advisors shared a silent toast.[90]

WHY DIDN'T THE Senate convict the deeply unpopular president and, thereby, remove him from the presidency? Many factors helped, but four stand out: the weak presentation for impeachment, presidential promises and payoffs, Republican concerns about Johnson's replacement, and anticipation of the next election.

First, the managers didn't present their case well. The articles themselves were weak, mostly relying on Johnson's violation of a law that many observers suspected wouldn't pass judicial review. It took a while, but the Supreme Court did, in fact, rule decades later that presidents don't need Senate approval to dismiss previously appointed officers. One representative who'd voted for impeachment in the House later said it was "the cause of subsequent humiliation to all who had taken part in its enactment."[91] The floor speeches themselves often underwhelmed. One spectator called a manager's speech "so bitter, and yet so almost theatrical, that it seemed unreal." He likened it to a "violent attack" in which "blameless incidents were made to seem traitorous."[92]

Second, at least a few undecided senators made it clear that they wanted to get something tangible for going against the Radical Republican tidal wave. Government jobs went to some senators' associates or constituents. Johnson's supporters had assembled at least one pile of cash, which circumstantial evidence suggests made its way into the hands of at least one senator. And several acquittal votes probably depended on quiet White House pledges that the president would stop obstructing congressional Reconstruction plans.[93]

Third, existing succession law directed that, in the absence of a vice president, the highest office in the land would go to the Senate's president pro tempore. In 1868, that was Ohio's Benjamin Wade, who was, to put it mildly, unsuited for the presidency. For years, he dared challengers to attack him in the Senate, having prominently placed two loaded pistols on his desk when he came into the chamber.[94] During the Civil War, he had held back a line of Union soldiers fleeing the disastrous first battle of Bull Run, threatening them with a squirrel rifle and vowing to "stop this damned run-away."[95] Republican representative (and future president) James Garfield of Ohio wrote to a friend, "I have no doubt that the personal dislike of Mr. Wade had more power over them than they are aware of."[96] Another representative reflected the views of many on Capitol Hill when he told a colleague, "Johnson in the White House is bad enough, but we know what we have. Lord knows what we would get with old Ben Wade there."[97]

Fourth, many Republicans weren't looking for a post-impeachment wild card because they were in a strong position to take the White House in the fall with a widely popular candidate, Ulysses

Grant. One Republican representative had advised back in 1867 that the party should not risk a sure thing with the general: "Maintain things as they are and nothing can prevent Grant from being the next President."[98]

Johnson's conflict with Congress would settle down a bit as he fulfilled his patronage promises and stopped interfering with new Southern state constitutions that guaranteed voting rights for former slaves. Although legislators didn't let him function freely despite the acquittal, they avoided the shock to the system a constitutional removal would have brought. Senator Fessenden of Maine, one of the Republicans who voted against conviction, was clear about this logic at the time, saying impeachment and removal should be reserved for only "extreme cases, and then only upon clear and unquestionable grounds" with "no suspicion upon the motives of those who inflict the penalty."[99] Law professor Brian Kalt puts it more simply: "He was acquitted because there was some institutional self-restraint."[100]

DURING THE SEVENTY-FIVE years after Johnson's acquittal, two presidents heard calls for their impeachment formally offered in the House of Representatives. Congressmen submitted such resolutions against both Grover Cleveland and Herbert Hoover; neither initiative, though, made it to the Judiciary Committee, much less to the floor for a full vote.[101] Things got a little more interesting after mid-century, but no serious actions moved forward on impeachment until just before the new century began.

HARRY TRUMAN WAS LIVID. Managing the Korean War was hard enough without an exceptionally popular general trying to publicly force a new strategy on him.

Douglas MacArthur, a hero from World War II, was now leading US forces in the Far East and military actions in Korea, where China had intervened to escalate the conflict. On March 7, 1951, while acknowledging that he didn't make the ultimate decisions, MacArthur told reporters there would be "savage slaughter" unless

Truman accepted his policy suggestions. Then, on March 24, the general issued a statement calling on the United States to take the war *to* China, "through an expansion of our military operations to its coastal areas and interior bases."[102] At a minimum, he put his commander in chief on the spot. Many saw it as insubordination against civil authority.

"It was my duty to act," Truman later wrote, so he did.[103] On April 11, the president relieved MacArthur of his commands, elevating General Matthew Ridgway in his place. Before flying back to the United States, MacArthur told Ridgway that Truman's "bewilderment and confusion of thought" placed in doubt the president's mental stability. He even implied that Truman was dying.[104] That conversation remained private for many years, but MacArthur's return home was far from quiet, featuring a speech to a joint session of Congress and massive parades in his honor in Washington and New York. Gallup reported that 69 percent of Americans supported the general in the dispute, with the president polling only 29 percent. "Many of my father's decisions had made headlines before," noted Margaret Truman, "but nothing compared to the uproar which now ensued."[105]

In the midst of it all, Republican legislators and conservative newspapers were preparing the ground for dramatic action. An Indiana senator asserted that the country had been taken over by "a secret inner coterie which is directed by agents of the Soviet Union. Our only choice is to impeach President Truman."[106] He "must be impeached and convicted," the editorial board of the *Chicago Tribune* announced. "His hasty and vindictive removal of General MacArthur is the culmination of a series of acts which have shown that he is unfit, morally and mentally, for his high office." The paper also cited as impeachable offenses the president's ordering of troops to Korea without a congressional declaration of war and "surrounding himself with grifters and incompetents."[107]

But before impeachment articles got drafted, something unexpected happened at MacArthur's testimony to a combined session of two Senate committees. His answers to the senators' questions raised serious doubts about *his* judgment, especially on big-picture matters. Chairman of the Joint Chiefs of Staff Omar Bradley, apolitical and even more widely respected than MacArthur, seemed to contradict MacArthur's assertions, saying, "The course of action often described as a 'limited war' with Red China would increase the risk we are taking by engaging too much of our power in an area that is not the strategic prize. . . . Frankly, in the opinion of the Joint Chiefs of Staff, this strategy would involve us in the wrong war, in the wrong place, at the wrong time and with the wrong enemy."[108] The shift was quick and decisive; MacArthur's credibility and appeal dropped rapidly while support grew around the president.[109]

That crisis faded, but Truman wasn't done with threats of impeachment yet. In 1952, four different representatives offered resolutions based on the president's seizure of steel mills before workers could go on strike. One of the measures harkened back to the earlier controversy by including, as an additional point, Truman's removal of MacArthur from his commands. The Judiciary Committee took no action on any of these resolutions.[110]

Two VERY DIFFERENT foreign policy initiatives during Ronald Reagan's administration drove impeachment talk. The first, the invasion of Grenada in 1983, spurred a resolution in the House claiming the president committed high crimes or misdemeanors when he violated congressional war power authority, violated treaty obligations, and—in a first for impeachment charges—"prevented news coverage of the invasion." Not surprisingly, this resolution received no formal action in the Judiciary Committee.[111]

The second involved an issue that had public hearings, intense public attention, and a cast of colorful characters but surprisingly little on the impeachment front. The scandal known as Iran-Contra involved arms sales to Iran, attempts to trade weapons sales for hostages, and funding for anti-Communist Contra rebels in Central America. But the most extensive investigation into the scandal, the Tower Commission, later concluded that the president was principally at fault for an overly delegative management style, with an irresponsible and undisciplined staff—not sufficient tinder for an impeachment fire.[112] Even at the time, prominent senators William

Cohen and George Mitchell jointly declared, "A foreign policy mistake did not demand a political beheading."[113]

Talk of impeachment came up on Capitol Hill briefly in June 1987, when a memorandum popped up that seemed to link Reagan to the diversion of profits from the arms sales to Iran. Congressman Lee Hamilton publicly called it a potential "smoking gun," noting that if the memo checked out and the president had, in fact, approved that diversion, "you would have a demand for impeachment hearings." But further investigation showed that memo did not relate to the Contras in Central America, and such talk faded fast.[114] That didn't stop one persistent congressman from trying. Back in March, he had introduced a resolution impeaching Reagan for high crimes and misdemeanors related to various aspects of the Iran-Contra scandal. Like so many other such measures throughout the history of House impeachment, it went to the Judiciary Committee—and sat there. But instead of giving up, Representative Henry Gonzalez took to the floor of the House nine separate times during the year to try to get someone to listen to his pleas to take action on his proposal.[115]

These failures don't mean the prospect of impeachment went without effect. The specter of Watergate and managing an at-risk presidency came into the mind of the White House chief of staff during the crisis.[116] After the Reagan administration was over, one of his former attorneys general admitted he'd thought about impeachment during the scandal—less because of the facts of the case than because of the opportunity it handed opponents of the president to use impeachment hearings to inflict political harm.[117] The possibility of impeachment can have a dark-matter effect, where even in its absence it can affect the behavior of the president and close advisors.

Reagan's successor, George H. W. Bush, would pardon six major players in the Iran-Contra scandal, including former secretary of defense Caspar Weinberger, before leaving office. But impeachment charges didn't come his way for that; instead, a Texas representative twice offered resolutions seeking to impeach Bush for supposed high crimes and misdemeanors related to the 1990–1991 Gulf War, in which the United States and its international coalition liberated

Kuwait after Iraq's invasion. The Judiciary Committee received both resolutions, and did nothing with them.[118]

WHEN DO LIES meet the threshold of impeachable high crimes and misdemeanors? The Nixon case showed that most legislators and most of the American people would have said lies told to cover up otherwise impeachable abuses of power counted. But it gets tricky when a chief executive lies to cover up personal indiscretions and to protect himself against civil actions that do not directly involve presidential powers—and even trickier when the president involved is personally popular and his enemies are seen as hyperpartisan.

THE INVESTIGATIONS THAT led to Bill Clinton's impeachment for high crimes and misdemeanors and his trial in the Senate began long before and far removed from White House interns and sex acts. It all went back to a complex series of real estate investments, illegal loans, and bank problems in Arkansas that involved Bill and Hillary Clinton. Eventually fifteen people—but not the Clintons—were convicted on a range of charges emerging from the Whitewater investigation.[119]

Independent counsels digging into these issues and related matters didn't even file charges against the Clintons on the core case.[120] But in his investigation, independent counsel Ken Starr found evidence that Bill Clinton lied about his sexual relationship with Monica Lewinsky, a White House intern, and about his attempts to help *her* cover up the affair and lie in a sexual harassment civil suit that Paula Jones had filed against the president. This activity occurred while he was president, raising interest in impeachment. Because Starr interpreted his mandate more akin to a truth commission than a conventional criminal inquiry, he sent to the House both an unwieldy amount of evidence and a report with a recommendation to impeach, which the House Judiciary Committee quickly translated into its own articles of impeachment for the full House to consider.[121]

Even Clinton's own lawyers thought things looked bad for him because of the lies he'd told in a Jones suit deposition. He'd claimed he couldn't recall ever being alone with Lewinsky—with whom he had, in fact, been alone several times starting in December 1995, inside the White House, to engage in sexual acts. Starr, and eventually the House Judiciary Committee, had plenty of proof about that relationship, too, not only from Lewinsky's eventual testimony and others' observations but also from one of her dresses that provided evidence of a sexual encounter. "It was beyond reasonable dispute," Ben Wittes writes, "that both Lewinsky and the president testified falsely in the Jones case."[122]

The Republican majority in the House generally viewed Clinton's behavior as both reprehensible and worthy of impeachment. But these were lies to cover up an unseemly relationship, different than the lies in the Nixon case about the president using his power to order federal agencies to obstruct justice. Consequently, the confidence level among Republicans going into the impeachment vote fell short of that among the Democrats in 1974 going into the comparable Nixon vote. "We've got to stop this," said Bob Livingston, the likely successor to Newt Gingrich as House Speaker before a sex scandal also stalled Livingston's career, the night before the full House weighed in. He was minutes away from calling a meeting of House Republicans to pull the plug on the impeachment vote before a staffer convinced him to go forward with it.[123]

Others on the Republican side were more certain. "Impeachment was not only the proper remedy," wrote the chief investigative counsel to the Judiciary Committee, whose views reflect those of many members, "it was the only constitutional remedy available to correct some of the most outrageous conduct ever engaged in by a president of the United States."[124] One of the eventual House managers argued, "The evidence shows clearly that the President engaged in a repeated and lengthy pattern of felonious conduct—conduct for which ordinary citizens can—and have—lost their liberty. . . . the solemnity of our sacred oath obliges us to do what the President regretfully has failed to do: defend the rule of law, and defend the concept that no person is above the law."[125]

Especially as the hearings and votes went on, Democrats on the Judiciary Committee and in the wider House came to see the issue primarily as one of trying to hide private sexual conduct—bad behavior, no doubt, but not a constitutional travesty. That vision of the case allowed politics to dominate quickly.[126] "Theirs was a circle-the-wagons mentality," a Republican member of the Judiciary Committee describes. "They chose defending the Clintons—at all costs—to ward off any collateral political damage to the Democratic Party."[127]

Clinton's lawyers and their client caught a lucky break. On December 19, 1998, the article of impeachment drawn up by the Judiciary Committee charging perjury for his Jones suit deposition, which would have been the hardest to disprove, failed to pass in the full House.[128] Another article of impeachment for abuse of power also failed to clear that hurdle. But the committee had written two other articles, one charging the president with perjury to a grand jury, another charging him with obstruction of justice in his attempts to cover things up. Those articles both passed.

Clinton, the forty-second president, became only the second chief executive impeached by the House of Representatives. Attention then shifted to the Senate, where constitutional interpretation and politics created a real mess.

TWO NARRATIVES HAD developed by the time the president's trial started on January 7, 1999. Most senators appeared to settle on one or the other quickly.

One frame portrayed the president's actions with Lewinsky and in covering up the relationship as unbecoming, even reprehensible, but not rising to the level of constitutional high crimes and misdemeanors. He did not, in other words, injure the "order of political society," as Conrad Black put it, because his acts did not relate ultimately to matters of state.

The other frame portrayed the president's actions of perjury and obstruction of justice as inherently conflicting with his article 2, section 3 duty to "take care that the laws be faithfully executed." He did, in other words, injure the "order of political society" because he betrayed the president's duty to uphold, and be held accountable to, the law. "Their view was that we have an established set of expectations about how presidents behave," Keith Whittington says, "and President Clinton had violated those."[129]

House managers delivered their opening statements on January 14–16 to make the case for impeachment, followed by the president's lawyers' statements on January 19–21. The chief justice reinforced the special nature of the event when he ruled that the senators should not be referred to as "jurors" because they were, in fact, not merely a jury but the entire court.[130]

Not a single senator went to the office building nearby to review evidence.[131] Because most senators had focused on the big-picture narratives more than the details, the opening statements actually opened some Democrats' eyes to the power of the case; this wasn't going to be as easy to dismiss as "just about sex" as they'd thought.[132] But there was no last-minute drama, no uncertain senators holding the president's fate in their hands as the vote was tallied. It was essentially over on January 27, when Senator Robert Byrd, seen as a leader for those Democrats still on the fence, called for a dismissal and an end to the trial. The final votes on February 12, 45-55 for the perjury article and 50-50 for the obstruction of justice one, didn't even get a majority, much less anything close to the two-thirds majority needed for conviction.

Through it all, despite their solemn vow, senators couldn't help but have one eye on the polls. Even before the impeachment, 65 percent of Americans in a Gallup poll thought the Republicans in Congress were attacking Clinton unfairly over a private matter; even 39 percent of Republicans agreed.[133] Through the impeachment proceedings, his approval ratings went *up*, not down; he garnered the highest approval ratings of his administration during the Senate trial.[134] It became hard for senators to see the key question for their vote as "Did he do the things he is accused of?" or "Are they high crimes and misdemeanors?" Instead, politics intruded. Many, if not most, saw a different question driving their votes: "Am I with this popular president or am I against him?"

THE CLINTON IMPEACHMENT opened up discussion of that option for each of his successors, but the process only moved forward for one of them. The most significant of the efforts occurred on June 10, 2008, when Dennis Kucinich and co-sponsor Robert Wexler introduced thirty-five impeachment articles against George W. Bush in the House.[135] Representatives voted 251-166 on June 11 to refer their resolution to the Judiciary Committee, where it stalled. Coming so late in his second term, it would have been quite a logistical challenge to arrange hearings, collect evidence, and so on even if it had made it through the committee.

The enduring lesson of the Johnson, Nixon, and Clinton impeachment proceedings, as well as the others that failed to get as far along as those did, seems to be that impeachment and, especially, removal will remain a very high bar to clear. Clearly heinous behavior may be necessary but insufficient. It's hard to imagine a successful conviction by two-thirds of a divided Senate without a deeply unpopular president who can be found definitively to have harmed the very institutions of government through malign action or inaction.

Chapter Eight

Shoved Aside at the Polls

It was desirable that the sense of the people
should operate in the choice of the person to whom
so important a trust was to be confided.[1]

—JAMES MADISON

ALTHOUGH THE FOUNDERS mentioned foreign intrigue as a concern while creating a new mechanism for electing the country's leaders, they didn't foresee a hostile country's internet-based interference in a presidential election some 230 years in the future. What may come to be seen as the most dramatic case of a preemptive removal from office was followed by a series of related indictments, talk of constitutional crises, and the most divisive administration since at least Andrew Johnson.

"WE ASSESS RUSSIAN PRESIDENT Vladimir Putin ordered an influence campaign in 2016 aimed at the US presidential election. Russia's goals were to undermine public faith in the US democratic process, denigrate Secretary Clinton, and harm her electability and potential presidency. We further assess Putin and the Russian Government developed a clear preference for President-elect Trump. We have high confidence in these judgments."[2]

The US Intelligence Community, with this statement on January 6, 2017, described the most recent attempt to remove a president pre-emptively: an attempt to manipulate an election. "We also assess," the statement continued, "Putin and the Russian Government aspired to help President-elect Trump's election chances when possible by discrediting Secretary Clinton and publicly contrasting her unfavorably to him. All three agencies agree with this judgment. CIA and FBI have high confidence in this judgment; NSA has moderate confidence." But the Intelligence Community stopped short of weighing in on the effects: "We did not make an assessment of the impact that Russian activities had on the outcome of the 2016 election. The US Intelligence Community is charged with monitoring and assessing the intentions, capabilities, and actions of foreign actors; it does not analyze US political processes or US public opinion."[3]

Claims of foreign interference in US presidential elections go back to 1800, when supporters of incumbent John Adams and those of challenger Thomas Jefferson accused opponents of taking assistance from the French and the British, respectively. It became a major campaign issue in 1888, as Benjamin Harrison's partisans sought to peel some Irish American voters away from the incumbent, Grover Cleveland, by making it look like he would do the bidding of the British government. They goaded the United Kingdom's minister in Washington, Sir Lionel Sackville-West, into writing a letter favoring Cleveland, embarrassing the president enough to tell Sir Lionel that he'd worn out his welcome in the United States and would have to go home.[4]

But such cases pale in comparison to 2016. The same Intelligence Community analysis just cited also declared that the Russian strategy blended "covert intelligence operations—such as cyber activity—with overt efforts by Russian Government agencies, state-funded media, third-party intermediaries, and paid social media users or 'trolls.'"[5] Just over a year later, the Justice Department charged thirteen Russians and three companies in a sweeping indictment for stealing US citizens' identities and manipulating divisive campaign issues.[6] According to the prosecutors, Russians in August 2016 even posed as Americans and coordinated with Trump campaign staff to

organize rallies in Florida.[7] And in July 2018, the Justice Department charged twelve Russian military officers for conspiring to hack
into computers, steal documents, release documents in an effort to
interfere with the election, and infiltrate computers of organizations
responsible for administering elections.[8]

Whether these Russian efforts actually steered the election results
will remain difficult to conclude with anything close to certainty.[9]
The byzantine interplay of campaign tactics and voters' perceptions,
compounded by the complex nature of social media influence, means
we will probably never know whether 2016 constitutes a case of preemptive removal.

IN A SENSE, every presidential election is a chance for the voting
public either to keep someone from getting into office in the first
place or to eject an incumbent. And each election presents opportunities for interested parties to try to manipulate voters.

Ten American presidents seeking reelection have been removed
at the polls; just three cases before 2016 show some of the most creative ways, from presidential branding to voodoo, opponents and
party bosses have tried to guide the result to remove a president after
four years.

JOHN QUINCY ADAMS had entered the White House in 1825, both
as the first son of a former president to win the presidency and
under a shadow for how he got into it. It wasn't that he lacked the
experience for the job. In fact, the younger Adams had served his
country for more than thirty years as a four-time ambassador, senator from Massachusetts, and two-term secretary of state. Few American presidents have come into office better prepared.

The problem, instead, was that he looked illegitimate. He'd won
both fewer popular votes and fewer electoral votes than leading
contender General Andrew Jackson. But the proliferation of major presidential candidates on Election Day had left Jackson well
short of the majority of electoral votes, throwing the choice to a

constitutionally directed one-vote-per-state decision in the House of Representatives. Speaker Henry Clay of Kentucky, no fan of Jackson, prodded enough delegations of states that had gone for the general in the popular vote to switch, giving Adams the win.[10]

Although fully constitutional, the perceived injustice of the action—especially when Adams turned around and nominated Clay for secretary of state, the most prestigious position in the administration—ignited cries of a "corrupt bargain" that had cheated Jackson out of the White House. Never mind that Clay had preferred Adams to Old Hickory even before the election shifted into the House and that no evidence of such a bargain came to light. And, even if it had occurred, it would hardly be the first time political positions would reward election support.

During the next four years, as "corrupt bargain" echoes followed his administration, Adams didn't help his cause by acting like a pompous ass. What supporters saw as integrity, erudition, and pride looked to most others like haughty arrogance or worse. "In his anxiety to be upright," wrote one nineteenth-century biographer, "he was undoubtedly prone to be needlessly disagreeable . . . an adept in alienation, a novice in conciliation. His magnetism was negative."[11] Everything he did publicly reinforced the notion that he was detached and aloof, leading opposition press to call him aristocratic and assert he held "no feelings in common with the mass of the people."[12]

The political landscape also shifted against Adams between 1824 and 1828. Voting rights, for one, expanded dramatically, from just over a quarter of adult white males when Adams won the election to virtually all of them four years later. Likewise, most of the states that had still tasked their legislatures with selecting electoral votes when Adams first took office had now shifted that duty to the people.[13] Both moves benefitted Jackson, bringing into presidential elections the nation's "forgotten men"—at least the white ones—who saw Andrew Jackson as their champion against the establishment and its political bosses.[14]

Their crucial support came early; only seven months after Adams's inauguration, the Tennessee legislature nominated Jackson for the next presidential contest. The general's allies, who began calling themselves "Democrats,"[15] got right to work, laying the groundwork for a campaign of character assassination to ensure Adams wouldn't get elected again.

The bruising battle of 1828 remains one of America's ugliest. The incumbent's detractors screamed "corrupt bargain" early and often, relentlessly berating the president as an anti-democratic monarchist despite his solid credentials as a dedicated public servant. Senator Thomas Hart Benton of Missouri noted that the Jackson campaign's emphasis on "the people's right to govern themselves" reflected public disgust with the House of Representatives' anti-democratic choice in 1825: "The sanction, or rebuke, of that violation was a leading question in the whole canvass."[16] Jacksonian propaganda spread outward from Washington, pushing consistent themes like never before.[17] While earlier elections rarely featured campaign-related objects to reinforce such themes, their use exploded in 1828 with mostly pro-Jackson fabrics, snuff boxes, flasks, small medals, combs, and even hickory poles—all designed to cement in voters' minds the image of Jackson as a hero to rescue the people from the corrupt Adams and Clay.[18]

When Election Day came, this manufactured public rage nearly doubled the turnout from four years earlier, leading to a Jackson landslide over Adams in both the popular vote and the electoral tally. For only the second time, the American people had gotten rid of an incumbent (who, both times, was an Adams). But the 1828 election had been built on a deception—as even Benton, Jackson's stalwart ally in the Senate, later admitted when he declared that the "corrupt bargain" charge had been used "unjustly in prejudicing the public mind against Mr. Adams and Mr. Clay."[19]

JACKSON'S SUCCESSOR IN 1837 was his second vice president, a masterful political technician nicknamed the "Little Magician," who was more responsible than anyone else for building the Democratic Party. Martin Van Buren's experience and skill as a politician might have helped him beat the odds and win another term in office despite a badly struggling economy. But his opponents beguiled the electorate with a trick the Little Magician couldn't top: putting forward an oversold military hero who said little about his policy preferences and instead just looked the part.

That man was General William Henry Harrison. Even a Van Buren supporter could see he was "a candidate more sure of being elected" than traditional leaders of his newly adopted Whig Party, who surely deserved the country's highest office more.[20] But there was little substance behind Harrison. Instead, it was all about his image. After his father had signed the Declaration of Independence and served as Virginia's governor, Harrison represented the Northwest Territory in Congress and served for more than a decade as the first governor of the Indiana Territory that Congress and President John Adams carved out from it.[21]

Echoing Jackson's frontier warrior persona, Harrison played up his battlefield experiences. Most notably, he had fought Native American incursions in a campaign that included the battle of Tippecanoe, not far from today's Lafayette, Indiana, in November 1811. There, a mystic Native American known as "the Prophet" convinced about five hundred tribesmen that he could blind and stupefy the group of around a thousand US soldiers encamped nearby, enabling a sneak attack. His spells clearly failed; a sentry fired upon the approaching marauders and a full fight ensued. Harrison emerged unscathed, but his troops took over 150 casualties, including almost seventy deaths, probably more than the smaller Native American forces suffered.[22] A victory, perhaps, but nothing stunning or particularly heroic.

The battle's mythology nevertheless expanded over the years. And Harrison's popularity grew when he saw action in the War of 1812, vanquished Native American leader Tecumseh,[23] and served as a state senator in Ohio, a US senator, and minister to Colombia. He achieved nothing truly remarkable during any of those positions, but this stately, genial gentleman projected an aura of confident command. That, more than his imprecise political philosophy, attracted the attention of the men forming the Whig Party. Harrison played along, parroting Whig policy positions and criticizing Jackson's executive overreach.[24] He finished in a strong second place to Van Buren in the 1836 election and geared up for a rematch.

Early in Van Buren's term, a major recession began. Ultimately, the Panic of 1837 and its aftermath would see the collapse of commodity prices, unemployment of up to 33 percent in some eastern cities, and bank collapses nationwide.[25] Whigs naturally blamed the incumbent for causing the country's troubles, labeling him "Martin Van Ruin."[26] Harrison lacked a detailed economic plan to fix things, but his image as a dignified former senior military officer by itself seemed reassuring enough that he might get into office just on that.

Whigs captured the public imagination with flashbacks to Harrison's supposed battlefield heroics at places like Tippecanoe River, marketing their candidate and his running mate, former Democrat John Tyler, like never before. The catchy campaign slogan "Tippecanoe and Tyler, Too!" was heard everywhere, supplemented by boisterous songs and frequent public presentations by the party faithful. When a Democratic newspaper suggested the aging Harrison should give up on his quest for the presidency and instead "sit the remainder of his days in his log cabin" with a pension and "a barrel of hard cider," his supporters smelled an opportunity, much as the revolutionary generation had accepted with pride the British taunt of "yankee." From that point on, imagery of log cabins and cider barrels dominated the campaign. A newspaper called *Log Cabin* soon led all Whig publications in circulation.[27] It kept emotions ahead of rational debate in voters' minds and highlighted how refreshing the supposed man of the people (Harrison) would be after four years of the man in the mansion (Van Buren).[28]

Eighty percent of eligible voters, a new record, went to the polls in November 1840, and the people booted Van Buren. By a solid lead in the popular vote and a resounding electoral vote, they replaced him with Harrison despite knowing little about what he stood for. Harrison occupied the presidency for less time than any other chief executive, a mere thirty-one days. He was one of the most presidential-looking men to win the office, which had been enough to get him into it.

IN 1912, REPUBLICAN William Howard Taft's reelection bid won him only two states and eight electoral votes, the worst defeat to that point of a sitting chief executive. He was removed almost entirely by the same man who'd put him there: Theodore Roosevelt.

The irony is that Taft hadn't sought the presidency much to begin with. He had served Roosevelt as war secretary but preferred the judicial realm to the political one, wanting, above all, a seat on the nation's highest bench. Taft's status-conscious wife, Nellie, had loftier ambitions for him, and she took them up with the man who mattered most, President Roosevelt. "It was true that once [Roosevelt] decided to appoint Mr. Taft to the Supreme Court," said long-serving White House usher Ike Hoover. "Mr. Taft himself approved, and it was only through the pleadings of Mrs. Taft that he was not appointed. I can remember the exact hour of the famous visit when Mrs. Taft, in the face of the opposition of both the President and her husband, the secretary of war, carried her point. From that time on the President seemed to feel that Mr. Taft should be his successor."[29] Taft, accepting the Republican nomination in 1908, sounded likely to follow through on the president's progressive agenda when he declared, "The chief function of the next administration is to complete and perfect the machinery" that Roosevelt had begun.[30]

Taft won that general election and started as president in March 1909, freeing Roosevelt to hunt and travel in Africa, true to his adventurous inclination, for a year. But their close relationship had already started to unravel. The new president failed to keep most of his predecessor's cabinet, prompting Roosevelt to tell a friend that his successor was "weak."[31] Roosevelt also expected that Taft would accept his recommendations for positions. He didn't.[32]

Even the outgoing First Family got in on the act. On the night before the inauguration, Roosevelt's daughter Alice sought to bring bad luck to the Tafts, digging a hole in the South Lawn of the White House to bury what she called a "bad little idol."[33]

Voodoo influence or not, Taft and Roosevelt drifted still further apart. The new president replaced his predecessor's activist, progressive approach with a strict constructionist view of presidential powers, backing away from any role in the legislation-crafting process. The one area his administration showed real energy in, antitrust cases, only exacerbated his conflict with Roosevelt. Taft's attorney general filed a case against U.S. Steel, a trust that Roosevelt himself had consented to when he had been in charge.[34]

Having served almost eight years as president and vowing not to run for another term, Roosevelt nonetheless entered the race in 1912 to do whatever it took to take down his former protégé. This was personal, and it would get ugly.[35] Taft first tried to blow it off. Then he tried to match Roosevelt barb for barb. The campaign descended into insult swapping between the former friends, especially after Taft won the Republican nomination and Roosevelt insisted on continuing his crusade on a new Progressive Party ticket. Publicly calling his successor names like "guinea-pig brain," Roosevelt caused his own wife to hold her nose during the campaign, "gloomy" at his decision to run and calling the whole situation "hateful."[36] Taft countered by labeling Roosevelt an "egotist" and "demagogue," eventually claiming that electing the former president "would hurry us into a condition which would find no parallel except in the French Revolution."[37]

Roosevelt through the summer failed to win over the bulk of the Republican establishment, which generally stuck with their nominee. It looked like Taft was gaining ground as autumn progressed. Then, on October 14, Roosevelt took an assailant's bullet in the chest before heading to a planned campaign event. The buff and tough ex-president went ahead anyway, telling frantic advisors, "This is my big chance, and I am going to make that speech if I die doing it." The former president revealed to the crowd that he'd been shot—proclaiming, "It takes more than that to kill a bull moose!"—and spoke for ninety minutes before finally agreeing to go to a hospital.[38] Roosevelt regained his lost support and finished the campaign strong as, well, a bull moose.

Woodrow Wilson exploited the divided Republicans to triumph in the electoral college despite winning less than 42 percent of the popular vote. Roosevelt finished second, the only time in US history a third-party candidate has beaten a major-party nominee. Roosevelt's supporters dismissed Republicans' claims that the former president had undermined Taft and, thus, his own party as "the veriest twaddle" and "bunk and peanuts."[39] Yet it was Roosevelt's personal vendetta against Taft for not following his policies closely enough that took down this president.

Chapter Nine

Presidents, Processes,

and the People

The government we mean to erect
is intended to last for ages.[1]
—JAMES MADISON

O UR GREAT NATIONAL experiment has endured precisely because
we can remove presidents as needed, whether by elections or
via more intrusive means.

One huge consequence of our boisterous, bruising, and sometimes bumbling system is that we haven't needed a revolution to
initiate a whole new system of government or a murder to displace
an officeholder each time we've had a bad experience with a leader.
Political parties have booted subpar presidents even before voters
have had the chance to reject them in the voting booth. Opponents
and sometimes even supposed allies have undermined them, effectively removing them in place by restricting their powers. Some have
been preemptively discarded, taken out before reaching office. Death
has played its part a few times. A declaration of disability or an impeachment and removal have stood ready.

But speeding up a leader's death, as four presidential assassins have
done, should never become acceptable in a constitutional republic

in which other means exist. Coup attempts and murder plots have emerged often in absolute monarchies because such governments lack legal means for subjects to get rid of horrific rulers. The United States of America doesn't have that system. Despite the stunning geographical, cultural, and political diversity across the United States, the assassins of Lincoln, Garfield, McKinley, and Kennedy won few fans, even among political opponents of the assassinated president. Instead, their acts repulsed overwhelming majorities.

Getting rid a chief executive at the point of a gun is a theft of the rights of the voters or their elected representatives. The choice to override all the other methods for removing presidents through violence also insults the toils and sacrifices of all Americans who have built, maintained, and defended that system through service in the military, work as a government employee, or participation in our democratic institutions. It is uncivil and alien to our political culture, and we remain best off not going there again.

THIS BOOK HAS looked at *how* America has chosen to get rid of its leaders, but behind the history of presidential defenestration is the more subtle question of *when* to eject a chief executive. The answer depends on whether the candidate for removal is primarily unpopular, unable, or unfit.

A PRESIDENT, BY THE founders' original design, must go before the voters and win another popularity contest to keep the office. The delegates in Philadelphia debated having a presidency without limit, or one with a term of seven years or longer, but both ideas lost out.

By choosing a four-year term, the delegates in Philadelphia ensured that any wildly *unpopular* president who loses the support of the vast majority of Americans would not stay in office long. The next election would boot that chief executive out and give someone else a shot at it. There should be a low bar for getting rid of unpopular presidents via an election. Americans, if antagonized by their elected leaders, must not succumb to apathy. Get out and vote.

But a high bar should stand in the way of removing a merely unpopular president by nonelectoral means. Using impeachment, for example, against a president primarily because his policies have proven unpopular was the mistake of Radical Republicans when they tried to remove Andrew Johnson. Legislative action, including many overrides of presidential vetoes, had effectively boxed Johnson in. He found himself unable to make into policy the most horrible things he sought to enact; Congress remained able to do what it thought best. All of that happened before the impeachment vote and Senate trial. The fact that the House managers could not obtain a guilty verdict by two-thirds of the Senate despite a two-thirds Republican majority shows that the system actually worked in this case.

Many observers argue that personal animus rather than constitutional concerns drove the Clinton impeachment. That example shows us the danger of trying to impeach a chief executive who retains high popularity despite having lied under oath and obstructed justice. If a significant percentage of the public remains strongly behind a president despite behavior that while repugnant, doesn't rise to the level of damaging the constitutional order itself, then undermining that president politically or just waiting for the next election to make a better case to the voters seem better strategies than impeachment. Undermining an unpopular president through means short of impeachment generally works; attempting prematurely to impeach a generally popular president risks damaging the whole political process.

If nothing else, relying on voters to remove unpopular incumbents gives those presidents' ultimate removals greater stamps of legitimacy. Former FBI director Jim Comey expressed a version of this when he said during an ABC News interview in April 2018 that impeaching and removing Donald Trump "would let the American people off the hook and have something happen indirectly that I believe they're duty bound to do directly."[2]

WHEN TO REMOVE a president who seems *unable* to do the job depends on the perceived degree of the disability. The Twenty-fifth Amendment helped immensely by providing the country with a much more useful tool than it had before 1967 for removing a disabled president.

Let's say the president falls into a coma, or loses his freedom when an enemy captures him. Even in peaceful times, the commander in chief would thereby lose the ability to exercise the powers and duties of the office. No rational person, under either scenario, can justify keeping the presidency as it is. Just as simple should be cases that obviously fail to justify a presidential disability. A pattern of usually long naps, a tendency to brag or bloviate, or abnormally frequent golf games that hamper efficient decision making all present cause for concern, but cannot plausibly justify removing the powers and duties of the presidency, even temporarily, against an occupant's will.

Between those extremes lie scenarios where the declaration of disability via section 4 might seem prudent but nevertheless would remain unlikely politically, either because the necessary medical information is unclear or because any sane vice president will seek to avoid looking like a power-grabbing usurper. Recall that Gerald Ford in 1974 didn't explore supplanting the commander in chief during the denouement of Richard Nixon's Watergate crisis, despite Ford's almost certain awareness of the president's severe depression and, perhaps, his increased drinking. George H. W. Bush in 1981 didn't want to appear eager for power while rushing to consult with top officials after the assassination attempt against Ronald Reagan. Even risky medical procedures are unlikely to spur a transfer of power against the president's wishes. No reasonable vice president or cabinet majority, for example, would today seek to displace the chief executive in a case like Grover Cleveland's oral surgery, short of clear evidence of true debilitation.

What if the president goes missing, and the Secret Service informs the vice president that communications have been lost? It seems unlikely that the vice president would instantly seek to invoke the Twenty-fifth Amendment instead of waiting a few more minutes or hours, maybe even days, for an update from authorities. Or perhaps if instead of seizing the commander in chief, foreign enemies or domestic terrorists were to kidnap the president's spouse or children. It's unfair and unreasonable to expect unimpaired presidential judgment at such a time. But if the president looks in the eyes of his vice president and each cabinet member and says, "I'm okay, I've got this," would we expect the vice president and majority of the cabinet to act on their concerns?

When in 1919–1920 should Woodrow Wilson have been declared disabled? Hindsight makes it clear he was unable to do his job. But, even now, it's easy to imagine a president staying in the residence for days or weeks, interacting with only two or three people while excluding all others, without unanimous agreement among those left out that the president must be replaced. That's especially true if the president's spouse and a respected physician both acknowledge the oddity but assert that all remains fine, just as Edith Wilson and Dr. Grayson did a century ago. It appears a vice president would remain less likely to grab power than to hold back and seek more information.

At a certain point, hope and faith kick in, as the legislators debating the Twenty-fifth Amendment foresaw some forty years ago. The House Speaker said then, "We cannot legislate for every human consideration that might occur in the future. All we can do is the best that we can under the circumstances."

TRICKIEST OF ALL is when to remove an *unfit* president.

Although impeachment and removal, the constitutional remedy for a truly unacceptable chief executive, has some inherent flexibility, those responsible for it should remain wary of stretching its scope. Gerald Ford in 1970 famously said, "An impeachable offense is whatever a majority of the House of Representatives considers it to be at a given moment in history."[3] While that carries a core truth—only the Senate, in deciding whether to convict, is in a position to judge if the House brought charges correctly—caution remains in order.

"Ford is right in putting his finger on the fact that this is ultimately a political process, and the founders had understood it to be a political process," constitutional expert Keith Whittington says. "On the other hand, the Constitution does try to create a standard, even if it's a very flexible and loosely defined one, for thinking about high crimes and misdemeanors. If we say that this is just an empty vessel to use however we want, we're going down the wrong path, encouraging the misuse of the impeachment power."[4] Law professor Brian Kalt agrees. "We have to think carefully about what a majority of the House would say it is. It's not like passing a resolution in support of National Burrito Week."[5]

But an incumbent leader who remains otherwise able and perhaps even still-popular but abuses the office by explicitly aiding an enemy, taking money for specific presidential acts, or clearly undermining the constitutional order deserves to be kicked out quickly. Ideally, political pressure from within the president's own party will spur a resignation, as it ultimately did with Richard Nixon. Without that, it gets difficult—as kicking a president out without the direct input of the people should be.

Just because the two successful impeachments, of Andrew Johnson and Bill Clinton, haven't resulted in conviction and removal (and several other attempts have fallen short of even the first step of impeachment itself) doesn't mean the idea should be taken off the table unless three hundred million people march into Washington with torches, pitchforks, and worse. "There are occasions where merely the impeachment itself is important to give a particularly strong form of censure," says Whittington. "It has become easy to frame an impeachment that doesn't result in removal as being a mistake—to say that the House never should have gone forward. To the extent we do that, we have lost some sense about the flexibility of the impeachment power and what it can accomplish."[6]

Personal dislike and policy differences alone are no grounds for impeachment. Yet, if reasonable evidence of treason, bribery, or high crimes and misdemeanors comes to light, it's not only acceptable but necessary for Congress to investigate. Unfortunately, no timely, efficient mechanism exists for it to do so. "When John Conyers was chairman of the Judiciary Committee," says John Dean, "he told me, 'John, the committee has zero capacity to investigate.' Take the Nixon impeachment. Before the special prosecutor gave the committee his road map, the committee was floundering." Dean has suggested a permanent select committee on impeachment to handle executive and judicial cases alike. Such an institution within the legislative branch would build up the expertise of staff and even members on impeachment investigation procedures to help avoid reinventing the wheel every few years when a potential presidential (and, more often, judicial) impeachment possibility arises. "It would make congressional oversight more meaningful," Dean asserts.[7]

Even absent structural reform, lawmakers should not fear the impeachment and removal process so much that they preemptively abjure the option, and, through that refusal, remove one of the essential constitutional checks on presidential power. If nothing else, a reasonable chance of impeachment can itself help prevent worse behavior, as the case of Richard Nixon revealed. "Every president, every day of his presidency," Kalt points out, "has been constrained by the possibility of impeachment."[8]

Also, such discussions almost exclusively neglect the third branch of government, because the judiciary often sits out of "political questions" between the competing authorities of the executive and legislative branches. But it need not be so, even on impeachment. "A happier approach is to submit a controversy between Congress and the President, arising out of conflicting claims to power, to the courts, as Andrew Johnson wished to do," argued legal historian Raoul Berger. "There are no legal obstacles to submission of such controversies to the courts. Conflicting boundary claims are preeminently suited to judicial arbitrament, the least disruptive of solutions."[9]

THE MOST DIFFICULT questions about when to get rid of a president come when unusual behavior raises concerns but falls short of indisputable unpopularity, inability, and lack of fitness, thus immobilizing regular institutions of removal, such that the people don't trust any method to work.

What do you do, for example, with a chief executive who manifests an indifference toward, or inability to discern, the difference between truth and untruth—a leader who makes policy solely by gut feeling and belief instead of any actual facts on the ground? That sounds neither like a high crime or misdemeanor nor like the kind of disability the framers of the Constitution and the authors of the Twenty-fifth Amendment, respectively, had in mind. And a significant percentage of the public might very well agree enough with the underlying instinct of the president to go along and jettison the truth. Clearly four years of this could damage a country's domestic tranquility and international alliances, perhaps even its governing norms.

Just such a "chaos candidate" has highlighted that danger. When Donald Trump entered the presidential race in June 2015—as a Republican, surprisingly, given his previous views and political donations—most observers viewed his candidacy more as a publicity stunt than as a serious bid. Just two months later, in the *Atlantic*, Jon Lovett pretended to look back at a Trump presidency, considered a virtual impossibility at that time. "Obviously, everyone knew, he could never actually get anywhere once the votes were cast," Lovett wrote, reflecting conventional wisdom. "American democracy was too robust to let that happen. He was too dangerous to win, and to win would be too dangerous. It couldn't happen because it couldn't happen. And then, just like that, it did."

The shock value of this "prediction" in August 2015 was balanced by a purported look back at how the system, before Trump's inauguration, would have jumped into high gear to place obstacles in the way of his potential violations of long-standing norms about the presidency. With overwhelming bipartisan support, in Lovett's alternative timeline, Congress passed, and then the outgoing president signed, a bill that "stripped away the presidential prerogatives that had accrued over the previous century." The chief justice, so the story went, had suggested publicly that the judiciary would uphold such a law. Lovett correctly foresaw the victory of this change agent, but the system's reaction played out quite differently than he had predicted. Instead of a coordinated effort to protect government institutions from a wrecking-ball president, legislators in the real world have largely shrugged, appearing to value the perceived benefits of acquiescence over constitutional checks and balances.

REMOVING PRESIDENTS HAS WORKED as a safety valve because our basic political structure and norms have been so strong. Truly tough times come when *any one president* seems to matter more than the role the *presidency as an institution* plays within the wider constitutional order; when the person matters more than the policy or even the party. With some speed bumps along the way, the country has generally done well on this score. Even the widely popular Franklin Roosevelt, for example, saw significant pushback from Congress and the public when he tried to pack the courts.

The proper course of action may require extraordinary courage to do what's in the best interests of the country, at the expense of perceived partisan gain. But even if the House of Representatives (for example, in the case of impeachment) proves unwilling to check the president, the people can replace the legislators through congressional elections—held twice as often as those for the presidency—and demand action. And when the system itself does not provide suitable legal means to cover the contingency, we can change the core law of the land by amending it. All twenty-seven constitutional amendments so far have started on Capitol Hill, but if Congress is part of the problem, federalism kicks in: the Constitution allows state legislatures to begin the amendment process by calling a constitutional convention.

Either way, those who argue that we must stick to what the Constitution says conveniently forget that fundamental parts of it have been amended, even repealed. If the founders' ideas are to be held sacred, then we must go back to the things that they clearly got wrong, like letting only white men vote and counting an enslaved African American as three-fifths of a person for representation purposes. Why should we treat the delegates' eccentric methods, created in a rush, as sacrosanct? Their solutions balanced the idiosyncratic circumstances of the time, primarily (but not exclusively) between small states and large states, between slaveholders and freemen, between believers in and skeptics of direct democracy, and between advocates and critics of strong central government. Their original solutions are neither flawless nor eternal. So if the paths to get rid of a president fail to meet the needs of the nation, we can mobilize our representatives to revise or add to them.

The founders, in particular, could not have predicted the role and impact of global technology and social media, and how those factors inhibit some of our ways of removing leaders. One reaction to new developments that raise difficult questions about our institutions is to throw our hands up and say that our 250-year-old methods can no longer address a troubled presidency. A better option is to amend the Constitution to adapt to modern circumstances. The system has a mechanism for change built into it. We must have the courage to use it to ensure that, as Abraham Lincoln said, "government of the people, by the people, for the people, shall not perish from the earth." Getting rid of a president is consistent with that.

Acknowledgments

This book proved easier to deliver than my first, *The President's Book of Secrets*, in a few ways; most of those are due to my great fortune to work again with much of the same team. Heartfelt thanks to my steadfast agent, Andrew Wylie; my champion and hands-on editor, Clive Priddle; and the rest of the extended PublicAffairs family, including Jamie Leifer, Lindsay Fradkoff, Kristina Fazzalaro, Melissa Raymond, Athena Bryan, and Miguel Cervantes. The brilliant cover, internal design, copyediting, and index came from a collection of real pros at this: Pete Garceau, Christine Marra, Jane Raese, Gray Cutler, Jeff Georgeson, and Donna Riggs.

Researching and retelling nearly 250 years of American political history challenged me like never before. Fortunately, support came from many quarters. My sincere gratitude goes to the many politicians, pundits, and expert scholars who agreed to share information and insights. Some of you are cited, but many more of you are not. Your absence from the endnotes reflects no lack of deep appreciation for your ideas and your time. I also give a shout-out to the employees at the presidential libraries and other archives that provided material appearing here or informing my judgments. I didn't get to see all of you face to face this time, but you all helped.

I tip my hat to the industrious and inspiring biographers of America's presidents, almost presidents, and other leading political figures. I enjoyed the opportunity to delve into primary sources—papers and autobiographies of participants in the stories told in these pages, related memoirs and oral histories, and interviews—but many authors cited in the footnotes dove deeply to bring alive the stories of their subjects. A diverse range of others provided food for thought, in conversations (and, often, also in their own writings): Paul Brandus, Bruce Carlson, Mark Cheathem, Susan Hennessey, Donald

Holloway, Brian Kalt, Ethan Scheiner, Julie Silverbrook, Shirley Anne Warshaw, Keith Whittington, and Benjamin Wittes. None of you deserve blame for my words; all of you bear some responsibility for influencing (or corrupting, your choice) the ideas behind them.

I researched and wrote this book during a particularly trying couple of years. So my family, friends, and mentors deserve special recognition. To Renee and Griffin: You contributed in every way to this book—and sacrificed for it, too. I'll never forget your consistent love and support. To Dianne: You offered not only your blunt feedback on various turns of phrase but also motivation, even while bravely facing your own struggles. I'll never forget your lessons on learning and on life. To Carter: You motivated me to press on and also conducted in-the-trenches research at presidential libraries to help. I'll never forget your persistence and positivity. To Cheryl: You inspired me with your patience and dignity. I'll never forget your grace under pressure, and I'll never match it—but you compel me to keep trying. To Maria: You supported me at every step along the way here. I'll never forget your kindness and your keen eye. To John: You shared insights and encouragement, from the genesis of this project to its conclusion. I'll never forget your intensity, your honest feedback, and most of all your ability to instantly set substance aside to simply be a caring human being when I needed it most. To Ann, Ashu, Ben, Bruce, Dave, Dean, Ethan, John, Mary, Meredith, Mike, Nancy, Paige, and Tim: Your friendship sustained me even as life kept us further apart than seemed fair. Finally, to Joe White, Fred Walk, John Wenum, Bob Leh, Mike Weis, Ole Holsti, Joe Grieco, and Peter Feaver: You have exceeded the expectations of what teachers could do and should be, and I owe more to you than I can repay.

Notes

Introduction. President-Eject

1. James G. Blaine, *Twenty Years of Congress: From Lincoln to Garfield*, vol. 2 (Norwich, CT: Henry Hill, 1886), 658.
2. Letter from Silas Deane to Benjamin Franklin (February 1, 1782), National Archives Founders Online, available at http://founders.archives .gov/documents/Franklin/01-36-02-0356.
3. Max Farrand, ed., *The Records of the Federal Convention of 1787*, vol. 1 (New Haven: Yale University Press, 1911), 65 (June 1).
4. Ibid., 66 (June 1).
5. Ibid., 83 (June 2).
6. Ibid., 103 (June 4).
7. Ibid., 109 (June 4).
8. Ibid., 101 (June 4).
9. Max Farrand, ed., *The Records of the Federal Convention of 1787*, vol. 2 (New Haven: Yale University Press, 1911), 29 (July 17).
10. Ibid., 33 (July 17).
11. Ibid., 55 (July 19).
12. Ibid., 33–36 (July 17).

Chapter One. Rejected by the Party

1. Gerald R. Ford, *A Time to Heal: The Autobiography of Gerald R. Ford* (New York: Harper & Row, 1979), 333.
2. Oliver Perry Chitwood, *John Tyler: Champion of the Old South* (Newtown, CT: American Political Biography Press, 1939), 117.
3. Marquis James, *The Life of Andrew Jackson: Complete in One Volume* (New York: Bobbs-Merrill, 1938), 620–21.
4. Oliver Perry Chitwood, *John Tyler: Champion of the Old South* (Newtown, CT: American Political Biography Press, 1939), 120.

5. Peter R. Levin, *Seven by Chance: The Accidental Presidents* (New York: Farrar, Straus, 1948), 19–20.

6. Oliver Perry Chitwood, *John Tyler: Champion of the Old South* (Newtown, CT: American Political Biography Press, 1939), 167–68.

7. Peter R. Levin, *Seven by Chance: The Accidental Presidents* (New York: Farrar, Straus, 1948), 26.

8. Oliver Perry Chitwood, *John Tyler: Champion of the Old South* (Newtown, CT: American Political Biography Press, 1939), 219.

9. Ibid., 202.

10. Peter R. Levin, *Seven by Chance: The Accidental Presidents* (New York: Farrar, Straus, 1948), 28–29.

11. Philip Abbott, *Accidental Presidents: Death, Assassination, Resignation, and Democratic Succession* (New York: Palgrave Macmillan, 2008), 27.

12. Edward P. Crapol, *John Tyler: The Accidental President* (Chapel Hill, NC: University of North Carolina Press, 2006), 10–13.

13. Peter R. Levin, *Seven by Chance: The Accidental Presidents* (New York: Farrar, Straus, 1948), 30.

14. Oliver Perry Chitwood, *John Tyler: Champion of the Old South* (Newtown, CT: American Political Biography Press, 1939), 211.

15. Michael F. Holt, *The Rise and Fall of the American Whig Party: Jacksonian Politics and the Onset of the Civil War* (New York: Oxford University Press, 1999), 128.

16. Oliver Perry Chitwood, *John Tyler: Champion of the Old South* (Newtown, CT: American Political Biography Press, 1939), 215.

17. Thomas Hart Benton, *Thirty Years' View*, vol. 2 (New York: D. Appleton, 1856), 318–28.

18. Ibid., 357.

19. Oliver Perry Chitwood, *John Tyler: Champion of the Old South* (Newtown, CT: American Political Biography Press, 1939), 273–77.

20. Aaron Scott Crawford, "'I am President:' John Tyler, Presidential Succession, the Crisis of Legitimacy, and the Defense of Presidential Power," in Jeffrey A. Engel and Thomas J. Knock, eds., *When Life Strikes the President: Scandal, Death, and Illness in the White House* (New York: Oxford University Press, 2017), 48.

21. Thomas Hart Benton, *Thirty Years' View*, vol. 2 (New York: D. Appleton, 1856), 359.

22. Michael F. Holt, *The Rise and Fall of the American Whig Party: Jacksonian Politics and the Onset of the Civil War* (New York: Oxford University Press, 1999), 149–50.

23. Thomas Hart Benton, *Thirty Years' View*, vol. 2 (New York: D. Appleton, 1856), 362.

24. Ibid., 594.

25. Jeffrey A. Engel and Thomas J. Knock, eds., *When Life Strikes the President: Scandal, Death, and Illness in the White House* (New York: Oxford University Press, 2017), 56.

26. Robert W. Merry, *A Country of Vast Designs: James K. Polk, the Mexican War, and the Conquest of the American Continent* (New York: Simon & Schuster, 2009), 103–4. A researcher who has examined Polk's presidential diary and all his correspondence found no wavering on his pledge to serve only one term. See Tom Chaffin, *Met His Every Goal? James K. Polk and the Legends of Manifest Destiny* (Knoxville, TN: University of Texas Press, 2014), 17.

27. K. Jack Bauer, *Zachary Taylor: Solider, Planter, Statesman of the Old Southwest* (Baton Rouge: Louisiana State University Press, 1985), 217.

28. Peter R. Levin, *Seven by Chance: The Accidental Presidents* (New York: Farrar, Straus, 1948), 68–75.

29. Robert J. Rayback, *Millard Fillmore: Biography of a President* (Buffalo, NY: Henry Steward, 1959), 199.

30. Michael J. Gerhardt, *The Forgotten Presidents: Their Untold Constitutional Legacy* (New York: Oxford University Press, 2013), 89.

31. Meade Minnigerode, *Presidential Years, 1787–1860* (New York, G. P. Putnam's Sons, 1928), 279.

32. Michael F. Holt, *The Rise and Fall of the American Whig Party: Jacksonian Politics and the Onset of the Civil War* (New York: Oxford University Press, 1999), 543, 551.

33. Peter R. Levin, *Seven by Chance: The Accidental Presidents* (New York: Farrar, Straus, 1948), 79.

34. Michael F. Holt, *The Rise and Fall of the American Whig Party: Jacksonian Politics and the Onset of the Civil War* (New York: Oxford University Press, 1999), 680–81.

35. Michael J. Gerhardt, *The Forgotten Presidents: Their Untold Constitutional Legacy* (New York: Oxford University Press, 2013), 93.

36. Michael F. Holt, *The Rise and Fall of the American Whig Party: Jacksonian Politics and the Onset of the Civil War* (New York: Oxford University Press, 1999), 680–82.

37. Ibid., 711–22.

38. Peter R. Levin, *Seven by Chance: The Accidental Presidents* (New York: Farrar, Straus, 1948), 81.

39. Peter A. Wallner, *Franklin Pierce: New Hampshire's Favorite Son* (Concord, NH: Plaidswede, 2004), 10–15; Roy Franklin Nichols, *Franklin Pierce: Young Hickory of the Granite Hills*, rev. ed. (Philadelphia: University of Pennsylvania Press, 1969), 9.

40. Michael F. Holt, "Personal Loss and Franklin Pierce's Presidency," in Jeffrey A. Engel and Thomas J. Knock, eds., *When Life Strikes the President: Scandal, Death, and Illness in the White House* (New York: Oxford University Press, 2017), 72.

41. Nathaniel Hawthorne, *The Life of Franklin Pierce* (Boston: Ticknor, Reed and Fields, 1852).

42. Roy Franklin Nichols, *Franklin Pierce: Young Hickory of the Granite Hills*, rev. ed. (Philadelphia: University of Pennsylvania Press, 1969), 224.

43. Brady Carlson, *Dead Presidents: An American Adventure into the Strange Deaths and Surprising Afterlives of Our Nation's Leaders* (New York: W. W. Norton, 2016), 213.

44. Roy Franklin Nichols, *Franklin Pierce: Young Hickory of the Granite Hills*, rev. ed. (Philadelphia: University of Pennsylvania Press, 1969), 225, 226.

45. Michael J. Gerhardt, *The Forgotten Presidents: Their Untold Constitutional Legacy* (New York: Oxford University Press, 2013), 100; Robert W. Johannsen, *Stephen A. Douglas* (Chicago: University of Illinois Press, 1997), 510, 533.

46. Meade Minnigerode, *Presidential Years, 1787–1860* (New York: G. P. Putnam's Sons, 1928), 312.

47. Robert W. Johanssen, *Stephen A. Douglas* (Chicago: University of Illinois Press, 1973), 507.

48. Ibid., 508–9.

49. Ibid., 518.

50. Philip S. Klein, *President James Buchanan: A Biography* (Newtown, CT: American Political Biography Press, 1962), 259.

51. David Holzel, "Five Amazing Facts About Franklin Pierce (in honor of his 203rd birthday)," *Mental Floss*, November 19, 2007, available at http://mentalfloss.com/article/17407/five-amazing-facts-about-franklin-pierce-honor-his-203rd-birthday.

52. Roy Franklin Nichols, *Franklin Pierce: Young Hickory of the Granite Hills*, rev. ed. (Philadelphia: University of Pennsylvania Press, 1969), 532.

53. Philip. S. Klein, *President James Buchanan: A Biography* (Newtown, CT: American Political Biography Press, 1962), 192–93.

54. Robert W. Merry, *A Country of Vast Designs: James K. Polk, the Mexican War, and the Conquest of the American Continent* (New York: Simon & Schuster, 2009), 190–92, 256–57; Philip S. Klein, *President James Buchanan: A Biography* (Newtown, CT: American Political Biography Press, 1962), 192.

55. Robert W. Merry, *A Country of Vast Designs: James K. Polk, the Mexican War, and the Conquest of the American Continent* (New York: Simon & Schuster, 2009), 135.

56. Philip S. Klein, *President James Buchanan: A Biography* (Newtown, CT: American Political Biography Press, 1962), 205.

57. Robert W. Johanssen, *Stephen A. Douglas* (Chicago: University of Illinois Press, 1973), 365.

58. Meade Minnigerode, *Presidential Years, 1787–1860* (New York: G. P. Putnam's Sons, 1928), 334.

59. Philip S. Klein, *President James Buchanan: A Biography* (Newtown, CT: American Political Biography Press, 1962), 272.

60. Ibid., 279.

61. Ibid., 331–32.

62. See David S. Reynolds, *John Brown, Abolitionist: The Man Who Killed Slavery, Sparked the Civil War, and Seeded Civil Rights* (New York: Alfred A. Knopf, 2005).

63. Philip S. Klein, *President James Buchanan: A Biography* (Newtown, CT: American Political Biography Press, 1962), 335–37.

64. Meade Minnigerode, *Presidential Years, 1787–1860* (New York: G. P. Putnam's Sons, 1928), 348–49.

65. Philip S. Klein, *President James Buchanan: A Biography* (Newtown, CT: American Political Biography Press, 1962), 340–41.

66. Meade Minnigerode, *Presidential Years, 1787–1860* (New York: G. P. Putnam's Sons, 1928), 364.

67. Robert W. Johanssen, *Stephen A. Douglas* (Chicago: University of Illinois Press, 1973), 811.

68. J. G. Randall and David Donald, *The Civil War and Reconstruction*, 2nd ed. (Lexington, MA: D. C. Heath, 1969), 473–74.

69. Michael Burlingame, *Abraham Lincoln: A Life*, vol. 2 (Baltimore, MD: Johns Hopkins University Press, 2008), 645.

70. J. G. Randall and David Donald, *The Civil War and Reconstruction*, 2nd ed. (Lexington, MA: D. C. Heath, 1969), 473–74.

71. David M. Jordan, *Roscoe Conkling of New York: Voice in the Senate* (Ithaca: Cornell University Press, 1971), 321.

72. William H. Crook, *Through Five Administrations* (New York: Harper & Brothers, 1910), 234–35.

73. Ronald C. White, *American Ulysses: A Life of Ulysses S. Grant* (New York: Random House, 2016), 617.

74. Peter R. Levin, *Seven by Chance: The Accidental Presidents* (New York: Farrar, Straus, 1948), 157–58.

75. George Frederick Howe, *Chester A. Arthur: A Quarter-Century of Machine Politics* (New York: Dodd, Mead, 1934), 109.

76. Peter R. Levin, *Seven by Chance: The Accidental Presidents* (New York: Farrar, Straus, 1948), 167.

77. Scott S. Greenberger, *The Unexpected President: The Life and Times of Chester A. Arthur* (New York: De Capo Press, 2017), 154–55.

78. George Frederick Howe, *Chester A. Arthur: A Quarter-Century of Machine Politics* (New York: Dodd, Mead, 1934), 151.

79. Ibid., 153.

80. Ibid., 154.

81. Ibid., 155.

82. Peter R. Levin, *Seven by Chance: The Accidental Presidents* (New York: Farrar, Straus, 1948), 168.

83. Michael J. Gerhardt, *The Forgotten Presidents: Their Untold Constitutional Legacy* (New York: Oxford University Press, 2013), 115–17.

84. George Frederick Howe, *Chester A. Arthur: A Quarter-Century of Machine Politics* (New York: Dodd, Mead, 1934), 213.

85. Justus D. Doenecke, *The Presidencies of James A. Garfield and Chester A. Arthur* (Lawrence, KS: University Press of Kansas, 1981), 102.

86. George Frederick Howe, *Chester A. Arthur: A Quarter-Century of Machine Politics* (New York: Dodd, Mead, 1934), 217.

87. Ibid., 254–55.

88. Scott S. Greenberger, *The Unexpected President: The Life and Times of Chester A. Arthur* (New York: De Capo Press, 2017), 199–200, 224.

89. David M. Jordan, *Roscoe Conkling of New York: Voice in the Senate* (Ithaca: Cornell University Press, 1971), 420.

90. Justus D. Doenecke, *The Presidencies of James A. Garfield and Chester A. Arthur* (Lawrence, KS: University Press of Kansas, 1981), 80.

91. William H. Crook, *Through Five Administrations* (New York: Harper & Brothers, 1910), 279–80.

92. George Frederick Howe, *Chester A. Arthur: A Quarter-Century of Machine Politics* (New York: Dodd, Mead, 1934), 262–64.

93. Scott S. Greenberger, *The Unexpected President: The Life and Times of Chester A. Arthur* (New York: De Capo Press, 2017), 227–28.

94. Justus D. Doenecke, *The Presidencies of James A. Garfield and Chester A. Arthur* (Lawrence, KS: University Press of Kansas, 1981), 182.

95. Doris Kearns Goodwin, *Lyndon Johnson and the American Dream* (New York: St. Martin's Griffin, 1976), 340.

96. Carl Solberg, *Hubert Humphrey: A Biography* (New York: W. W. Norton, 1984), 318.

97. Robert Dallek, *Flawed Giant: Lyndon Johnson and His Times, 1961–1973* (New York: Oxford University Press, 1998), 522.

98. Theodore H. White, *The Making of the President 1968* (New York: Atheneum House, 1969), 120.

99. Doris Kearns Goodwin, *Lyndon Johnson and the American Dream* (New York: St. Martin's Griffin, 1976), 340.

100. Robert Dallek, *Flawed Giant: Lyndon Johnson and His Times, 1961–1973* (New York: Oxford University Press, 1998), 515.

101. Lyndon Baines Johnson, *The Vantage Point: Perspectives of the Presidency, 1963–1969* (New York: Holt, Rinehart and Winston, 1971), 384.

102. Robert Dallek, *Flawed Giant: Lyndon Johnson and His Times, 1961–1973* (New York: Oxford University Press, 1998), 526.

103. Doris Kearns Goodwin, *Lyndon Johnson and the American Dream* (New York: St. Martin's Griffin, 1976), 343.

104. Lyndon Baines Johnson, *The Vantage Point: Perspectives of the Presidency, 1963–1969* (New York: Holt, Rinehart and Winston, 1971), 435.

105. Paul R. Henggeler, *In His Steps: Lyndon Johnson and the Kennedy Mystique* (Chicago, Ivan R. Dee, 1991), 243.

106. Theodore H. White, *The Making of the President 1968* (New York: Atheneum House, 1969), 132.

107. Lyndon Baines Johnson, *The Vantage Point: Perspectives of the Presidency, 1963–1969* (New York: Holt, Rinehart and Winston, 1971), 425–26.

108. Ibid., 427–28.

109. Robert Dallek, *Flawed Giant: Lyndon Johnson and His Times, 1961–1973* (New York: Oxford University Press, 1998), 544–45.

110. Ibid., 524.

111. Ibid., 528.

112. Ibid., 570.

113. Ibid., 548.

114. Ibid., 570–71.

115. Ibid., 572.

116. Ibid., 573.

117. Clint Hill with Lisa McCubbin, *Five Presidents: My Extraordinary Journey with Eisenhower, Kennedy, Johnson, Nixon, and Ford* (New York: Gallery Books, 2016), 303–5.

118. Lyndon Baines Johnson, *The Vantage Point: Perspectives of the Presidency, 1963–1969* (New York: Holt, Rinehart and Winston, 1971), 549.

119. Hugh Sidey, *A Very Personal Presidency: Lyndon Johnson in the White House* (New York: Atheneum, 1968), 278.

Chapter Two.
Undermined by Opponents or Subordinates

1. Hans Trefousse, *Andrew Johnson: A Biography* (New York: W. W. Norton, 1989), 335.

2. William H. Crook, *Through Five Administrations* (New York: Harper & Brothers, 1910), 83.

3. Gene Smith, *High Crimes and Misdemeanors: The Impeachment and Trial of Andrew Johnson* (New York: William Morrow, 1977), 47, 53.

4. Ibid., 60–64.

5. Hans Trefousse, *Andrew Johnson: A Biography* (New York: W. W. Norton, 1989), 190–91.

6. Ibid., 245.

7. Ibid., 227.

8. Adam Badeau, *Grant in Peace: From Appomattox to Mount McGregor* (Hartford, CT: S. S. Scranton, 1887), 33.

9. Hans Trefousse, *Andrew Johnson: A Biography* (New York: W. W. Norton, 1989), 236.

10. Ibid., 217.

11. William H. Rehnquist, *Grand Inquests: The Historic Impeachments of Justice Samuel Chase and President Andrew Johnson* (New York: Quill, 1992), 203.

12. Adam Badeau, *Grant in Peace: From Appomattox to Mount McGregor* (Hartford, CT: S. S. Scranton, 1887), 32.

13. Edward McPherson, *The Political History of the United States of America During the Period of Reconstruction* (Washington, DC: Philp & Solomons, 1870), 147–50.

14. Eric Foner, *Reconstruction: America's Unfinished Revolution* (New York: Harper & Row, 1988), 243–50; David O. Stewart, *Impeached: The Trial of President Andrew Johnson and the Fight for Lincoln's Legacy* (New York: Simon & Schuster, 2009), 51.

15. Gene Smith, *High Crimes and Misdemeanors: The Impeachment and Trial of Andrew Johnson* (New York: William Morrow, 1977), 164; Hans Trefousse, *Andrew Johnson: A Biography* (New York: W. W. Norton, 1989), 253.

16. James G. Blaine, *Twenty Years of Congress: From Lincoln to Garfield*, vol. 2 (Norwich, CT: Henry Hill, 1886), 179.

17. J. G. Randall and David Donald, *The Civil War and Reconstruction*, 2nd ed. (Lexington, MA: D. C. Heath, 1969), 581–84.

18. David O. Stewart, *Impeached: The Trial of President Andrew Johnson and the Fight for Lincoln's Legacy* (New York: Simon & Schuster, 2009), 54.

19. Adam Badeau, *Grant in Peace: From Appomattox to Mount McGregor* (Hartford, CT: S. S. Scranton, 1887), 38–39.

20. Gene Smith, *High Crimes and Misdemeanors: The Impeachment and Trial of Andrew Johnson* (New York: William Morrow, 1977), 181.

21. Hans Trefousse, *Andrew Johnson: A Biography* (New York: W. W. Norton, 1989), 266.

22. David O. Stewart, *Impeached: The Trial of President Andrew Johnson and the Fight for Lincoln's Legacy* (New York: Simon & Schuster, 2009), 65.

23. Adam Badeau, *Grant in Peace: From Appomattox to Mount McGregor* (Hartford, CT: S. S. Scranton, 1887), 53–54.

24. David O. Stewart, *Impeached: The Trial of President Andrew Johnson and the Fight for Lincoln's Legacy* (New York: Simon & Schuster, 2009), 70.

25. Adam Badeau, *Grant in Peace: From Appomattox to Mount McGregor* (Hartford, CT: S. S. Scranton, 1887), 47.

26. Ibid., 86.

27. Hans Trefousse, *Andrew Johnson: A Biography* (New York: W. W. Norton, 1989), 280–81, 291.

28. Ibid., 273.

29. Adam Badeau, *Grant in Peace: From Appomattox to Mount McGregor* (Hartford, CT: S. S. Scranton, 1887), 86.

30. Ibid., 46.

31. Ron Chernow, *Grant* (New York: Penguin, 2017), 586–87.

32. Hans Trefousse, *Andrew Johnson: A Biography* (New York: W. W. Norton, 1989), 277.

33. Ibid., 304.

34. Ron Chernow, *Grant* (New York: Penguin, 2017), 590.

35. William H. Rehnquist, *Grand Inquests: The Historic Impeachments of Justice Samuel Chase and President Andrew Johnson* (New York: Quill, 1992), 213–15.

36. Hans Trefousse, *Andrew Johnson: A Biography* (New York: W. W. Norton, 1989), 315.

37. Adam Badeau, *Grant in Peace: From Appomattox to Mount McGregor* (Hartford, CT: S. S. Scranton, 1887), 137.

38. Hans Trefousse, *Andrew Johnson: A Biography* (New York: W. W. Norton, 1989), ch. 18.

39. Ibid., 324–25.

40. Ibid., 340–42.

41. William H. Crook, *Through Five Administrations* (New York: Harper & Brothers, 1910), 68.

42. Gene Smith, *High Crimes and Misdemeanors: The Impeachment and Trial of Andrew Johnson* (New York: William Morrow, 1977), 300.

43. Hans Trefousse, *Andrew Johnson: A Biography* (New York: W. W. Norton, 1989), 347.

44. Alexander Clarence Flick, *Samuel Jones Tilden: A Study in Political Sagacity* (New York: Dodd, Mead, 1939), 175–79.

45. Stephen F. Knott and Tony Williams, *Washington and Hamilton: The Alliance That Forged America* (Naperville, IL: Sourcebooks, 2015), 206–8.

46. Harlow Giles Unger, *The Last Founding Father: James Monroe and a Nation's Call to Greatness* (New York: Da Capo Press, 2009), 309–10.

47. Ibid., 311.

48. Ibid., 320.

49. Michael J. Gerhardt, *The Forgotten Presidents: Their Untold Constitutional Legacy* (New York: Oxford University Press, 2013), 58.

50. Thomas Hart Benton, *Thirty Years' View*, vol. 2 (New York: D. Appleton, 1856), 418.

51. Michael F. Holt, *The Rise and Fall of the American Whig Party: Jacksonian Politics and the Onset of the Civil War* (New York: Oxford University Press, 1999), 146–47.

52. Oliver Perry Chitwood, *John Tyler: Champion of the Old South* (Newtown, CT: American Political Biography Press, 1939), 300.

53. Thomas Hart Benton, *Thirty Years' View*, vol. 2 (New York: D. Appleton, 1856), 418.

54. Michael J. Gerhardt, *The Forgotten Presidents: Their Untold Constitutional Legacy* (New York: Oxford University Press, 2013), 57.

55. Oliver Perry Chitwood, *John Tyler: Champion of the Old South* (Newtown, CT: American Political Biography Press, 1939), 250.

56. Michael F. Holt, *The Rise and Fall of the American Whig Party: Jacksonian Politics and the Onset of the Civil War* (New York: Oxford University Press, 1999), 137.

57. Oliver Perry Chitwood, *John Tyler: Champion of the Old South* (Newtown, CT: American Political Biography Press, 1939), 318.

58. Philip H. Melanson, *The Secret Service: The Hidden History of an Enigmatic Agency* (New York: MJF Books, 2002), 135–36.

59. John Whitcomb and Claire Whitcomb, *Real Life at the White House: Two Hundred Years of Daily Life at the World's Most Famous Residence* (New York: Routledge, 2002), 84, 94.

60. "The First Congressional Override of a Presidential Veto," History, Art & Archives page of the United States House of Representatives website, available at http://history.house.gov/Historical-Highlights/1800-1850/The -first-congressional-override-of-a-presidential-veto/.

61. K. Jack Bauer, *Zachary Taylor: Solider, Planter, Statesman of the Old Southwest* (Baton Rouge, LA: Louisiana State University Press, 1985), 259.

62. Michael F. Holt, *The Rise and Fall of the American Whig Party: Jacksonian Politics and the Onset of the Civil War* (New York: Oxford University Press, 1999), 421.

63. Michael J. Gerhardt, *The Forgotten Presidents: Their Untold Constitutional Legacy* (New York: Oxford University Press, 2013), 74.

64. K. Jack Bauer, *Zachary Taylor: Solider, Planter, Statesman of the Old Southwest* (Baton Rouge, LA: Louisiana State University Press, 1985), 257.

65. Michael J. Gerhardt, *The Forgotten Presidents: Their Untold Constitutional Legacy* (New York: Oxford University Press, 2013), 76–77.

66. Michael Burlingame, *Abraham Lincoln: A Life*, vol. 2 (Baltimore, MD: Johns Hopkins University Press, 2008), 450–58, 459–61.

67. Ibid., 468–73.

68. "Order to General Scott," issued April 27 1861, in John G. Nicolay and John Hay, eds., *Abraham Lincoln: Complete Works, Comprising His Speeches, Letters, State Papers, and Miscellaneous Writings*, vol. 2 (New York: Century, 1894), 39.

69. Todd Brewster, *Lincoln's Gamble: The Tumultuous Six Months That Gave America the Emancipation Proclamation and Changed the Course of the Civil War* (New York: Scribner, 2014), 152–58.

70. Michael Burlingame, *Abraham Lincoln: A Life*, vol. 2 (Baltimore, MD: Johns Hopkins University Press, 2008), 152–53.

71. Robert Sobel, *Coolidge: An American Enigma* (Washington, DC: Regnery, 1998), 350–51.

72. Robert H. Ferrell, *Frank B. Kellogg and Henry L. Stimson* (New York: Cooper Square, 1963), 292; Lorenzo Meyer, *Mexico and the United States in the Oil Controversy, 1917–1942* (Austin, TX: University of Texas Press, 1972), 127–28.

73. "Reinforcing Marines Banned by the Senate," *New York Times*, June 17, 1932, 8.

74. Lars Schoultz, *Beneath the United States: A History of U.S. Policy toward Latin America* (Cambridge, MA: Harvard University Press, 1998), 270.

75. George B. Galloway, "Presidential Commissions," *Editorial research reports 1931*, vol. 1 (Washington, DC: CQ Press, 1931). Available at http://library.cqpress.com/cqresearcher/cqresrre1931052800.

76. Conrad Black, *Franklin Delano Roosevelt: Champion of Freedom* (New York: PublicAffairs, 2003), 352, 377–78.

77. William E. Leuchtenburg, "When Franklin Roosevelt Clashed with the Supreme Court—and Lost," *Smithsonian Magazine*, May 2005.

78. Conrad Black, *Franklin Delano Roosevelt: Champion of Freedom* (New York: PublicAffairs, 2003), 407–9

79. William E. Leuchtenburg, "When Franklin Roosevelt Clashed with the Supreme Court—and Lost," *Smithsonian Magazine*, May 2005.

80. Conrad Black, *Franklin Delano Roosevelt: Champion of Freedom* (New York: PublicAffairs, 2003), 412–18.

81. Ibid., 577–80.

82. James MacGregor Burns, *Roosevelt: The Soldier of Freedom, 1940–1945* (New York: History Book Club, 2006), 11–13.

83. Conrad Black, *Franklin Delano Roosevelt: Champion of Freedom* (New York: PublicAffairs, 2003), 605–7.

84. James MacGregor Burns, *Roosevelt: The Soldier of Freedom, 1940–1945* (New York: History Book Club, 2006), 45–46.

85. Ibid., 49.

86. Conrad Black, *Franklin Delano Roosevelt: Champion of Freedom* (New York: PublicAffairs, 2003), 623.

87. H. R. Haldeman, *The Haldeman Diaries: Inside the Nixon White House* (New York: G. P. Putnam's Sons, 1994), 62.

88. Ibid., 63.

89. John A. Farrell, *Richard Nixon: The Life* (New York: Doubleday, 2017), 358.

90. H. R. Haldeman, *The Haldeman Diaries: Inside the Nixon White House* (New York: G. P. Putnam's Sons, 1994), 63.

91. Ibid., passim.

92. Ibid., 330.

93. "Tapes Show Nixon Ordering Theft of Files," *New York Times*, November 22, 1996.

94. John Dean, interview by the author, May 2018.

95. Neil A. Lewis, "Nixon Tape Shows a Vendetta of '72," *New York Times*, May 18, 1993.

96. John A. Farrell, *Richard Nixon: The Life* (New York: Doubleday, 2017), 358–59.

97. John Dean, interview by the author, May 2018.

98. Robert Dallek, *Nixon and Kissinger: Partners in Power* (New York: HarperCollins, 2007), 520–23.

99. Henry Kissinger, *Crisis: The Anatomy of Two Major Foreign Policy Crises* (New York: Simon & Schuster, 2003), 343.

100. Alistair Horne, *Kissinger: 1973, the Crucial Year* (New York: Simon & Schuster, 2009), 302–3.

101. Walter Isaacson, *Kissinger: A Biography* (New York: Simon & Schuster, 1992), 532; Robert Dallek, *Nixon and Kissinger: Partners in Power* (New York: HarperCollins, 2007), 530–31.

102. Quoted in Tim Weiner, "That Time the Middle East Exploded—and Nixon Was Drunk," *Politico*, June 15, 2015, available at https://www.politico.com/magazine/story/2015/06/richard-nixon-watergate-drunk-yom-kippur-war-119021.

103. Barry Werth, *31 Days: Gerald Ford, the Nixon Pardon, and a Government in Crisis* (New York: Anchor Books, 2007), 17; but see Jonathan Aiken, *Nixon: A Life* (Washington, DC: Regnery, 1993), 520, and Stanley Kutler, "The Imaginings of James R. Schlesinger," *Huffington Post*, April 1, 2014, available at https://www.huffingtonpost.com/stanley-kutler/the-imaginings-of-james-r_b_5066130.html.

104. Garrett M. Graff, *Raven Rock: The Story of the U.S. Government's Secret Plan to Save Itself—While the Rest of Us Die* (New York: Simon & Schuster, 2017), xiv.

105. Jon Huntsman and Joseph Lieberman, "The Republican SCOTUS Blockade Is 'Not Acceptable,'" *Time*, March 25, 2016, available at http://time.com/4271942/supreme-court-compromise/.

106. Jess Bravin, "Former Government Lawyers on Supreme Court Nominee Garland," *Wall Street Journal*, May 5, 2016, available at https://blogs.wsj.com/washwire/2016/05/05/former-government-lawyers-on-supreme-court-nominee-garland-supremely-qualified/.

107. Debra Cassens Weiss, "Merrick Garland Gets ABA's 'Well-Qualified' Rating," *ABA Journal*, June 21, 2016, available at http://www.abajournal.com/news/article/merrick_garland_gets_a_well_qualified_rating_from_aba/.

108. Timothy B. Lee, "At Least 14 Supreme Court Justices Have Been Confirmed During Election Years," *Vox*, February 13, 2016, available at https://www.vox.com/2016/2/13/10987692/14-supreme-court-confirmations; Steve Benen, "Justice Kennedy's Confirmation Debunks Key GOP Talking Point," *MSNBC.com*, February 15, 2016, available at http://www.msnbc.com/rachel-maddow-show/justice-kennedys-confirmation-debunks-key-gop-talking-point.

109. Donald B. Cole, *Martin Van Buren and the American Political System* (Princeton, N.J.: Princeton University Press, 1984), 276.

Chapter Three. Dismissed Preemptively

1. Marquis James, *The Life of Andrew Jackson: Complete in One Volume* (New York: Bobbs-Merrill, 1938), 738.

2. David S. Heidler and Jeanne T. Heidler, *Henry Clay: The Essential American* (New York: Random House, 2010), xiii.

3. Ibid., 116–17.

4. Harlow Giles Unger, *Henry Clay: America's Greatest Statesman* (Philadelphia: De Capo Press, 2015), 83–84.

5. Harlow Giles Unger, *The Last Founding Father: James Monroe and a Nation's Call to Greatness* (Boston: Da Capo Press, 2009), 290–94.

6. David S. Heidler and Jeanne T. Heidler, *Henry Clay: The Essential American* (New York: Random House, 2010), 141–42.

7. Ibid., 142–43.

8. H. W. Brands, *Andrew Jackson: His Life and Times* (New York: Anchor Books, 2006), 354–55; David S. Heidler and Jeanne T. Heidler, *Henry Clay: The Essential American* (New York: Random House, 2010), 146–48.

9. Marquis James, *The Life of Andrew Jackson: Complete in One Volume* (New York: Bobbs-Merrill, 1938), 442.

10. Meade Minnigerode, *Presidential Years, 1787–1860* (New York: G. P. Putnam's Sons, 1928), 151.

11. Marquis James, *The Life of Andrew Jackson: Complete in One Volume* (New York: Bobbs-Merrill, 1938), 443.

12. Epes Sargent, *The Life and Public Services of Henry Clay* (New York: Greeley & McElrath, 1848), 87.

13. Marquis James, *The Life of Andrew Jackson: Complete in One Volume* (New York: Bobbs-Merrill, 1938), 445.

14. Harlow Giles Unger, *Henry Clay: America's Greatest Statesman* (Philadelphia: De Capo Press, 2015), 55.

15. Ibid., 132–35.

16. Thomas Hart Benton, *Thirty Years' View*, vol. 1 (New York: D. Appleton, 1854), 77.

17. Mark Cheathem, interview by the author, October 2017.

18. Michael F. Holt, *The Rise and Fall of the American Whig Party: Jacksonian Politics and the Onset of the Civil War* (New York: Oxford University Press, 1999), 18.

19. Thomas Hart Benton, *Thirty Years' View*, vol. 1 (New York: D. Appleton, 1854), 269.

20. David S. Heidler and Jeanne T. Heidler, *Henry Clay: The Essential American* (New York: Random House, 2010), 251–56.

21. Thomas Hart Benton, *Thirty Years' View*, vol. 1 (New York: D. Appleton, 1854), 402.

22. David S. Heidler and Jeanne T. Heidler, *Henry Clay: The Essential American* (New York: Random House, 2010), 266.

23. Thomas Hart Benton, *Thirty Years' View*, vol. I (New York: D. Appleton, 1854), 423.

24. Ibid., 425–26.

25. Mark Cheathem, interview by the author, October 2017.

26. David S. Heidler and Jeanne T. Heidler, *Henry Clay: The Essential American* (New York: Random House, 2010), 273.

27. Michael F. Holt, *The Rise and Fall of the American Whig Party: Jacksonian Politics and the Onset of the Civil War* (New York: Oxford University Press, 1999), 103.

28. Thomas Hart Benton, *Thirty Years' View*, vol. 2 (New York: D. Appleton, 1856), 204.

29. Mark Cheathem, interview by the author, October 2017.

30. Glyndon G. Van Duesen, *The Life of Henry Clay* (Boston: Little, Brown, 1937), 338–39.

31. Mark R. Cheathem, *The Coming of Democracy: Presidential Campaigning in the Age of Jackson* (Baltimore: Johns Hopkins University Press, 2018), 173.

32. David S. Heidler and Jeanne T. Heidler, *Henry Clay: The Essential American* (New York: Random House, 2010), 341.

33. Harlow Giles Unger, *Henry Clay: America's Greatest Statesman* (Boston, MA: De Capo Press, 2015), 223.

34. Mark Cheathem, interview by the author, October 2017.

35. Joseph Cummins, *Anything for a Vote: Dirty Tricks, Cheap Shots, and October Surprises in U.S. Presidential Campaigns* (Philadelphia: Quirk Books, 2015), 76.

36. Thomas Hart Benton, *Thirty Years' View*, vol. 2 (New York: D. Appleton, 1856), 626.

37. Meade Minnigerode, *Presidential Years, 1787–1860* (New York: G. P. Putnam's Sons, 1928), 183.

38. Scott Farris, *Almost President: The Men Who Lost the Race but Changed the Nation*, paperback ed. (Guilford, CT: Lyons Press, 2013), 45.

39. David S. Heidler and Jeanne T. Heidler, *Henry Clay: The Essential American* (New York: Random House, 2010), 464.

40. Ibid., xvii.

41. Harlow Giles Unger, *Henry Clay: America's Greatest Statesman* (Boston: Da Capo Press, 2015), 268.

42. William H. Rehnquist, *Centennial Crisis: The Disputed Election of 1876* (New York: Knopf, 2004), 66–72.

43. Paul Leland Haworth, *The Hayes-Tilden Disputed Presidential Election of 1876* (Cleveland, OH: Burrow Brothers, 1906), 28; Alexander Clarence Flick, *Samuel Jones Tilden: A Study in Political Sagacity* (New York: Dodd, Mead, 1939), 165.

44. Alexander Clarence Flick, *Samuel Jones Tilden: A Study in Political Sagacity* (New York: Dodd, Mead, 1939), 177.

45. Ibid., 188.

46. William H. Rehnquist, *Centennial Crisis: The Disputed Election of 1876* (New York: Knopf, 2004), 77.

47. Alexander Clarence Flick, *Samuel Jones Tilden: A Study in Political Sagacity* (New York: Dodd, Mead, 1939), 200–1.

48. Ibid., 207–8.

49. Mark Weston, *The Runner-Up Presidency: The Elections That Defied America's Popular Will (and How Our Democracy Remains in Danger)* (Guilford, CT: Lyons Press, 2016), 33.

50. Alexander Clarence Flick, *Samuel Jones Tilden: A Study in Political Sagacity* (New York: Dodd, Mead, 1939), 220.

51. Ibid., 225–29.

52. Paul Leland Haworth, *The Hayes-Tilden Disputed Presidential Election of 1876* (Cleveland, OH: Burrow Brothers, 1906), 29; Alexander Clarence Flick, *Samuel Jones Tilden: A Study in Political Sagacity* (New York: Dodd, Mead, 1939), 260–61.

53. James G. Blaine, *Twenty Years of Congress: From Lincoln to Garfield*, vol. 2 (Norwich, CT: Henry Hill, 1886), 573, 576–77.

54. Joseph Cummins, *Anything for a Vote: Dirty Tricks, Cheap Shots, and October Surprises in U.S. Presidential Campaigns* (Philadelphia: Quirk Books, 2015), 117–18.

55. H. J. Eckenrode, *Rutherford B. Hayes: Statesman of Reunion* (New York: Dodd, Mead, 1930), 139, 150.

56. Alexander Clarence Flick, *Samuel Jones Tilden: A Study in Political Sagacity* (New York: Dodd, Mead, 1939), 310.

57. James G. Blaine, *Twenty Years of Congress: From Lincoln to Garfield*, vol. 2 (Norwich, CT: Henry Hill, 1886), 579; Paul Leland Haworth, *The Hayes-Tilden Disputed Presidential Election of 1876* (Cleveland, OH: Burrow Brothers, 1906), 37–38.

58. H. J. Eckenrode, *Rutherford B. Hayes: Statesman of Reunion* (New York: Dodd, Mead, 1930), 141–43.

59. Alexander Clarence Flick, *Samuel Jones Tilden: A Study in Political Sagacity* (New York: Dodd, Mead, 1939), 317–18.

60. Ibid., 320.

61. Paul Leland Haworth, *The Hayes-Tilden Disputed Presidential Election of 1876* (Cleveland, OH: Burrow Brothers, 1906), 30, 38.

62. Robert G. Caldwell, *James A. Garfield: Party Chieftain* (New York: Dodd, Mead, 1931), 251.

63. H. J. Eckenrode, *Rutherford B. Hayes: Statesman of Reunion* (New York: Dodd, Mead, 1930), 178.

64. J. G. Randall and David Donald, *The Civil War and Reconstruction*, 2nd ed. (Lexington, MA: D. C. Heath, 1969), 687.

65. Paul Leland Haworth, *The Hayes-Tilden Disputed Presidential Election of 1876* (Cleveland, OH: Burrow Brothers, 1906), 51.

66. Ibid., chs. 6–8.

67. Roy Morris, Jr., *Fraud of the Century: Rutherford B. Hayes, Samuel Tilden, and the Stolen Election of 1876* (New York: Simon & Schuster, 2003), 197–98.

68. James Monroe, "The Hayes-Tilden Electoral Commission," *Atlantic*, October 1893, available at https://www.theatlantic.com/magazine/archive/1893/10/the-hayes-tilden-electoral-commission/523971/; Alexander Clarence Flick, *Samuel Jones Tilden: A Study in Political Sagacity* (New York: Dodd, Mead, 1939), 415.

69. James Monroe, "The Hayes-Tilden Electoral Commission," *Atlantic*, October 1893, available at https://www.theatlantic.com/magazine/archive/1893/10/the-hayes-tilden-electoral-commission/523971/.

70. Willard L. King, *Lincoln's Manager: David Davis* (Cambridge, MA: Harvard University Press, 1960), 89–92.

71. Roy Morris, Jr., *Fraud of the Century: Rutherford B. Hayes, Samuel Tilden, and the Stolen Election of 1876* (New York: Simon & Schuster, 2003), 218–19.

72. Paul Leland Haworth, *The Hayes-Tilden Disputed Presidential Election of 1876* (Cleveland, OH: Burrow Brothers, 1906), 169.

73. Lloyd Robinson, *The Stolen Election: Hayes versus Tilden—1876* (New York: Tom Doherty Associates, 2001), 192.

74. Paul Leland Haworth, *The Hayes-Tilden Disputed Presidential Election of 1876* (Cleveland, OH: Burrow Brothers, 1906), 188.

75. Ibid., 241.

76. Eric Foner, *Reconstruction: America's Unfinished Revolution, 1863–1877* (New York: Harper & Row, 1988), 577.

77. Alexander Clarence Flick, *Samuel Jones Tilden: A Study in Political Sagacity* (New York: Dodd, Mead, 1939), 330–31.

78. James Monroe, "The Hayes-Tilden Electoral Commission," *Atlantic*, October 1893, available at https://www.theatlantic.com/magazine/archive/1893/10/the-hayes-tilden-electoral-commission/523971/.

79. Lloyd Robinson, *The Stolen Election: Hayes versus Tilden—1876* (New York: Tom Doherty Associates, 2001), 195–96.

80. Roy Morris, Jr., *Fraud of the Century: Rutherford B. Hayes, Samuel Tilden, and the Stolen Election of 1876* (New York: Simon & Schuster, 2003), 188–89, 250.

81. Lloyd Robinson, *The Stolen Election: Hayes versus Tilden—1876* (New York: Tom Doherty Associates, 2001), 207.

82. Eric Foner, *Reconstruction: America's Unfinished Revolution, 1863–1877* (New York: Harper & Row, 1988), 581.

83. James Monroe, "The Hayes-Tilden Electoral Commission," *Atlantic*, October 1893, available at https://www.theatlantic.com/magazine/archive/1893/10/the-hayes-tilden-electoral-commission/523971/.

84. Lloyd Robinson, *The Stolen Election: Hayes versus Tilden—1876* (New York: Tom Doherty Associates, 2001), 206.

85. James P. Boyd, *Life and Public Services of Hon. James G. Blaine: The Illustrious American Orator, Diplomat and Statesman* (Philadelphia: Publishers' Union, 1893), 239.

86. William H. Crook, *Through Five Administrations* (New York: Harper & Brothers, 1910), 260–61.

87. Edward Stanwood, *James Gillespie Blaine* (New York: Houghton, Mifflin, 1905), 64.

88. Theodore Clark Smith, *The Life and Letters of James Abram Garfield*, vol. 2 (New Haven, CT: Yale University Press, 1925), 957.

89. David M. Jordan, *Roscoe Conkling of New York: Voice in the Senate* (Ithaca: Cornell University Press, 1971), 72.

90. Charles W. Calhoun, *Minority Victory: Gilded Age Politics and the Front Porch Campaign of 1888* (Lawrence, KS: University Press of Kansas, 2008), 74.

91. David M. Jordan, *Roscoe Conkling of New York: Voice in the Senate* (Ithaca: Cornell University Press, 1971), 80.

92. Ron Chernow, *Grant* (New York: Penguin, 2017), 752–53.

93. Edward P. Crapol, *James G. Blaine: Architect of Empire* (Wilmington, DE: Scholarly Resources, 2000), 44.

94. James P. Boyd, *Life and Public Services of Hon. James G. Blaine: The Illustrious American Orator, Diplomat and Statesman* (Philadelphia: Publishers' Union, 1893), 524.

95. Ibid., 528.

96. Theodore Clark Smith, *The Life and Letters of James Abram Garfield*, vol. 2 (New Haven, CT: Yale University Press, 1925), 1166.

97. Ron Chernow, *Grant* (New York: Penguin, 2017), 932.

98. David M. Jordan, *Roscoe Conkling of New York: Voice in the Senate* (Ithaca: Cornell University Press, 1971), 420–21.

99. Denis Tilden Lynch, *Grover Cleveland: A Man Four-Square* (New York: Horace Liveright, 1932), 247.

100. Allan Nevins, *Grover Cleveland: A Study in Courage* (New York: Dodd, Mead, 1932), 169.

101. Ibid., 162–66.

102. Mark Wahlgren Summers, *Rum, Romanism, and Rebellion: The Making of a President, 1884* (Chapel Hill, NC: University of North Carolina Press, 2000), 184.

103. Allan Nevins, *Grover Cleveland: A Study in Courage* (New York: Dodd, Mead, 1932), 182.

104. David M. Jordan, *Roscoe Conkling of New York: Voice in the Senate* (Ithaca: Cornell University Press, 1971), 421.

105. Charles W. Calhoun, *Minority Victory: Gilded Age Politics and the Front Porch Campaign of 1888* (Lawrence, KS: University Press of Kansas, 2008), 76.

106. David M. Jordan, *Roscoe Conkling of New York: Voice in the Senate* (Ithaca: Cornell University Press, 1971), 421.

Chapter Four. Displaced by Death

1. Michael J. Gerhardt, *The Forgotten Presidents: Their Untold Constitutional Legacy* (New York: Oxford University Press, 2013), 25.

2. Robert Gray Gunderson, *The Log-Cabin Campaign* (Lexington, KY: University Press of Kentucky, 1957), 223.

3. Ibid., 70, 74.

4. Mark R. Cheathem, *The Coming of Democracy: Presidential Campaigning in the Age of Jackson* (Baltimore: Johns Hopkins University Press, 2018), 171.

5. Robert Gray Gunderson, *The Log-Cabin Campaign* (Lexington, KY: University Press of Kentucky, 1957), 261–62.

6. John D. Feerick, *From Failing Hands: The Story of Presidential Succession* (New York: Fordham University Press, 1965), 89.

7. William Henry Harrison, "Inaugural Address," March 4, 1841, available at http://www.presidency.ucsb.edu/ws/index.php?pid=25813.

8. Merrill D. Peterson, *The Great Triumvirate: Webster, Clay, and Calhoun* (New York: Oxford University Press, 1987), 298–301.

9. Thomas Hart Benton, *Thirty Years' View*, vol. 2 (New York: D. Appleton, 1856), 210.

10. Merrill D. Peterson, *The Great Triumvirate: Webster, Clay, and Calhoun* (New York: Oxford University Press, 1987), 301.

11. Michael J. Gerhardt, *The Forgotten Presidents: Their Untold Constitutional Legacy* (New York: Oxford University Press, 2013), 33.

12. Jane McHugh and Philip A. Mackowiak, "Death in the White House: President William Henry Harrison's Atypical Pneumonia," *Clinical Infectious Diseases* 59, no. 7 (October 1, 2014), 990–95.

13. Oliver Perry Chitwood, *John Tyler: Champion of the Old South* (Newtown, CT: American Political Biography Press, 1939), 201–2.

14. Jane McHugh and Philip A. Mackowiak, "Death in the White House: President William Henry Harrison's Atypical Pneumonia," *Clinical Infectious Diseases* 59, no. 7 (October 1, 2014), 990–95.

15. Thomas Hart Benton, *Thirty Years' View*, vol. 2 (New York: D. Appleton, 1856), 210.

16. Marquis James, *The Life of Andrew Jackson: Complete in One Volume* (New York: Bobbs-Merrill, 1938), 745; Mark R. Cheathem, *The Coming of Democracy: Presidential Campaigning in the Age of Jackson* (Baltimore: Johns Hopkins University Press, 2018), 173.

17. Robert E. Gilbert, *The Mortal Presidency: Illness and Anguish in the White House* (New York: Basic Books, 1992), 1.

18. James Thomas Flexner, *Washington: The Indispensible Man* (Boston: Little, Brown, 1974), 271.

19. John D. Feerick, *The Twenty-Fifth Amendment: Its Complete History and Applications*, 3rd ed. (New York: Fordham University Press, 2014), 4–5; David S. Heidler and Jeanne T. Heidler, *Henry Clay: The Essential American* (New York: Random House, 2010), 106.

20. Oliver Perry Chitwood, *John Tyler: Champion of the Old South* (Newtown, CT: American Political Biography Press), 397–98.

21. Thomas Hart Benton, *Thirty Years' View*, vol. 2 (New York: D. Appleton, 1856), 568.

22. Paul F. Boller, *Presidential Campaigns: From George Washington to George W. Bush* (New York: Oxford University Press, 2004), 86.

23. K. Jack Bauer, *Zachary Taylor: Soldier, Planter, Statesman of the Old Southwest* (Baton Rouge: Louisiana State University Press, 1985), 269–70.

24. "A Tale of Arsenic and Old Lace," *Newsweek*, June 30, 1991, available at http://www.newsweek.com/tale-arsenic-and-old-Zach-204102.

25. Michael F. Holt, *The Rise and Fall of the American Whig Party: Jacksonian Politics and the Onset of the Civil War* (New York: Oxford University Press, 1999), 418–19.

26. Ibid., 438–39, 457.

27. K. Jack Bauer, *Zachary Taylor: Soldier, Planter, Statesman of the Old Southwest* (Baton Rouge: Louisiana State University Press, 1985), 300–1, 307.

28. Michael F. Holt, *The Rise and Fall of the American Whig Party: Jacksonian Politics and the Onset of the Civil War* (New York: Oxford University Press, 1999), 419.

29. Thomas Hart Benton, *Thirty Years' View*, vol. 2 (New York: D. Appleton,, 1856), 765.

30. K. Jack Bauer, *Zachary Taylor: Soldier, Planter, Statesman of the Old Southwest* (Baton Rouge: Louisiana State University Press, 1985), 314.

31. Ibid., 314.

32. Elbert B. Smith, *The Presidencies of Zachary Taylor and Millard Fillmore* (Lawrence, KS: University Press of Kansas, 1988), 156.

33. William R. Maples, PhD, and Michael Browning, *Dead Men Do Tell Tales: The Strange and Fascinating Cases of a Forensic Anthropologist* (New York: Main Street Books, 1994), 223.

34. K. Jack Bauer, *Zachary Taylor: Soldier, Planter, Statesman of the Old Southwest* (Baton Rouge: Louisiana State University Press, 1985), 315–16.

35. Thomas Hart Benton, *Thirty Years' View*, vol. 2 (New York: D. Appleton, 1856), 765.

36. Brady Carlson, *Dead Presidents: An American Adventure into the Strange Deaths and Surprising Afterlives of Our Nation's Leaders* (New York: W. W. Norton, 2016), 67.

37. Eric Harrison, "Zachary Taylor Did Not Die of Arsenic Poisoning, Tests Indicate," *Los Angeles Times*, June 27, 1971, available at http://article.latimes.com/1991-06-27/news/Man-2064_1_zachary-taylor.

38. William R. Maples, PhD, and Michael Browning, *Dead Men Do Tell Tales: The Strange and Fascinating Cases of a Forensic Anthropologist* (New York: Main Street Books, 1994), 225–26.

39. Eric Harrison, "Zachary Taylor Did Not Die of Arsenic Poisoning, Tests Indicate," *Los Angeles Times*, June 27, 1971, available at http://article.latimes.com/1991-06-27/news/Man-2064_1_zachary-taylor.

40. William R. Maples, PhD, and Michael Browning, *Dead Men Do Tell Tales: The Strange and Fascinating Cases of a Forensic Anthropologist* (New York: Main Street Books, 1994), 235–36.

41. Robert K. Murray, *The Harding Era: Warren G. Harding and His Administration* (Newtown, CT: American Political Biography Press, 1969), 25.

42. Ibid., 51.

43. Ibid., 121.

44. Edmund W. Starling, as told to Thomas Sugrue, *Starling of the White House* (New York: Simon and Schuster, 1946), 167.

45. Robert K. Murray, *The Harding Era: Warren G. Harding and His Administration* (Newtown, CT: American Political Biography Press, 1969), 113–14.

46. Ibid., 418.

47. Ibid, 438–39.

48. Richard H. Hansen, *The Year We Had No President* (Lincoln, NE: University of Nebraska Press, 1962), 49.

49. Edmund W. Starling, as told to Thomas Sugrue, *Starling of the White House* (New York: Simon and Schuster, 1946), 189–91.

50. Ibid., 196.

51. Robert K. Murray, *The Harding Era: Warren G. Harding and His Administration* (Newtown, CT: American Political Biography Press, 1969), 439–41.

52. Ibid., 446.

53. Ibid., 448–49.

54. Edmund W. Starling, as told to Thomas Sugrue, *Starling of the White House* (New York: Simon and Schuster, 1946), 200.

55. Richard H. Hansen, *The Year We Had No President* (Lincoln, NE: University of Nebraska Press, 1962), 50.

56. Robert K. Murray, *The Harding Era: Warren G. Harding and His Administration* (Newtown, CT: American Political Biography Press, 1969), 451.

57. Gaston B. Means as told to May Dixon Thacker, *The Strange Death of President Harding* (New York: Guild, 1930), 260.

58. A. S. Goldman et al., "What was the cause of Franklin Delano Roosevelt's paralytic illness?" *Journal of Medical Biography* 11, no. 4 (November 2003), 232–40, available at https://www.ncbi.nlm.nih.gov/pubmed/14562158.

59. Geoffrey C. Ward, *A First-Class Temperament: The Emergence of Franklin Roosevelt* (New York: Harper & Row, 1989), 783.

60. Michael F. Reilly, as told to William J. Slouch, *Reilly of the White House* (New York: Simon and Schuster, 1947), 15–16.

61. Grace Tully, *F.D.R.: My Boss* (Chicago: Peoples Book Club, 1949), 236.

62. James Roosevelt, interview by the author, October 2017.

63. Grace Tully, *F.D.R.: My Boss* (Chicago: Peoples Book Club, 1949), 253.

64. James Roosevelt, interview by the author, October 2017.

65. Grace Tully, *F.D.R.: My Boss* (Chicago: Peoples Book Club, 1949), 273–74.

66. Charles E. Bohlen, *Witness to History: 1929–1969* (New York: W. W. Norton, 1973), 143–44.

67. David M. Jordan, *FDR, Dewey, and the Election of 1944* (Indianapolis: Indiana University Press, 2011), 130.

68. Jim Bishop, *FDR's Last Year: April 1944–April 1945* (New York: William Morrow, 1974), 4–7.

69. Frank Costigliola, "The Splendid Deception of 'Doctor' Roosevelt," in Jeffrey A. Engel and Thomas J. Knock, eds., *When Life Strikes the President: Scandal, Death, and Illness in the White House* (New York: Oxford University Press, 2017), 161–87.

70. Turner Catledge, *My Life and the Times* (New York: Harper & Row, 1971), 144.

71. James Roosevelt, interview by the author, October 2017.

72. Paul Sparrow, interview by the author, September 2017.

73. Ibid.

74. Jim Bishop, *FDR's Last Year: April 1944–April 1945* (New York: William Morrow, 1974), 127–28.

75. Ibid., 157–58.

76. Harry H. Vaughan, Truman Library oral history, January 14, 1963, available online at https://www.trumanlibrary.org/oralhist/vaughan.htm.

77. Paul Sparrow, interview by the author, September 2017.

78. Jim Bishop, *FDR's Last Year: April 1944–April 1945* (New York: William Morrow, 1974), 383.

79. Robert E. Gilbert, *The Mortal Presidency: Illness and Anguish in the White House* (New York: Basic Books, 1992), 67.

80. Alfred Steinberg, *Sam Rayburn: A Biography* (New York, Hawthorn Books, 1975), 224.

81. Jim Bishop, *FDR's Last Year: April 1944–April 1945* (New York: William Morrow, 1974), 497–99, 516.

82. Alfred Steinberg, *Sam Rayburn: A Biography* (New York, Hawthorn Books, 1975), 225.

83. Michael F. Reilly, as told to William J. Slouch, *Reilly of the White House* (New York: Simon and Schuster, 1947), 230.

Chapter Five. Taken Out by Force

1. Max Farrand, ed., *The Records of the Federal Convention of 1787*, vol. 2 (New Haven: Yale University Press, 1911), 65 (July 20).

2. United States Department of the Treasury, "Public Report of the White House Security Review" (1995), ch. 4, available at https://fas.org/irp/agency/ustreas/usss/t1pubrpt.html.

3. Edward Steers, Jr., *Blood on the Moon: The Assassination of Abraham Lincoln* (Lexington: University Press of Kentucky, 2001), 16.

4. Michael Burlingame, *Abraham Lincoln: A Life*, vol. 2 (Baltimore: Johns Hopkins University Press, 2008), 33.

5. Ibid., 32–33.

6. Ibid., 32–34.

7. Ibid., 34.

8. Ibid.

9. "A Brief History of Presidential Protection," Appendix VII in President's Commission on the Assassination of President John F. Kennedy (Warren Commission), *Report of the President's Commission on the Assassination of John F. Kennedy* (Washington, DC: U.S. Government Printing Office, 1964), 505–6.

10. Ibid., 506.

11. J. G. Randall and David Donald, *The Civil War and Reconstruction*, 2nd ed. (Lexington, MA: D. C. Heath, 1969), 163, 307–9, 473.

12. United States Department of the Treasury, "Public Report of the White House Security Review" (1995), ch. 4, available at https://fas.org/irp/agency/ustreas/usss/t1pubrpt.html.

13. William H. Crook, *Through Five Administrations* (New York: Harper & Brothers, 1910), 3.

14. Ibid., 6.

15. Michael W. Kauffman, *American Brutus: John Wilkes Booth and the Lincoln Conspiracies* (New York: Random House, 2004), 135–36.

16. William H. Crook, *Through Five Administrations* (New York: Harper & Brothers, 1910), 1–2.

17. Ronald L. Feinman, *Assassinations, Threats, and the American Presidency: From Andrew Jackson to Barack Obama* (New York: Rowman and Littlefield, 2015), 18.

18. William H. Crook, *Through Five Administrations* (New York: Harper & Brothers, 1910), 42–43, 45–46.

19. Ibid., 54.

20. Asia Booth Clarke, *The Elder and the Younger Booth* (Boston: James R. Osgood, 1882), 54, 65.

21. Ibid., 131, 152, and passim.

22. Stanley Kimmel, *The Mad Booths of Maryland*, 2nd ed. (New York, Dover Publications, 1969), 149.

23. Asia Booth Clarke, *The Elder and the Younger Booth* (Boston: James R. Osgood, 1882), 159.

24. Ibid., 110.

25. Ibid., 122–23.

26. Stanley Kimmel, *The Mad Booths of Maryland*, 2nd ed. (New York, Dover Publications, 1969), 149–53.

27. Edward Steers, Jr., *Blood on the Moon: The Assassination of Abraham Lincoln* (Lexington: University Press of Kentucky, 2001), 36.

28. Stanley Kimmel, *The Mad Booths of Maryland*, 2nd ed. (New York, Dover Publications, 1969), 156.

29. Michael W. Kauffman, *American Brutus: John Wilkes Booth and the Lincoln Conspiracies* (New York: Random House, 2004), 121.

30. Ibid., 134–35.

31. James L. Swanson, *Manhunt: The Twelve-Day Chase for Lincoln's Killer* (New York: Harper Perennial, 2007), 25.

32. Michael W. Kauffman, *American Brutus: John Wilkes Booth and the Lincoln Conspiracies* (New York: Random House, 2004), 184–85.

33. Edward Steers, Jr., *Blood on the Moon: The Assassination of Abraham Lincoln* (Lexington: The University Press of Kentucky, 2001), 91.

34. William H. Crook, *Through Five Administrations* (New York: Harper & Brothers, 1910), 62.

35. Ibid., 66.

36. Edward Steers, Jr., *Blood on the Moon: The Assassination of Abraham Lincoln* (Lexington: The University Press of Kentucky, 2001), 108.

37. Ben Pitman, *The Assassination of President Lincoln and the Trial of the Conspirators* (New York: Moore, Wilstach & Baldwin, 1865), 73–74.

38. Ibid., 77.

39. Ibid., 78.

40. William H. Crook, *Through Five Administrations* (New York: Harper & Brothers, 1910), 72.

41. Ben Pitman, *The Assassination of President Lincoln and the Trial of the Conspirators* (New York: Moore, Wilstach & Baldwin, 1865), 78.

42. Ibid., 78.

43. Ibid., 76–77.

44. Michael W. Kauffman, *American Brutus: John Wilkes Booth and the Lincoln Conspiracies* (New York: Random House, 2004), 9.

45. Edward Steers, Jr., *Blood on the Moon: The Assassination of Abraham Lincoln* (Lexington: University Press of Kentucky, 2001), 166–67.

46. Michael W. Kauffman, *American Brutus: John Wilkes Booth and the Lincoln Conspiracies* (New York: Random House, 2004), 203.

47. Edward Steers, Jr., *Blood on the Moon: The Assassination of Abraham Lincoln* (Lexington: University Press of Kentucky, 2001), 126.

48. Ben Pitman, *The Assassination of President Lincoln and the Trial of the Conspirators* (New York: Moore, Wilstach & Baldwin, 1865), 81.

49. Lindsay Porter, *Assassination: A History of Political Murder* (New York: Overlook Press, 2010), 150–51.

50. United States Department of the Treasury, "Public Report of the White House Security Review" (1995), ch. 4, available at https://fas.org/irp/agency/ustreas/usss/t1pubrpt.html.

51. Ibid.

52. "A Brief History of Presidential Protection," Appendix VII in President's Commission on the Assassination of President John F. Kennedy (Warren Commission), *Report of the President's Commission on the Assassination of John F. Kennedy* (Washington, DC: U.S. Government Printing Office, 1964), 505.

53. Robert J. Donovan, *The Assassins* (London: Elek Books, 1956), 70.

54. Robert Remini, *Andrew Jackson* (New York: Twayne, 1966), 200–1.

55. Marquis James, *The Life of Andrew Jackson: Complete in One Volume* (New York: Bobs Merrill, 1938), 636.

56. Robert J. Donovan, *The Assassins* (London: Elek Books, 1956), 71.

57. John Meacham, *American Lion: Andrew Jackson in the White House* (New York: Random House, 2008), 255.

58. Robert J. Donovan, *The Assassins* (London: Elek Books, 1956), 70.

59. John Meacham, *American Lion: Andrew Jackson in the White House* (New York: Random House, 2008), 255.

60. Thomas Hart Benton, *Thirty Years' View*, vol. 1 (New York: D. Appleton, 1883), 521.

61. Marquis James, *The Life of Andrew Jackson, Complete in One Volume* (New York: Bobbs-Merrill, 1938), 685.

62. Thomas Hart Benton, *Thirty Years' View*, vol. 2 (New York: D. Appleton, 1883), 521.

63. Ibid., 521.

64. Marquis James, *The Life of Andrew Jackson, Complete in One Volume* (New York: Bobbs-Merrill, 1938), 685.

65. Thomas Hart Benton, *Thirty Years' View*, vol. 1 (New York: D. Appleton, 1883), 522.

66. Ibid., 523.

67. Ibid.

68. Robert J. Donovan, *The Assassins* (London: Elek Books, 1956), 68.

69. Thomas Hart Benton, *Thirty Years' View*, vol. 1 (New York: D. Appleton, 1883), 523.

70. Ibid., 523–24.

71. Robert J. Donovan, *The Assassins* (London: Elek Books, 1956), 78–79.

72. Oliver Perry Chitwood, *John Tyler: Champion of the Old South* (Newtown, CT: American Political Biography Press, 1939), 229.

73. Ibid., 229, 447.

74. James G. Blaine, *Twenty Years of Congress: From Lincoln to Garfield*, vol. 2 (Norwich, CT: Henry Hill, 1886), 182.

75. William H. Crook, *Through Five Administrations* (New York: Harper & Brothers, 1910), 92–93.

76. Ron Chernow, *Grant* (New York: Penguin, 2017), 650.

77. H. J. Eckenrode, *Rutherford B. Hayes: Statesman of Reunion* (New York: Dodd, Mead, 1930), 235.

78. H. G. Hayes and C. J. Hayes, *A Complete History of the Trial of Guiteau, Assassin of President Garfield* (Philadelphia: Hubbard Bros., 1882), 308.

79. Ibid., 143.

80. Robert J. Donovan, *The Assassins* (London: Elek Books, 1956), 48.

81. H. G. Hayes and C. J. Hayes, *A Complete History of the Trial of Guiteau, Assassin of President Garfield* (Philadelphia: Hubbard Bros., 1882), 46–47.

82. Ron Chernow, *Grant* (New York: Penguin, 2017), 910.

83. H. G. Hayes and C. J. Hayes, *A Complete History of the Trial of Guiteau, Assassin of President Garfield* (Philadelphia: Hubbard Bros., 1882), 47–48.

84. Ibid., 48.

85. William H. Crook, *Through Five Administrations* (New York: Harper & Brothers, 1910), 266–68.

86. H. G. Hayes and C. J. Hayes, *A Complete History of the Trial of Guiteau, Assassin of President Garfield* (Philadelphia: Hubbard Bros., 1882), 137–38.

87. Ibid., 139.

88. Ibid., 51.

89. Candice Millard, *Destiny of the Republic: A Tale of Madness, Medicine, and the Murder of a President* (New York: Anchor Books, 2012), 143–44.

90. H. G. Hayes and C. J. Hayes, *A Complete History of the Trial of Guiteau, Assassin of President Garfield* (Philadelphia: Hubbard Bros., 1882), 13.

91. Robert J. Donovan, *The Assassins* (London: Elek Books, 1956), 47.

92. H. G. Hayes and C. J. Hayes, *A Complete History of the Trial of Guiteau, Assassin of President Garfield* (Philadelphia: Hubbard Bros., 1882), 54–57.

93. Ibid., 17.

94. Theodore Clark Smith, *The Life and Letters of James Abram Garfield*, vol. 2 (New Haven, CT: Yale University Press, 1925), 1179.

95. Candice Millard, *Destiny of the Republic: A Tale of Madness, Medicine, and the Murder of a President* (New York: Anchor Books, 2012), 160–61, 165.

96. William H. Crook, *Through Five Administrations* (New York: Harper & Brothers, 1910), 273.

97. Brady Carlson, *Dead Presidents: An American Adventure into the Strange Deaths and Surprising Afterlives of Our Nation's Leaders* (New York: W. W. Norton, 2016), 56.

98. H. G. Hayes and C. J. Hayes, *A Complete History of the Trial of Guiteau, Assassin of President Garfield* (Philadelphia: Hubbard Bros., 1882), 27.

99. Ibid., 62, 91, 134, 186, and passim.

100. James W. Clarke, *American Assassins: The Darker Side of Politics* (Princeton, NJ: Princeton University Press, 1982), 214.

101. Irwin Hood (Ike) Hoover, *Forty-Two Years in the White House* (New York: Houghton Mifflin, 1934), 313–14.

102. Philip H. Melanson, *The Secret Service: The Hidden History of an Enigmatic Agency* (New York: MJF Books, 2002), 24.

103. "A Brief History of Presidential Protection," Appendix VII in President's Commission on the Assassination of President John F. Kennedy (Warren Commission), *Report of the President's Commission on the Assassination of John F. Kennedy* (Washington, DC: U.S. Government Printing Office, 1964), 509.

104. James W. Clarke, *American Assassins: The Darker Side of Politics* (Princeton, NJ: Princeton University Press, 1982), 44–47.

105. Ibid., 52–53.

106. Scott Miller, *The President and the Assassin: McKinley, Terror, and Empire at the Dawn of the American Century* (New York: Random House, 2011), 264.

107. Quoted in Robert W. Merry, *President McKinley: Architect of the American Century* (New York: Simon & Schuster, 2017), 478.

108. L. Vernon Briggs, *The Manner of Man That Kills* (Boston: Gorham Press, 1921), 321–22.

109. Scott Miller, *The President and the Assassin: McKinley, Terror, and Empire at the Dawn of the American Century* (New York: Random House, 2011), 297–300.

110. A. Wesley Johns, *The Man Who Shot McKinley* (New York: A. S. Barnes, 1970), 89–90.

111. James W. Clarke, *American Assassins: The Darker Side of Politics* (Princeton, NJ: Princeton University Press, 1982), 57.

112. A. Wesley Johns, *The Man Who Shot McKinley* (New York: A. S. Barnes, 1970), 94–95.

113. Robert W. Merry, *President McKinley: Architect of the American Century* (New York: Simon & Schuster, 2017), 480–82.

114. L. Vernon Briggs, *The Manner of Man That Kills* (Boston: Gorham Press, 1921), 241–43.

115. "A Brief History of Presidential Protection," Appendix VII in President's Commission on the Assassination of President John F. Kennedy (Warren Commission), *Report of the President's Commission on the Assassination of John F. Kennedy* (Washington, DC: U.S. Government Printing Office, 1964), 510–11.

116. Rufus W. Youngblood, *20 Years in the Secret Service: My Life with Five Presidents* (New York: Simon and Schuster, 1973), 27.

117. Irwin Hood (Ike) Hoover, *Forty-Two Years in the White House* (New York: Houghton Mifflin, 1934), 314–15.

118. "A Brief History of Presidential Protection," Appendix VII in President's Commission on the Assassination of President John F. Kennedy (Warren Commission), *Report of the President's Commission on the Assassination of John F. Kennedy* (Washington, DC: U.S. Government Printing Office, 1964), 511.

119. Edmund W. Starling, as told to Thomas Sugrue, *Starling of the White House* (New York: Simon and Schuster, 1946), 31, 91.

120. Ibid., 117, 120–21.

121. Irwin Hood (Ike) Hoover, *Forty-Two Years in the White House* (New York: Houghton Mifflin, 1934), 234.

122. Ibid., 315.

123. Blaise Picchi, *The Five Weeks of Giuseppe Zangara: The Man Who Would Assassinate FDR* (Chicago: Academy Chicago, 1998), 13, 15–16.

124. Sally Denton, *The Plots Against the President: FDR, a Nation in Crisis, and the Rise of the American Right* (New York: Bloomsbury, 2012), 78.

125. Blaise Picchi, *The Five Weeks of Giuseppe Zangara: The Man Who Would Assassinate FDR* (Chicago: Academy Chicago, 1998), 67.

126. Sally Denton, *The Plots Against the President: FDR, a Nation in Crisis, and the Rise of the American Right* (New York: Bloomsbury, 2012), 84.

127. Frank J. Wilson and Beth Day, *Special Agent: Twenty-Five Years with the U.S. Treasury Department and Secret Service* (London: Frederick Muller Limited, 1966), 214.

128. Blaise Picchi, *The Five Weeks of Giuseppe Zangara: The Man Who Would Assassinate FDR* (Chicago: Academy Chicago, 1998), 203.

129. James W. Clarke, *American Assassins: The Darker Side of Politics* (Princeton, NJ: Princeton University Press, 1982), 171–72.

130. Robert Donovan, "Annals of Crime: The Long Stomach Ache," *New Yorker*, November 27, 1954, 120.

131. Conrad Black, *Franklin Delano Roosevelt: Champion of Freedom* (New York: PublicAffairs, 2003), 264.

132. Michael F. Reilly, as told to William J. Slouch, *Reilly of the White House* (New York: Simon and Schuster, 1947), 16–21.

133. Frank J. Wilson and Beth Day, *Special Agent: Twenty-Five Years with the U.S. Treasury Department and Secret Service* (London: Frederick Muller Limited, 1965), 110.

134. Michael F. Reilly, as told to William J. Slouch, *Reilly of the White House* (New York: Simon and Schuster, 1947), 101–3.

135. Sally Denton, *The Plots Against the President: FDR, a Nation in Crisis, and the Rise of the American Right* (New York: Bloomsbury, 2012), 186–217; Jules Archer, *The Plot to Seize the White House: The Shocking True Story of the Conspiracy to Overthrow F.D.R.* (New York: Skyhorse, 2007).

136. Michael F. Reilly, as told to William J. Slouch, *Reilly of the White House* (New York: Simon and Schuster, 1947), 4, 26.

137. Frank J. Wilson and Beth Day, *Special Agent: Twenty-Five Years with the U.S. Treasury Department and Secret Service* (London: Frederick Muller Limited, 1965), 142.

138. Grace Tully, *F.D.R.: My Boss* (Chicago: Peoples Book Club, 1949), 258–59.

139. Frank J. Wilson and Beth Day, *Special Agent: Twenty-Five Years with the U.S. Treasury Department and Secret Service* (London: Frederick Muller Limited, 1965), 149.

140. Paul Sparrow, interview by the author, September 2017.

141. Michael F. Reilly, as told to William J. Slouch, *Reilly of the White House* (New York: Simon and Schuster, 1947), 39, 43.

142. Frank J. Wilson and Beth Day, *Special Agent: Twenty-Five Years with the U.S. Treasury Department and Secret Service* (London: Frederick Muller Limited, 1965), 127–33.

143. Michael F. Reilly, as told to William J. Slouch, *Reilly of the White House* (New York: Simon and Schuster, 1947), 177; Bill Yenne, *Operation Long Jump: Stalin, Roosevelt, Churchill, and the Greatest Assassination Plot in History* (Washington: Regnery History, 2015), 115–17, 176–79.

144. Bill Yenne, *Operation Long Jump: Stalin, Roosevelt, Churchill, and the Greatest Assassination Plot in History* (Washington: Regnery History, 2015), xxv.

145. Michael F. Reilly, as told to William J. Slouch, *Reilly of the White House* (New York: Simon and Schuster, 1947), 182.

146. Mel Alton, *Hunting the President: Threats, Plots, and Assassination Attempts—From FDR to Obama* (New York: Regnery, 2014), 24.

147. A. J. Baime, *The Accidental President: Harry S. Truman and the Four Months That Changed the World* (New York: Houghton Mifflin Harcourt, 2017), 237–38.

148. See the account in ibid., 352–53.

149. Paul Brandus, *Under This Roof: The White House and the Presidency—21 Presidents, 21 Rooms, 21 Inside Stories* (Guilford, CT: Lyons Press, 2015), 191–92.

150. Margaret Truman, *Harry S. Truman* (New York: William Morrow, 1973), 488.

151. Stephen Hunter and John Bainbridge, Jr., *American Gunfight: The Plot to Kill President Truman—and the Shoot-out That Stopped It* (New York: Simon & Schuster, 2005), 90–91.

152. U. E. Baughman with Leonard Wallace Robinson, *Secret Service Chief* (New York: Harper & Brothers, 1962), 113.

153. A brief description of the gunfight appears in David McCullough, *Truman* (New York: Simon & Schuster, 1992), 809–11. A much more detailed account is Stephen Hunter and John Bainbridge, Jr., *American Gunfight: The Plot to Kill President Truman—and the Shoot-out That Stopped It* (New York: Simon & Schuster, 2005).

154. "The President's News Conference," November 2, 1950, *Public Papers, Harry S. Truman, 1945–1953*, available at https://www.trumanlibrary.org/publicpapers/index.php?pid=908.

155. Margaret Truman, *Harry S. Truman* (New York: William Morrow, 1973), 488.

156. Stephen Hunter and John Bainbridge, Jr., *American Gunfight: The Plot to Kill President Truman—and the Shoot-out That Stopped It* (New York: Simon & Schuster, 2005), 317.

157. U. E. Baughman with Leonard Wallace Robinson, *Secret Service Chief* (New York: Harper & Brothers, 1962), 181.

158. Rufus W. Youngblood, *20 Years in the Secret Service: My Life with Five Presidents* (New York: Simon and Schuster, 1973), 41–42.

159. Ibid., 43.

160. Mel Alton, *Hunting the President: Threats, Plots, and Assassination Attempts—From FDR to Obama* (New York: Regnery, 2014), 57.

161. Garland Blaine with Lisa McCubbin, *The Kennedy Detail: JFK's Secret Service Agents Break Their Silence* (New York: Gallery Books, 2010), 51–52.

162. U. E. Baughman with Leonard Wallace Robinson, *Secret Service Chief* (New York: Harper & Brothers, 1962), 9–10.

163. President's Commission on the Assassination of President John F. Kennedy (Warren Commission), *Report of the President's Commission on the Assassination of John F. Kennedy* (Washington, DC: U.S. Government Printing Office, 1964), 42.

164. The most detailed, yet easily read, description of Oswald's upbringing and youth as it relates to his later actions remains in Vincent Bugliosi, *Reclaiming History: The Assassination of President John F. Kennedy* (New York: W. W. Norton, 2007), at 515–788. My short summary here, supplemented by other sources separately cited, represents just the tip of the iceberg that Bugliosi lays out.

165. President's Commission on the Assassination of President John F. Kennedy (Warren Commission), *Report of the President's Commission on the Assassination of John F. Kennedy* (Washington, DC: U.S. Government Printing Office, 1964), 681.

166. Ibid., 689.

167. Ibid., 689–713.

168. James L. Swanson, *End of Days: The Assassination of John F. Kennedy* (New York: William Morrow, 2013), 15.

169. Ibid., 39–51.

170. President's Commission on the Assassination of President John F. Kennedy (Warren Commission), *Report of the President's Commission on the Assassination of John F. Kennedy* (Washington, DC: U.S. Government Printing Office, 1964), 299–310.

171. See the first-person account in Clint Hill with Lisa McCubbin, *Five Presidents: My Extraordinary Journey with Eisenhower, Kennedy, Johnson, Nixon, and Ford* (New York: Gallery Books, 2016), 154–55; see also Vincent Bugliosi, *Reclaiming History: The Assassination of President John F. Kennedy* (New York: W. W. Norton, 2007), 467–97.

172. Vincent Bugliosi, *Reclaiming History: The Assassination of President John F. Kennedy* (New York: W. W. Norton, 2007), xviii.

173. Fred Blumenthal, "The New President and the Secret Service," *Parade*, January 19, 1969, 24.

174. Los Angeles Police Department, *1969 Final Report*, available online at http://www.sos.ca.gov/archives/collections/rfk.

175. Robert Cushman, interview by Thomas Soapes, March 1977, Dwight D. Eisenhower Library, available online at https://www.dwightd eisenhower.com/DocumentCenter/View/1414/Cushman-Robert-PDF.

176. U. E. Baughman with Leonard Wallace Robinson, *Secret Service Chief* (New York: Harper & Brothers, 1962), 247–48.

177. Mel Alton, *Hunting the President: Threats, Plots, and Assassination Attempts—From FDR to Obama* (New York: Regnery, 2014), 91.

178. Ibid., 99–106.

179. Mike Endicott, interview by the author, July 2016.

180. Jess Bravin, *Squeaky: The Life and Times of Lynette Alice Fromme* (New York: St. Martin's Press, 1997), 285.

181. Gerald R. Ford, *A Time to Heal: The Autobiography of Gerald R. Ford* (New York: Harper & Row, 1979), 309.

182. Jess Bravin, *Squeaky: The Life and Times of Lynette Alice Fromme* (New York: St. Martin's Press, 1997), 8.

183. James W. Clarke, *American Assassins: The Darker Side of Politics* (Princeton, NJ: Princeton University Press, 1982), 152–54.

184. Gerald R. Ford, *A Time to Heal: The Autobiography of Gerald R. Ford* (New York: Harper & Row, 1979), 311.

185. Jess Bravin, *Squeaky: The Life and Times of Lynette Alice Fromme* (New York: St. Martin's Press, 1997), 284–85.

186. Philip H. Melanson, *The Secret Service: The Hidden History of an Enigmatic Agency* (New York: MJF Books, 2002), 102–3.

187. "Reported Carter-Assassination Plot Given Credibility by New Evidence," *New York Times*, May 12, 1979.

188. Del Quentin Wilber, *Rawhide Down: The Near Assassination of Ronald Reagan* (New York: Henry Holt, 2011), 80–85.

189. Ibid., 88–91.

190. Ibid., 97–98, 111.

191. Ronald Reagan, *The Reagan Diaries*, Douglas Brinkley, ed., (New York: HarperCollins, 2007), 12.

192. Del Quentin Wilber, *Rawhide Down: The Near Assassination of Ronald Reagan* (New York: Henry Holt, 2011), 178–79.

193. Ronald Reagan, *An American Life* (New York: Simon and Schuster, 1990), 262.

194. Maureen Dowd, "Crash at the White House," *New York Times*, September 13, 1994.

195. Mel Ayton, *Hunting the President: Threats, Plots, and Assassination Attempts—From FDR to Obama* (Washington, DC: Regnery History, 2014), 200–1.

196. "The Case of the Failed Hand Grenade Attack," Federal Bureau of Investigation website, January 11, 2006, available at https://archives.fbi.gov/archives/news/stories/2006/january/grenade_attack011106.

197. Carol D. Leonnig, "Secret Service fumbled response after gunman hit White House residence in 2011," *Washington Post*, September 27, 2014.

198. Kate Andersen Brower, *The Residence: Inside the Private World of the White House* (New York: Harper, 2015), 114.

199. Carol D. Leonnig, "Secret Service fumbled response after gunman hit White House residence in 2011," *Washington Post*, September 27, 2014.

200. Jonathan Wackrow, interview by the author, September 2017.

201. Kate Andersen Brower, *The Residence: Inside the Private World of the White House* (New York: Harper, 2015), 115.

202. Jonathan Wackrow, interview by the author, September 2017.

Chapter Six. Declared Unable to Serve

1. Lyndon Baines Johnson, *The Vantage Point: Perspectives of the Presidency, 1963–1969* (New York: Holt, Rinehart and Winston, 1971), 425.

2. Gene Smith, *When the Cheering Stopped: The Last Years of Woodrow Wilson* (New York: William Morrow, 1964), 96.

3. John D. Feerick, *From Failing Hands: The Story of Presidential Succession* (New York: Fordham University Press, 1965), 167–70.

4. Irwin Hood (Ike) Hoover, *Forty-Two Years in the White House* (New York: Houghton Mifflin, 1934), 97.

5. Ibid., 98–99.

6. Edith Boling Wilson, *My Memoir* (New York: Bobbs-Merrill, 1938), 273.

7. John Dos Passos, *Mr. Wilson's War* (Garden City, New York: Doubleday, 1962), 485.

8. Edmund W. Starling, as told to Thomas Sugrue, *Starling of the White House* (New York: Simon and Schuster, 1946), 148.

9. John Dos Passos, *Mr. Wilson's War* (Garden City, New York: Doubleday, 1962), 486.

10. Edith Boling Wilson, *My Memoir* (New York: Bobbs-Merrill, 1938), 273.

11. Ibid., 283.

12. Edmund W. Starling, as told to Thomas Sugrue, *Starling of the White House* (New York: Simon and Schuster, 1946), 151–52.

13. Edith Boling Wilson, *My Memoir* (New York: Bobbs-Merrill, 1938), 283–84.

14. Gene Smith, *When the Cheering Stopped: The Last Years of Woodrow Wilson* (New York: William Morrow, 1964), 84.

15. Ibid., 91.

16. Edith Boling Wilson, *My Memoir* (New York: Bobbs-Merrill, 1938), 283–84.

17. Ibid., 286–87.

18. John Milton Cooper, Jr., *Woodrow Wilson: A Biography* (New York: Alfred A. Knopf, 2009), 533–34.

19. Irwin Hood (Ike) Hoover, *Forty-Two Years in the White House* (New York: Houghton Mifflin, 1934), 103.

20. Edith Boling Wilson, *My Memoir* (New York: Bobbs-Merrill, 1938), 289.

21. William Hazelgrove, *Madam President: The Secret Presidency of Edith Wilson* (Washington, DC: Regnery History, 2016), 66.

22. John D. Feerick, *From Failing Hands: The Story of Presidential Succession* (New York: Fordham University Press, 1965), 170–72.

23. Thomas R. Marshall, *A Hoosier Salad: Recollections of Thomas R. Marshall, Vice-President and Hoosier Philosopher* (Bobbs-Merrill, 1925), 368.

24. Gene Smith, *When the Cheering Stopped: The Last Years of Woodrow Wilson* (New York: William Morrow, 1964), 101–4.

25. John Milton Cooper, Jr., *Woodrow Wilson: A Biography* (New York: Alfred A. Knopf, 2009), 540.

26. Gene Smith, *When the Cheering Stopped: The Last Years of Woodrow Wilson* (New York: William Morrow, 1964), 101–4.

27. Phyllis Lee Levin, *Edith and Woodrow: The Wilson White House* (New York: Scribner, 2001), 428–33; William Hazelgrove, *Madam President: The Secret Presidency of Edith Wilson* (Washington, DC: Regnery History, 2016), ch. 17.

28. Herbert Hoover, *The Memoirs of Herbert Hoover: The Cabinet and the Presidency, 1920–1933* (New York: MacMillan, 1952), 15.

29. Gene Smith, *When the Cheering Stopped: The Last Years of Woodrow Wilson* (New York: William Morrow, 1964), 107.

30. John D. Feerick, *From Failing Hands: The Story of Presidential Succession* (New York: Fordham University Press, 1965), 176–79.

31. Irwin Hood (Ike) Hoover, *Forty-Two Years in the White House* (New York: Houghton Mifflin, 1934), 103.

32. Ibid., 95.

33. Edmund W. Starling, as told to Thomas Sugrue, *Starling of the White House* (New York: Simon and Schuster, 1946), 159.

34. William Hazelgrove, *Madam President: The Secret Presidency of Edith Wilson* (Washington, DC: Regnery History, 2016), 274.

35. Max Farrand, ed., *The Records of the Federal Convention of 1787*, vol. 2 (New Haven: Yale University Press, 1911), 427 (August 27).

36. John D. Feerick, *From Failing Hands: The Story of Presidential Succession* (New York: Fordham University Press, 1965), 46–49.

37. Harlow Giles Unger, *The Last Founding Father: James Monroe and a Nation's Call to Greatness* (Boston: Da Capo Press, 2009), 233.

38. Adam Goodheart, "Washington Burning: The 220th Anniversary of The War of 1812," *Washingtonian*, July 19, 2012, available at https://www.washingtonian.com/2012/07/19/washington-burning-the-200th-anniversary-of-the-war-of-1812.

39. Ibid.

40. Steve Vogel, *Through the Perilous Fight: Six Weeks That Saved the Nation* (New York: Random House, 2013), 157–58.

41. Adam Goodheart, "Washington Burning: The 220th Anniversary of The War of 1812," *Washingtonian*, July 19, 2012, available at https://www.washingtonian.com/2012/07/19/washington-burning-the-200th-anniversary-of-the-war-of-1812.

42. Harlow Giles Unger, *The Last Founding Father: James Monroe and a Nation's Call to Greatness* (Boston: Da Capo Press, 2009), 246–47.

43. Thomas Hart Benton, *Thirty Years' View*, vol. 1(New York: D. Appleton, 1854), 77–78.

44. Andrew Glass, "Former Speaker Langdon Cheves dies, June 26, 1857," *Politico*, June 26, 2016, available at https://www.politico.com/story/2016/06/former-speaker-langdon-cheves-dies-june-26-1857-224660.

45. J. R. Davidson, K. M, Connor, and M. Swartz, "Mental illness in U.S. Presidents between 1776 and 1974: a review of biographical sources," *Journal of Nervous and Mental Disease* 194, no. 1 (January 2006), 47–51.

46. William Lee Miller, *Lincoln's Virtues: An Ethical Biography* (New York: Vintage Books, 2003), 54, 57.

47. Michael Burlingame, *Abraham Lincoln: A Life*, vol. 1 (Baltimore: Johns Hopkins University Press, 2008), 100.

48. Sidney Blumenthal, *A Self-Made Man: The Political Life of Abraham Lincoln, 1809–1849* (New York: Simon & Schuster, 2016), 78.

49. Michael Burlingame, *Abraham Lincoln: A Life*, vol. 1 (Baltimore: Johns Hopkins University Press, 2008), 101.

50. Sidney Blumenthal, *A Self-Made Man: The Political Life of Abraham Lincoln, 1809–1849* (New York: Simon & Schuster, 2016), 223.

51. Michael Burlingame, *Abraham Lincoln: A Life*, vol. 1 (Baltimore: Johns Hopkins University Press, 2008), 183–4.

52. Sidney Blumenthal, *Wrestling with His Angel: The Political Life of Abraham Lincoln, 1849–1856*, vol. 2 (New York: Simon & Schuster, 2017), 132–33.

53. Doris Kearns Goodwin, *Team of Rivals: The Political Genius of Abraham Lincoln* (New York: Simon & Schuster, 2005), 100–1.

54. Sidney Blumenthal, *Wrestling with His Angel: The Political Life of Abraham Lincoln, 1849–1856*, vol. 2 (New York: Simon & Schuster, 2017), 131.

55. Michael Burlingame, *Abraham Lincoln: A Life*, vol. 1 (Baltimore: Johns Hopkins University Press, 2008), 247.

56. Sidney Blumenthal, *Wrestling with His Angel: The Political Life of Abraham Lincoln, 1849–1856*, vol. 2 (New York: Simon & Schuster, 2017), 131–2.

57. Michael Burlingame, *Abraham Lincoln: A Life*, vol. 2 (Baltimore: Johns Hopkins University Press, 2008), 220.

58. Todd Brewster, *Lincoln's Gamble: The Tumultuous Six Months that Gave America the Emancipation Proclamation and Changed the Course of the Civil War* (New York: Scribner, 2014), 24.

59. Ibid., 287 n24.

60. Michael Burlingame, *Abraham Lincoln: A Life*, vol. 2 (Baltimore: Johns Hopkins University Press, 2008), 446.

61. Michael Burlingame, "Abraham Lincoln and the Death of His Son Willie," in Jeffrey A. Engel and Thomas J. Knock, eds., *When Life Strikes the President: Scandal, Death, and Illness in the White House* (New York: Oxford University Press, 2017), 87–89.

62. Ibid., 95.

63. Ibid., 91.

64. Jules Abels, *In the Time of Silent Cal* (New York: G. P. Putnam's Sons, 1969), 35–36.

65. Calvin Coolidge, *The Autobiography of Calvin Coolidge* (New York: Cosmopolitan Book Corporation, 1929), 126–27.

66. Calvin Coolidge, *Have Faith in Massachusetts: A Collection of Speeches and Messages* (New York: Houghton Mifflin, 1919), 223.

67. Calvin Coolidge, *The Autobiography of Calvin Coolidge* (New York: Cosmopolitan Book Corporation, 1929), 161–64.

68. Edmund W. Starling, as told to Thomas Sugrue, *Starling of the White House* (New York: Simon and Schuster, 1946), 209.

69. Jules Abels, *In the Time of Silent Cal* (New York: G. P. Putnam's Sons, 1969), 36.

70. Edmund W. Starling, as told to Thomas Sugrue, *Starling of the White House* (New York: Simon and Schuster, 1946), 221.

71. Jared Rhoads, "The Medical Context of Calvin Jr.'s Untimely Death," Calvin Coolidge Presidential Foundation online, July 7, 2014, at https://coolidgefoundation.org/blog/the-medical-context-of-calvin-jr-s -untimely-death.

72. Calvin Coolidge, *The Autobiography of Calvin Coolidge* (New York: Cosmopolitan Book Corporation, 1929), 190.

73. Edmund W. Starling, as told to Thomas Sugrue, *Starling of the White House* (New York: Simon and Schuster, 1946), 224.

74. Amity Shlaes, *Coolidge* (New York: HarperCollins, 2013), 316.

75. James David Barber, *The Presidential Character* (Englewood Cliffs, NJ: Prentice-Hall, 1977), 147; Calvin Coolidge, *The Autobiography of Calvin Coolidge* (New York: Cosmopolitan Book Corporation, 1929), 202.

76. Edmund W. Starling, as told to Thomas Sugrue, *Starling of the White House* (New York: Simon and Schuster, 1946), 235, 237–38.

77. Quoted in Amity Shlaes, "Calvin Coolidge," in Jeffrey A. Engel and Thomas J. Knock, eds., *When Life Strikes the President: Scandal, Death, and Illness in the White House* (New York: Oxford University Press, 2017), 150.

78. Claude M. Fuess, *Calvin Coolidge: The Man from Vermont* (Westport, CT: Greenwood Press, 1976), 351.

79. Calvin Coolidge, *The Autobiography of Calvin Coolidge* (New York: Cosmopolitan Book Corporation, 1929), 190.

80. This case is made in Amity Shlaes, "Calvin Coolidge," in Jeffrey A. Engel and Thomas J. Knock, eds., *When Life Strikes the President: Scandal, Death, and Illness in the White House* (New York: Oxford University Press, 2017), 131–59.

81. Donald R. McCoy, *Calvin Coolidge: The Quiet President* (Newtown, CT: American Political Biography Press, 2000), 267.

82. Jules Abels, *In the Time of Silent Cal* (New York: G. P. Putnam's Sons, 1969), 27.

83. Ibid., 34.

84. Calvin Coolidge, *The Autobiography of Calvin Coolidge* (New York: Cosmopolitan Book Corporation, 1929), 246.

85. Robert Gilbert, *The Tormented President: Calvin Coolidge, Death and Clinical Depression* (Westport, CT: Praeger, 2003), 3.

86. Edmund W. Starling, as told to Thomas Sugrue, *Starling of the White House* (New York: Simon and Schuster, 1946), 249.

87. William W. Keen, *The Surgical Operations on President Cleveland in 1893* (Philadelphia: George W. Jacobs, 1917), 30–31.

88. Matthew Algeo, *The President Is a Sick Man* (Chicago: Chicago Review Press, 2011), 39–40.

89. Ronald C. White, *American Ulysses: A Life of Ulysses S. Grant* (New York: Random House, 2016), 636.

90. Matthew Algeo, *The President Is a Sick Man* (Chicago: Chicago Review Press, 2011), 41.

91. Quoted in William W. Keen, *The Surgical Operations on President Cleveland in 1893* (Philadelphia: George W. Jacobs, 1917), 17.

92. William W. Keen, *The Surgical Operations on President Cleveland in 1893* (Philadelphia: George W. Jacobs, 1917), 32.

93. Denis Tilden Lynch, *Grover Cleveland: A Man Four-Square* (New York: Horace Liverlight, 1932), 424.

94. Matthew Algeo, *The President Is a Sick Man* (Chicago: Chicago Review Press, 2011), 79.

95. William W. Keen, *The Surgical Operations on President Cleveland in 1893* (Philadelphia: George W. Jacobs, 1917), 35.

96. Matthew Algeo, *The President Is a Sick Man* (Chicago: Chicago Review Press, 2011), 88–90.

97. William W. Keen, *The Surgical Operations on President Cleveland in 1893* (Philadelphia: George W. Jacobs, 1917), 32.

98. Ibid., 37.

99. Ibid., 37–40.

100. Matthew Algeo, *The President Is a Sick Man* (Chicago: Chicago Review Press, 2011), 95.

101. William W. Keen, *The Surgical Operations on President Cleveland in 1893* (Philadelphia: George W. Jacobs, 1917), 37–40.

102. Ibid., 42.

103. Matthew Algeo, *The President Is a Sick Man* (Chicago: Chicago Review Press, 2011), 96–97, 104.

104. William W. Keen, *The Surgical Operations on President Cleveland in 1893* (Philadelphia: George W. Jacobs, 1917), 41.

105. Matthew Algeo, *The President Is a Sick Man* (Chicago: Chicago Review Press, 2011), 106–8.

106. Horace Samuel Merrill, *Bourbon Leader: Grover Cleveland and the Democratic Party* (Boston: Little, Brown, 1957), 178.

107. Matthew Algeo, *The President Is a Sick Man* (Chicago: Chicago Review Press, 2011), chs. 7–10.

108. Denis Tilden Lynch, *Grover Cleveland: A Man Four-Square* (New York: Horace Liverlight, 1932), 424.

109. Robert E. Gilbert, *The Mortal Presidency: Illness and Anguish in the White House* (New York: Basic Books, 1992), 86–91.

110. Sherman Adams, *Firsthand Report: The Story of the Eisenhower Administration* (New York: Harper & Brothers, 1961), 181.

111. Richard M. Nixon, *Six Crises* (Garden City, NY: Doubleday, 1962), 139.

112. Ibid., 143.

113. Ibid., 148–51.

114. Robert E. Gilbert, *The Mortal Presidency: Illness and Anguish in the White House* (New York: Basic Books, 1992), 90–93.

115. Richard M. Nixon, *Six Crises* (Garden City, NY: Doubleday, 1962), 132.

116. Robert E. Gilbert, *The Mortal Presidency: Illness and Anguish in the White House* (New York: Basic Books, 1992), 80–84.

117. Sean Braswell, "President Eisenhower's $14 Billion Heart Attack," *OZY*, April 13, 2016, available at http://www.ozy.com//flashback/president-eisenhowers-14-billion-heart-attack/65157.

118. John D. Feerick, *From Failing Hands: The Story of Presidential Succession* (New York: Fordham University Press, 1965), 223–25.

119. Dwight D. Eisenhower, *Waging Peace: 1956–1961* (Garden City, NY: Doubleday, 1965), 226–28.

120. Sherman Adams, *Firsthand Report: The Story of the Eisenhower Administration* (New York: Harper & Brothers, 1961), 196.

121. Richard M. Nixon, *Six Crises* (Garden City, NY: Doubleday, 1962), 174.

122. Ibid., 171.

123. Dwight D. Eisenhower, *Waging Peace: 1956–1961* (Garden City, NY: Doubleday, 1965), 230.

124. Ibid., 233.

125. Richard M. Nixon, *Six Crises* (Garden City, NY: Doubleday, 1962), 139, 179.

126. John D. Feerick, *From Failing Hands: The Story of Presidential Succession* (New York: Fordham University Press, 1965), 228.

127. Ibid., 228.

128. Ibid., 228.

129. Ibid., 229.

130. "Transcript of Television and Radio Interview Conducted by Representatives of Major Broadcast Services," March 15, 1964, available at http://www.presidency.ucsb.edu/ws/index.php?pid=26108.

131. John D. Feerick, *From Failing Hands: The Story of Presidential Succession* (New York: Fordham University Press, 1965), 229.

132. Rufus W. Youngblood, *20 Years in the Secret Service: My Life with Five Presidents* (New York: Simon and Schuster, 1973), 187–88.

133. John D. Feerick, *The Twenty-Fifth Amendment: Its Complete History and Applications*, 3rd ed. (New York: Fordham University Press, 2014), 105n.

134. Birch Bayh, *One Heartbeat Away: Presidential Disability and Succession* (New York: Bobbs-Merrill, 1968), 6.

135. John D. Feerick, *The Twenty-Fifth Amendment: Its Complete History and Applications*, 3rd ed. (New York: Fordham University Press, 2014), 116.

136. Brian C. Kalt, *Constitutional Cliffhangers: A Legal Guide for Presidents and Their Enemies* (New Haven, CT: Yale University Press, 2012), ch. 3.

137. Julie Silverbrook, interview by the author, December 2017.

138. Brian Kalt, interview by the author, October 2017.

139. Herbert Brownell, et al., "Final Report of the Commission on Presidential Disability and the Twenty-Fifth Amendment" (1988), available at https://ir.lawnet.fordham.edu/cgi/viewcontent.cgi?article=1003&context=twentyfifth_amendment_executive_materials.

140. David Blumenthal and James A. Morone, *The Heart of Power: Health and Politics in the Oval Office* (Berkeley, CA: University of California Press, 2009), 206–13; John A. Farrell, *Richard Nixon: The Life* (New York: Doubleday, 2017), 241.

141. Robert Dallek, *Nixon and Kissinger: Partners in Power* (New York: HarperCollins, 2007), 93.

142. Ibid., 93.

143. John A. Farrell, *Richard Nixon: The Life* (New York: Doubleday, 2017), 411.

144. Bob Woodward and Carl Bernstein, *The Final Days* (New York; Simenon & Schuster, 1976), 103–4.

145. John A. Farrell, *Richard Nixon: The Life* (New York: Doubleday, 2017), 412.

146. Bob Woodward and Carl Bernstein, *The Final Days* (New York; Simenon & Schuster, 1976), 395.

147. John A. Farrell, *Richard Nixon: The Life* (New York: Doubleday, 2017), 527.

148. John Dean, interview by the author, May 2018.

149. Del Quentin Wilber, *Rawhide Down: The Near Assassination of Ronald Reagan* (New York: Henry Holt, 2011), 131–33.

150. Fred Fielding, interview by the author, October 2017.

151. Ibid.

152. Herbert Brownell, et al., "Final Report of the Commission on Presidential Disability and the Twenty-Fifth Amendment" (1988), available at https://ir.lawnet.fordham.edu/cgi/viewcontent.cgi?article=1003&context =twentyfifth_amendment_executive_materials.

153. Laurence I. Barrett, *Gambling with History: Ronald Reagan in the White House* (Garden City, NY: Doubleday, 1983), 114–15.

154. Del Quentin Wilber, *Rawhide Down: The Near Assassination of Ronald Reagan* (New York: Henry Holt, 2011), 165.

155. Cass R. Sunstein, *Impeachment: A Citizen's Guide* (Cambridge, MA: Harvard University Press, 2017), 138–39.

156. Fred Fielding, interview by the author, October 2017.

157. Del Quentin Wilber, *Rawhide Down: The Near Assassination of Ronald Reagan* (New York: Henry Holt, 2011), 201, 205.

158. Lou Cannon, *President Reagan: The Role of a Lifetime* (New York: PublicAffairs, 2000), 126.

159. Fred Fielding, interview by the author, October 2017.

160. Lawrence K. Altman, "Presidential Power: Reagan Doctor Says He Erred," *New York Times*, February 20, 1989, available at https://www .nytimes.com/1989/02/20/us/presidential-power-reagan-doctor-says -he-erred.html.

161. Herbert Brownell, et al., "Final Report of the Commission on Presidential Disability and the Twenty-Fifth Amendment" (1988), available at https://ir.lawnet.fordham.edu/cgi/viewcontent.cgi?article=1003&context =twentyfifth_amendment_executive_materials.

162. Lou Cannon, *President Reagan: The Role of a Lifetime* (New York: PublicAffairs, 2000), 543.

163. Fred Fielding, interview by the author, October 2017.

164. John D. Feerick, *The Twenty-Fifth Amendment: Its Complete History and Applications*, 3rd ed. (New York: Fordham University Press, 2014), 197.

165. Fred F. Fielding, "An Eyewitness Account of Executive 'Inability,'" *Fordham Law Review*, 79, no. 3 (2011), 831, available at: http://ir.lawnet .fordham.edu/flr/vol79/iss3/3.

166. Ibid.

167. Fred Fielding, interview by the author, October 2017.

168. Lawrence E. Walsh, *Firewall: The Iran-Contra Conspiracy and Cover-up* (New York: W. W. Norton, 1997), 355.

169. Quoted in John D. Feerick, *The Twenty-Fifth Amendment: Its Complete History and Applications*, 3rd ed. (New York: Fordham University Press, 2014), 199.

170. Robert E. Gilbert, *The Mortal Presidency: Illness and Anguish in the White House* (New York: Basic Books, 1992), xi–xiii.

171. Marlin Fitzwater, *Call the Briefing! Bush and Reagan, Sam and Helen: A Decade with Presidents and the Press* (New York: Times Books, 1995), 284–91.

172. Robert E. Gilbert, *The Mortal Presidency: Illness and Anguish in the White House* (New York: Basic Books, 1992), xiv.

173. Ann McDaniel, "25 Years Ago Today, George H. W. Bush Vomited on the Prime Minister of Japan," *Newsweek*, January 8, 2017, available at http:// www.newsweek.com/25-years-ago-today-george-h-w-bush-vomited -prime-minister-japan-538581.

174. Robert E. Gilbert, *The Mortal Presidency: Illness and Anguish in the White House* (New York: Basic Books, 1992), xiv–xvi.

175. Michael Wines, "Bush in Japan: Bush Collapses at State Dinner with the Japanese," *New York Times*, January 9, 1992, available at https:// www.nytimes.com/1992/01/09/world/bush-in-japan-bush-collapses-at -state-dinner-with-the-japanese.html.

176. John D. Feerick, *The Twenty-Fifth Amendment: Its Complete History and Applications*, 3rd ed. (New York: Fordham University Press, 2014), 202.

177. Fred Fielding, interview by the author, October 2017.

178. Fred F. Fielding, "An Eyewitness Account of Executive 'Inability,'" *Fordham Law Review* 79, no. 3 (2011), 833, available at: http://ir.lawnet .fordham.edu/flr/vol79/iss3/3.

179. John D. Feerick, *The Twenty-Fifth Amendment: Its Complete History and Applications*, 3rd ed. (New York: Fordham University Press, 2014), 203.

180. Sheryl Gay Stolberg, "Cheney Pens Letter While Acting as POTUS," *New York Times*, July 30, 2007, available at https://thecaucus.blogs.nytimes.com/2007/07/30/cheney-pens-letter-while-acting-as-potus/.

Chapter Seven. Impeached and Removed

1. "Federalist No. 65," Alexander Hamilton, James Madison and John Jay, *The Federalist Papers* (New York: Mentor, 1961), 396.

2. Stephen W. Stathis and David C. Huckabee, Congressional Research Service, "Congressional Resolutions on Presidential Impeachment: A Historical Overview," *CRS Report for Congress* 98-763 GOV, September 16, 1998, 14–18.

3. John W. Dean, *The Nixon Defense: What He Knew and When He Knew It* (New York: Viking, 2014), 36.

4. Ibid., 35–50.

5. Ibid., 56–60.

6. John A. Farrell, *Richard Nixon: The Life* (New York: Doubleday, 2017), 479.

7. John W. Dean, *The Nixon Defense: What He Knew and When He Knew It* (New York: Viking, 2014), 123.

8. Ibid., 308–17.

9. Ibid., 321.

10. John Dean, interview by the author, May 2018.

11. John W. Dean, *The Nixon Defense: What He Knew and When He Knew It* (New York: Viking, 2014), 416.

12. Howard Fields, *High Crimes and Misdemeanors* (New York: W. W. Norton, 1978), 32.

13. Available at https://www.congress.gov/bill/93rd-congress/house-resolution/513.

14. Available at https://www.congress.gov/bill/93rd-congress/house-resolution/625.

15. Stephen W. Stathis and David C. Huckabee, Congressional Research Service, "Congressional Resolutions on Presidential Impeachment: A Historical Overview," *CRS Report for Congress* 98-763 GOV, September 16, 1998, 12–14.

16. John A. Farrell, *Richard Nixon: The Life* (New York: Doubleday, 2017), 518.

17. John Dean, interview by the author, May 2018.

18. Stanley I. Kutler, *The Wars of Watergate: The Last Crisis of Richard Nixon* (New York: W. W. Norton, 1990), 407.

19. Howard Fields, *High Crimes and Misdemeanors* (New York: W. W. Norton, 1978), 37.

20. Ibid., 52.

21. Ibid., 110.

22. Ibid., 247.

23. Ibid., 147.

24. Ibid., 156–7.

25. Ibid., 178.

26. John A. Farrell, *Richard Nixon: The Life* (New York: Doubleday, 2017), 529.

27. Bob Woodward and Carl Bernstein, *The Final Days* (New York: Simon & Schuster, 1976), 293–94.

28. Brian Kalt, interview by the author, October 2017.

29. Keith Whittington, interview by the author, October 2017.

30. Howard Fields, *High Crimes and Misdemeanors* (New York: W. W. Norton, 1978), 293.

31. Ibid., 292.

32. Stephen W. Stathis and David C. Huckabee, Congressional Research Service, "Congressional Resolutions on Presidential Impeachment: A Historical Overview," *CRS Report for Congress* 98-763 GOV, September 16, 1998, 14.

33. Howard Fields, *High Crimes and Misdemeanors* (New York: W. W. Norton, 1978), 295.

34. Max Farrand, ed., *The Records of the Federal Convention of 1787*, vol. 2 (New Haven: Yale University Press, 1911), 64 (July 20).

35. Ibid., 65 (July 20).

36. Ibid., 65 (July 20).

37. Ibid., 66 (July 20).

38. Ibid., 134 (August 6).

39. Ibid., 186 (August 6).

40. Ibid., 499 (September 4).

41. Ibid., 550 (September 8).

42. Ibid., 545, 550 (September 8).

43. Ibid., 551 (September 8).
44. Ibid., 547, 551 (September 8).
45. Ibid., 65–66 (July 20).
46. Raoul Berger, *Impeachment: The Constitutional Problems* (Cambridge, MA: Harvard University Press, 1973), 60.
47. Charles L. Black, Jr., *Impeachment: A Handbook* (New Haven, CT: Yale University Press, 1974), 29.
48. Ibid., 39–40.
49. Julie Silverbrook, interview by the author, December 2017.
50. Florence Weston, *The Presidential Election of 1828* (Washington, DC: Ruddick Press, 1938), 127.
51. Jon Meacham, *American Lion: Andrew Jackson in the White House* (New York: Random House, 2008), 188.
52. Ibid., 49.
53. Ibid., 188–89.
54. Michael J. Gerhardt, *The Forgotten Presidents: Their Untold Constitutional Legacy* (New York: Oxford University Press, 2013), 41–43.
55. Thomas Hart Benton, *Thirty Years' View*, vol. 2 (New York: D. Appleton, 1856), 318–28, 357.
56. Ibid., 416–17.
57. Ibid., 418–19.
58. Oliver Perry Chitwood, *John Tyler: Champion of the Old South* (Newtown, CT: American Political Biography Press, 1939), 301–2.
59. Thomas Hart Benton, *Thirty Years' View*, vol. 2 (New York: D. Appleton, 1856), 418–19.
60. Oliver Perry Chitwood, *John Tyler: Champion of the Old South* (Newtown, CT: American Political Biography Press, 1939), 303; Stephen W. Stathis and David C. Huckabee, Congressional Research Service, "Congressional Resolutions on Presidential Impeachment: A Historical Overview," *CRS Report for Congress* 98-763 GOV, September 16, 1998, 2–3.
61. James G. Blaine, *Twenty Years of Congress: From Lincoln to Garfield*, vol. 2 (Norwich, CT: Henry Hill, 1886), 181.
62. Stephen W. Stathis and David C. Huckabee, Congressional Research Service, "Congressional Resolutions on Presidential Impeachment: A Historical Overview," *CRS Report for Congress* 98-763 GOV, September 16, 1998, 4.
63. J. G. Randall and David Donald, *The Civil War and Reconstruction*, 2nd ed. (Lexington, MA: D. C. Heath, 1969), 595–99.

64. Hans Trefousse, *Andrew Johnson: A Biography* (New York: W. W. Norton, 1989), 274, 288.

65. James G. Blaine, *Twenty Years of Congress: From Lincoln to Garfield*, vol. 2 (Norwich, CT: Henry Hill, 1886), 343.

66. Stephen W. Stathis and David C. Huckabee, Congressional Research Service, "Congressional Resolutions on Presidential Impeachment: A Historical Overview," *CRS Report for Congress* 98-763 GOV, September 16, 1998, 4.

67. David O. Stewart, *Impeached: The Trial of President Andrew Johnson and the Fight for Lincoln's Legacy* (New York: Simon & Schuster, 2009), 77; Chernow, *Grant* (New York: Penguin, 2017), 586.

68. James G. Blaine, *Twenty Years of Congress: From Lincoln to Garfield*, vol. 2 (Norwich, CT: Henry Hill, 1886), 270.

69. Gene Smith, *High Crimes and Misdemeanors: The Impeachment and Trial of Andrew Johnson* (New York: William Morrow, 1977), 212–13.

70. J. G. Randall and David Donald, *The Civil War and Reconstruction*, 2nd ed. (Lexington, MA: D. C. Heath, 1969), 603.

71. Hans Trefousse, *Andrew Johnson: A Biography* (New York: W. W. Norton & Company, 1989), 306.

72. Adam Badeau, *Grant in Peace: From Appomattox to Mount McGregor* (Hartford, CT: S. S. Scranton, 1887), 111–12.

73. Ibid., 110.

74. David O. Stewart, *Impeached: The Trial of President Andrew Johnson and the Fight for Lincoln's Legacy* (New York: Simon & Schuster, 2009), 124.

75. J. G. Randall and David Donald, *The Civil War and Reconstruction*, 2nd ed. (Lexington, MA: D. C. Heath, 1969), 604.

76. Hans Trefousse, *Andrew Johnson: A Biography* (New York: W. W. Norton, 1989), 312–13.

77. Ibid., 313.

78. Gene Smith, *High Crimes and Misdemeanors: The Impeachment and Trial of Andrew Johnson* (New York: William Morrow, 1977), 235.

79. Keith Whittington, interview by the author, October 2017.

80. Hans Trefousse, *Andrew Johnson: A Biography* (New York: W. W. Norton, 1989), 315.

81. Stephen W. Stathis and David C. Huckabee, Congressional Research Service, "Congressional Resolutions on Presidential Impeachment: A Historical Overview," *CRS Report for Congress* 98-763 GOV, September 16, 1998, 5–6.

82. James G. Blaine, *Twenty Years of Congress: From Lincoln to Garfield*, vol. 2 (Norwich, CT: Henry Hill, 1886), 358.

83. Gene Smith, *High Crimes and Misdemeanors: The Impeachment and Trial of Andrew Johnson* (New York: William Morrow, 1977), chs. 12–13.

84. Ibid., 287.

85. Hans Trefousse, *Andrew Johnson: A Biography* (New York: W. W. Norton, 1989), 325.

86. Gene Smith, *High Crimes and Misdemeanors: The Impeachment and Trial of Andrew Johnson* (New York: William Morrow, 1977), 287–93.

87. Ibid., 296.

88. Stephen W. Stathis and David C. Huckabee, Congressional Research Service, "Congressional Resolutions on Presidential Impeachment: A Historical Overview," *CRS Report for Congress* 98-763 GOV, September 16, 1998, 7.

89. Hans Trefousse, *Andrew Johnson: A Biography* (New York: W. W. Norton, 1989), 332–33.

90. William H. Crook, *Through Five Administrations* (New York: Harper & Brothers, 1910), 134.

91. James G. Blaine, *Twenty Years of Congress: From Lincoln to Garfield*, vol. 2 (Norwich, CT: Henry Hill, 1886), 274.

92. William H. Crook, *Through Five Administrations* (New York: Harper & Brothers, 1910), 126.

93. David O. Stewart, *Impeached: The Trial of President Andrew Johnson and the Fight for Lincoln's Legacy* (New York: Simon & Schuster, 2009), 292–99.

94. H. L. Trefousse, *Benjamin Franklin Wade: Radical Republican from Ohio* (New York: Twayne, 1963), 102–3.

95. Ibid., 150–51.

96. Margaret Leech and Harry J. Brown, *The Garfield Orbit* (New York: Harper & Row, 1978), 264.

97. Gene Smith, *High Crimes and Misdemeanors: The Impeachment and Trial of Andrew Johnson* (New York: William Morrow, 1977), 241.

98. Hans Trefousse, *Andrew Johnson: A Biography* (New York: W. W. Norton, 1989), 303.

99. David O. Stewart, *Impeached: The Trial of President Andrew Johnson and the Fight for Lincoln's Legacy* (New York: Simon & Schuster, 2009), 281.

100. Brian Kalt, interview by the author, October 2017.

101. Stephen W. Stathis and David C. Huckabee, Congressional Research Service, "Congressional Resolutions on Presidential Impeachment:

A Historical Overview," *CRS Report for Congress* 98-763 GOV, September 16, 1998, CRS-7-CRS-9.

102. Harry S. Truman, *Memoirs by Harry S. Truman, Volume Two: Years of Trial and Hope* (Garden City, NY: Doubleday, 1956), 440–42.

103. Ibid., 445.

104. H. W. Brands, *The General vs. the President: MacArthur and Truman at the Brink of Nuclear War* (New York: Doubleday, 2016), 304–6.

105. Margaret Truman, *Harry S. Truman* (New York: William Morrow, 1973), 516.

106. Ibid., 516.

107. H. W. Brands, *The General vs. the President: MacArthur and Truman at the Brink of Nuclear War* (New York: Doubleday, 2016), 313.

108. Ibid., 362.

109. David McCullough, *Truman* (New York: Simon & Schuster, 1992), 854–55.

110. Stephen W. Stathis and David C. Huckabee, Congressional Research Service, "Congressional Resolutions on Presidential Impeachment: A Historical Overview," *CRS Report for Congress* 98-763 GOV, September 16, 1998, 9–11.

111. Ibid., 19.

112. David E. Kyvig, *The Age of Impeachment: American Constitutional Culture since 1960* (Lawrence, KS: University of Kansas Press, 2008), 247.

113. William S. Cohen and George J. Mitchell, *Men of Zeal: A Candid Inside Story of the Iran-Contra Hearings* (New York: Penguin, 1988), 45.

114. Mark Hertsgaard, *On Bended Knee: The Press and the Reagan Presidency* (New York: Schocken Books, 1988), 333.

115. Ibid., 333.

116. Lawrence E. Walsh, *Firewall: The Iran-Contra Conspiracy and Cover-Up* (New York: Norton, 1997), 360.

117. Lou Cannon, *President Reagan: The Role of a Lifetime* (New York: PublicAffairs, 2000), 704.

118. Stephen W. Stathis and David C. Huckabee, Congressional Research Service, "Congressional Resolutions on Presidential Impeachment: A Historical Overview," *CRS Report for Congress* 98-763 GOV, September 16, 1998, CRS-20-CRS-21.

119. Benjamin Wittes, *Starr: A Reassessment* (New Haven, CT: Yale University Press, 2002), 97–103.

120. Ibid., 97–103.

121. Ibid, xi.

122. Ibid., 149.

123. Peter Baker, *The Breach: Inside the Impeachment and Trial of William Jefferson Clinton* (New York: Scribner, 2000), 15–17.

124. David P. Schippers with Alan P. Henry, *Sellout: The Inside Story of President Clinton's Impeachment* (Washington, DC: Regnery, 2000), 3.

125. James R. Rogan, *Catching Our Flag: Behind the Scenes of a Presidential Impeachment* (New York: WND Books, 2011), 396.

126. David E. Kyvig, *The Age of Impeachment: American Constitutional Culture since 1960* (Lawrence, KS: University of Kansas Press, 2008), 31.

127. James R. Rogan, *Catching Our Flag: Behind the Scenes of a Presidential Impeachment* (New York: WND Books, 2011), 187.

128. Peter Baker, *The Breach: Inside the Impeachment and Trial of William Jefferson Clinton* (New York: Scribner, 2000), 264–65.

129. Keith Whittington, interview by the author, October 2017.

130. Peter Baker, *The Breach: Inside the Impeachment and Trial of William Jefferson Clinton* (New York: Scribner, 2000), 309–10.

131. David P. Schippers with Alan P. Henry, *Sellout: The Inside Story of President Clinton's Impeachment* (Washington, DC: Regnery, 2000), 262.

132. Peter Baker, *The Breach: Inside the Impeachment and Trial of William Jefferson Clinton* (New York: Scribner, 2000), 305.

133. David E. Kyvig, *The Age of Impeachment: American Constitutional Culture since 1960* (Lawrence, KS: University of Kansas Press, 2008), 335.

134. Frank Newport, "Presidential Job Approval: Bill Clinton's High Ratings in the Midst of Crisis, 1998," Gallup, June 4, 1999, available at http://news.gallup.com/poll/4609/presidential-job-approval-bill-clintons -high-ratings-midst.aspx.

135. Text of impeachment charges available at https://www.congress .gov/bill/110th-congress/house-resolution/1258/text.

Chapter Eight. Shoved Aside at the Polls

1. Alexander Hamilton, James Madison and John Jay, "Federalist No. 68," *The Federalist Papers* (New York: Mentor, 1961), 412.

2. Office of the Director of National Intelligence, "Assessing Russian Activities and Intentions in Recent US Elections," Intelligence Community

Assessment ICD-2017-01D, January 6, 2017, available at https://www
.dni.gov/files/documents/ICA_2017_01.pdf.

3. Ibid.

4. Allan Nevins, *Grover Cleveland: A Study in Courage, To the Loss of the Presidency, 1837–1888* (Newtown, CT: American Political Biography Press, 1932), 428–31.

5. Office of the Director of National Intelligence, "Assessing Russian Activities and Intentions in Recent US Elections," Intelligence Community Assessment ICD-2017-01D, January 6, 2017, available at https://www
.dni.gov/files/documents/ICA_2017_01.pdf. For more details, see Malcolm Nance, *The Plot to Hack America* (New York: Skyhorse, 2016).

6. Matt Apuzzo and Sharon LaFranierre, "13 Russians Indicted as Mueller Reveals Effort to Aid Trump Campaign," February 16, 2018, available at https://www.nytimes.com/2018/02/16/us/politics/russians-indicted
-mueller-election-interference.html.

7. Ibid.

8. "Deputy Attorney General Rod J. Rosenstein Delivers Remarks Announcing the Indictment of Twelve Russian Intelligence Officers for Conspiring to Interfere in the 2016 Presidential Election Through Computer Hacking and Related Offenses," July 13, 2018, available at https://
www.justice.gov/opa/speech/deputy-attorney-general-rod-j-rosenstein
-delivers-remarks-announcing-indictment-twelve.

9. Jonathan Allen and Amie Parnes, *Shattered: Inside Hillary Clinton's Doomed Campaign* (New York: Crown, 2017), 80–81.

10. Marquis James, *The Life of Andrew Jackson: Complete in One Volume* (New York: Bobbs-Merrill, 1938), 439–40.

11. John T. Morse, Jr., *John Quincy Adams* (New York: Houghton Mifflin, 1882), 202–3.

12. Florence Weston, *The Presidential Election of 1828* (Washington, DC: Ruddick Press, 1938), 49.

13. Michael F. Holt, *The Rise and Fall of the American Whig Party: Jacksonian Politics and the Onset of the Civil War* (New York: Oxford University Press, 1999), 8.

14. Florence Weston, *The Presidential Election of 1828* (Washington, DC: Ruddick Press, 1938), 3, 7.

15. Mark R. Cheathem, *The Coming of Democracy: Presidential Campaigning in the Age of Jackson* (Baltimore: Johns Hopkins University Press, 2018), 37.

16. Thomas Hart Benton, *Thirty Years' View*, vol. 1 (New York: D. Appleton, 1854), 111.

17. Michael F. Holt, *The Rise and Fall of the American Whig Party: Jacksonian Politics and the Onset of the Civil War* (New York: Oxford University Press, 1999), 9.

18. Mark R. Cheathem, *The Coming of Democracy: Presidential Campaigning in the Age of Jackson* (Baltimore: Johns Hopkins University Press, 2018), 57–58.

19. Thomas Hart Benton, *Thirty Years' View*, vol. 1 (New York: D. Appleton, 1854), 48.

20. Thomas Hart Benton, *Thirty Years' View*, vol. 2 (New York: D. Appleton, 1856), 204.

21. Robert Gray Gunderson, *The Log-Cabin Campaign* (Westport, CT: Greenwood Press, 1957), 111.

22. Robert M. Owens, *Mr. Jefferson's Hammer: William Henry Harrison and the Origins of American Indian Policy* (Norman, OK: University of Oklahoma Press, 2007), 217–18.

23. Ibid., 223.

24. Michael F. Holt, *The Rise and Fall of the American Whig Party: Jacksonian Politics and the Onset of the Civil War* (New York: Oxford University Press, 1999), 41.

25. Donald B. Cole, *Martin Van Buren and the American Political System* (Princeton, NJ: Princeton University Press, 1984), 348–49.

26. Michael F. Holt, *The Rise and Fall of the American Whig Party: Jacksonian Politics and the Onset of the Civil War* (New York: Oxford University Press, 1999), 108; Donald B. Cole, *Martin Van Buren and the American Political System* (Princeton, NJ: Princeton University Press, 1984), 377.

27. Donald B. Cole, *Martin Van Buren and the American Political System* (Princeton, NJ: Princeton University Press, 1984), 369.

28. Robert Gray Gunderson, *The Log-Cabin Campaign* (Westport, CT: Greenwood Press, 1957), 74–77; Mark R. Cheathem, *The Coming of Democracy: Presidential Campaigning in the Age of Jackson* (Baltimore: Johns Hopkins University Press, 2018), 136–38.

29. Irwin Hood (Ike) Hoover, *Forty-Two Years in the White House* (New York: Houghton Mifflin, 1934), 37–38.

30. Michael J. Gerhardt, *The Forgotten Presidents: Their Untold Constitutional Legacy* (New York: Oxford University Press, 2013), 173.

31. Carl Sferrazza Anthony, *Nellie Taft: The Unconventional First Lady of the Ragtime Era* (New York: William Morrow, 2005), 221.

32. Irwin Hood (Ike) Hoover, *Forty-Two Years in the White House* (New York: Houghton Mifflin, 1934), 39.

33. Alice Roosevelt Longworth, *Crowded Hours* (New York: Charles Scribner's Sons, 1933), 158.

34. Michael J. Gerhardt, *The Forgotten Presidents: Their Untold Constitutional Legacy* (New York: Oxford University Press, 2013), 172–80.

35. Oscar King Davis, *Released for Publication: Some Inside Political History of Theodore Roosevelt and His Times, 1898–1918* (New York: Houghton Mifflin, 1925), 261.

36. Carl Sferrazza Anthony, *Nellie Taft: The Unconventional First Lady of the Ragtime Era* (New York: William Morrow, 2005), 343; Kathleen Dalton, *Theodore Roosevelt: A Strenuous Life* (New York: Vintage, Books, 2002), 379.

37. Carl Sferrazza Anthony, *Nellie Taft: The Unconventional First Lady of the Ragtime Era* (New York: William Morrow, 2005), 343; Kathleen Dalton, *Theodore Roosevelt: A Strenuous Life* (New York: Vintage, Books, 2002), 385.

38. Oscar King Davis, *Released for Publication: Some Inside Political History of Theodore Roosevelt and His Times, 1898–1918* (New York: Houghton Mifflin, 1925), 377–86.

39. Ibid., 407.

Chapter Nine. Presidents, Processes, and the People

1. Max Farrand, ed., *The Records of the Federal Convention of 1787*, vol. 1 (New Haven: Yale University Press, 1911), 431 (June 26).

2. Transcript available at https://abcnews.go.com/Site/transcript-james -comeys-interview-abc-news-chief-anchor/story?id=54488723.

3. "Impeachment," United States Senate website, available at https:// www.senate.gov/artandhistory/history/common/briefing/Senate_ Impeachment_Role.htm.

4. Keith Whittington, interview by the author, October 2017.

5. Brian Kalt, interview by the author, October 2017.

6. Keith Whittington, interview by the author, October 2017.

7. John Dean, interview by the author, May 2018.

8. Brian Kalt, interview by the author, October 2017.

9. Raoul Berger, *Impeachment: The Constitutional Problems* (Cambridge, MA: Harvard University Press, 1973), 300.

Index

About the Author

RENEE PRIESS

David Priess is author of *The President's Book of Secrets: The Untold Story of Intelligence Briefings to America's Presidents*. He has a PhD in political science from Duke University and served at the CIA during the presidencies of Bill Clinton and George W. Bush as an intelligence officer, manager, and daily intelligence briefer, and at the State Department. Priess writes, speaks, and appears often on broadcast media about the presidency and national security.

PublicAffairs is a publishing house founded in 1997. It is a tribute to the standards, values, and flair of three persons who have served as mentors to countless reporters, writers, editors, and book people of all kinds, including me.

I. F. STONE, proprietor of *I. F. Stone's Weekly*, combined a commitment to the First Amendment with entrepreneurial zeal and reporting skill and became one of the great independent journalists in American history. At the age of eighty, Izzy published *The Trial of Socrates*, which was a national bestseller. He wrote the book after he taught himself ancient Greek.

BENJAMIN C. BRADLEE was for nearly thirty years the charismatic editorial leader of *The Washington Post*. It was Ben who gave the *Post* the range and courage to pursue such historic issues as Watergate. He supported his reporters with a tenacity that made them fearless and it is no accident that so many became authors of influential, best-selling books.

ROBERT L. BERNSTEIN, the chief executive of Random House for more than a quarter century, guided one of the nation's premier publishing houses. Bob was personally responsible for many books of political dissent and argument that challenged tyranny around the globe. He is also the founder and longtime chair of Human Rights Watch, one of the most respected human rights organizations in the world.

. . .

For fifty years, the banner of Public Affairs Press was carried by its owner Morris B. Schnapper, who published Gandhi, Nasser, Toynbee, Truman, and about 1,500 other authors. In 1983, Schnapper was described by *The Washington Post* as "a redoubtable gadfly." His legacy will endure in the books to come.

Peter Osnos, *Founder*